K·I·S·S

The Only Guides You'll Ever Need!

THIS SERIES IS YOUR TRUSTED GUIDE through all of life's stages and situations. Want to learn how to surf the Internet or care for your new dog? Or maybe you'd like to become a wine connoisseur or an expert gardener? The solution is simple: Just pick up a K.I.S.S. Guide and turn to the first page.

Expert authors will walk you through the subject from start to finish, using simple blocks of knowledge to build your skills one step at a time. Build upon these learning blocks and by the end of the book, you'll be an expert yourself! Or, if you are familiar with the topic but want to learn more, it's easy to dive in and pick up where you left off.

The K.I.S.S. Guides deliver what they promise: Simple access to all the information you'll need on one subject. Other titles you might want to check out include: Gardening, Online Investing, Pregnancy, Selling, and many more to come.

GUIDE TO THE

Kama Sutra

ANNE HOOPER

A Dorling Kindersley Book

LONDON, NEW YORK, MUNICH, MELBOURNE, DELHI

DK Publishing, Inc.
Series Editor Jennifer Williams
Editor Matthew X. Kiernan
Copyeditor Pamela Thomas

Dorling Kindersley Limited
Project Editor Jane Sarluis
Managing Editor Maxine Lewis
Managing Art Editor Heather McCarry

Production Heather Hughes
Category Publisher Mary Thompson

Produced for Dorling Kindersley by **Cooling Brown**
9–11 High Street, Hampton, Middlesex TW12 2SA

Creative Director Arthur Brown
Senior Editor Amanda Lebentz

Art Editors Pauline Clarke, Elly King, Alistair Plumb
Editors Patsy North, Kate Sheppard

First American Edition, 2001

00 01 02 03 04 05 10 9 8 7 6 5 4 3 2 1

Published in the United States by
DK Publishing, Inc.
375 Hudson Street,
New York, NY 10014

Hooper, Anne, 1941-
    K.I.S.S. guide to the Kama Sutra / Anne Hooper.-- 1st American ed.
    p. cm. -- (Keep it simple series)
"A Dorling Kindersley Book."
Includes index.
        ISBN 0-7894-8381-5 (alk. paper)
        1. Sex instruction. 2. Kissing. 3. Vatsyayana. Kamasutra.
    I Title: KISS guide to the Kama Sutra. II. Title: Guide to the Kama
    Sutra. III. Title. IV. Series.
HQ31 .H7445 2002
613.9'6--dc21
                                                                    2001005040

Color reproduction by ColourScan, Singapore
Printed and bound by Printer Industria Grafica, S.A., Barcelona, Spain

See our complete product line at

Contents at a Glance

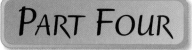

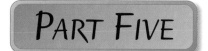

CONTENTS

PART TWO Building Up to Divine Sex

PART FIVE Timeless Kama Sutra Skills

APPENDICES

Introduction

WHEN I WAS FIRST ASKED to write a version of the Kama Sutra, I was less than enthusiastic. Although I am fascinated by human nature, I am not very interested in sex gymnastics-style and I didn't feel there was much I could relate to in the text.

However, when – with some reluctance – I sat down and read Burton and Arbuthnot's original 1883 version of the Kama Sutra (which is extensively quoted in this book), I was surprised to find that I'd been quite wrong in my opinion of the book. For a start, I discovered lots of intriguing advice about managing your personal life as well as valuable instruction on how to do sex well.

I began to understand the humor behind some of the more exotic poses and realized that many of the poses are not just about sex – they are also about the union of mind and body. Some sex poses are yoga positions and many are forerunners of the concept of Tantric sexuality. What's more, the goal of both yoga and Tantra is to achieve mental and physical harmony. In the 21st century nearly all of us, in our own way, are looking to achieve this – and it seems to have become increasingly difficult to reach!

Not only was the book a veritable sex manual, telling men how to arouse timid women or provide seriously deep pleasure, it also dispensed advice on alleviating male sexual problems such as a reluctant erection or a lack of stamina. It even contained its own health section at the back, featuring some truly poisonous-sounding remedies, not to mention a plethora of spells and incantations guaranteed to make men such amazing lovers that women would never be able to get enough of them!

The chapters providing instruction on how to be a good wife in a household containing several other wives were fascinating. Although far-removed from our modern lives, some of the pyschologically adroit advice (which I have included) is still *helpful to those of us who have to cope with jealousy, remarriage,*

or ex-spouses' new partners.

I felt that the way forward with a new edition of the Kama Sutra

was not only to reproduce the familiar language of Sir Richard

Burton, the Victorian author, but also to provide a 21st-century

commentary. If I could demonstrate that this centuries-old

manual might have practical relevance to our sex lives today,

the whole volume would become instantly accessible to modern

men and women.

As I researched Sir Richard Burton, I discovered him to be a lion

of a man, a famous explorer, a poet, a lover of women, and

eventually a British consul. Thanks to his enormously romantic

character, I have included a fascinating section on what motivated

this giant individual and what his legacy to us, 150 years later,

has been. It makes for intriguing reading.

So what might you gain from the Kama Sutra? The answer depends on your priorities. If you want to enjoy gorgeous lovemaking, all the ingredients to enable you to do so are within these pages. If you're looking for some help or advice, you'll find it here too. And if, like many people today, you believe that sex is very special indeed and that it provides rather more than physical relief, then the idea of using loving sex as a gateway to spirituality will appeal enormously.

And ultimately, like all sex books worth browsing, I hope you, the reader, gain some new insights into your own character and behavior and pick up some wonderful practical tips to enable you to make truly amazing love to your adored partner. With any luck, you will feel some of the gain too – first hand!

Anne J. Hooper

PS. You can e-mail me at anne@annehooper.com

ANNE HOOPER

What's Inside?

THE WAY IN WHICH the information in the K.I.S.S. *Guide to the Kama Sutra is arranged may surprise you, in that sex positions come before the advice on courtship and seduction – but this is exactly how the original book was set out.*

PART ONE

Part One looks at the history of the *Kama Sutra* and the philosophy behind Vatsyayana's writings. We'll be finding out how the Indian classic reached the Western world, how it created a storm in Victorian times, and how the *Kama Sutra* has remained popular as our attitudes to sex have changed.

PART TWO

In Part Two, we'll focus on the physical build-up to sex. The *Kama Sutra* was very clear on the importance of cleanliness, so we'll be talking about preparing the body and setting the scene for your tryst. Then we'll move on to find out how to caress, touch, and kiss your partner into a frenzy of desire.

PART THREE

This is the part for which the *Kama Sutra* is most famous: the love positions. I'll take you through the wide variety of postures described by Vatsyayana – from the simple to the more convoluted – and to complement these, you'll also find poses featured from two more classic books, the *Ananga Ranga* and *The Perfumed Garden*.

PART FOUR

In Part Four we leave the physical behind and focus on seducing the emotions. Find out how to build trust and confidence in a partner and inflame their desire. Vatsyayana also gives advice on dealing with multiple wives and conducting affairs, aspects of which, despite being far-removed from our present-day lives, still have some relevance today.

PART FIVE

In Part Five we'll look at the skills taught by the *Kama Sutra* that have stood the test of time. We'll discover the importance of understanding your partner's character and two-way communication and find out about ancient (and modern) treatments for sexual health problems. Finally, we'll learn why the *Kama Sutra* is still so relevant today.

The Extras

THROUGHOUT THE BOOK, *you will notice a number of boxes and symbols. They are there to emphasize certain points I want you to pay special attention to, because they are important to your understanding and improvement. You'll find:*

Very Important Point

This symbol points out a topic I believe deserves careful attention. You really need to know this information before continuing.

Complete No-No

This is a warning, something I want to advise you not to do or to be aware of.

Getting Technical

When the information is about to get a bit technical, I'll let you know so that you can read carefully.

Inside Scoop

These are special suggestions and pieces of information that come from the wisdom of my experience.

You'll also find some little boxes that include information I think is important, useful, or just plain fun.

Trivia...

These are simply fun facts that will give you an extra appreciation of the uniqueness of the Kama Sutra.

DEFINITION

Here I'll define words and terms for you in an easy-to-understand style. You'll also find a glossary at the back of the book packed with useful terms.

INTERNET

www.dk.com

Since this is the computer age, I've scouted out some web sites that will add to your understanding of the Kama Sutra and sexual issues.

PART ONE

THE *KAMA SUTRA* IS A CLASSIC MIX OF SEX AND POETRY

WHAT IS THE KAMA SUTRA?

TODAY'S SEX MANUALS are designed to appeal to men and women who want to experience joyful, satisfactory sexual relationships. These sensual human beings live in many different parts of the world, but share a common desire – to experience *great sex*.

The *Kama Sutra* is no different from the present-day volumes that seek to help us improve and enhance an already enjoyable sex life. The original readers of the *Kama Sutra* were not much different to us – they simply lived in the 4th century rather than in the 21st. Yet why should one particular sex book survive over so many centuries? Perhaps the great secret of its success lies in its *extraordinary poetic* descriptions – they have made this early work a great *classic* of all time.

Chapter 1

The Story of the Book

THE *KAMA SUTRA* IS FIRMLY rooted in ancient Indian tradition, which revered sex as a sacred practice. As a result, the idea that sex can bring you closer to heaven if you are lucky enough to do it really well is always in the background. Yet there's also a well-grounded aspect to the book. At the time that this great classic was written, sex was believed to be one of the keystones of personal success. In practical terms, this meant that if you wanted a brilliant career, you needed to enjoy a superb love life.

In this chapter...

✓ Who wrote the Kama Sutra?

✓ The golden age of Indian history

✓ Who was the Kama Sutra written for?

✓ The women who stood to gain from men's karma

THE *KAMA SUTRA* WAS COMPILED PRIMARILY TO INSTRUCT MEN IN THE SKILLS OF LOVE

Who wrote the Kama Sutra?

THE KAMA SUTRA was written by not one but many authors and has been edited often, throughout time. The most famous editor, named Vatsyayana, is thought to have lived some time between AD 100–400. His book forms the basis of the many versions we see on sale today.

The Kama Sutra is a compilation of writings by various authors about sex. It is not a pornographic book but a simple statement of how sex — one of the most important aspects of ancient Indian life — can be enjoyed. The book, in its present form, has endured for at least 1,600 years and is regarded as one of the great Indian classics.

Vatsyayana

Unfortunately we don't know much about Vatsyayana, but we can make some educated guesses. He appears to have been an educated Brahmin and probably lived in the city of Pataliputra at a time of cultural renaissance during an era known as the Gupta period.

Vatsyayana collected writings about sex that had been transcribed some 600–700 years previously. Deciding it was time they were brought up to date, he reworked them into the order and format that are still familiar to readers today. In fact, without Vatsyayana's skill in knowing what to bring to young people's attention, the individual books and papers would have faded into obscurity.

INTERNET

www.bibliomania.com /2/1/76/123/flameset. html

www.here-now4u. de/.eng/the_kamasutra_ of_vatsyayana.htm

Bibliomania's site provides literature from all over the world for free, including the Kama Sutra. Click on here-now4u's web address to read an overall view of the book.

The Vedas

The information that formed the basis of the *Kama Sutra* was the *Vedas*. *Vedas* were wise maxims that were passed by word of mouth in the absence of writing skills. Due to a wave of Aryan invasions much earlier in India's history, the ability to write had been lost and didn't make a comeback

> **DEFINITION**
>
> *A Brahmin was a priest; next to the king, Brahmins made up the highest social class in Hindu India. Brahmins were venerated because people believed that they were "purer" than members of other castes and that they alone were capable of performing certain vital religious tasks. Because of their high prestige and learning, Brahmins wielded influence, not only in religious circles but in all spheres. Even today Brahmins are still priests, particularly in southern India.*

until about 800 BC. When literacy re-emerged, the *Vedas* were written down on paper. Its various authors probably included Nandi, Babhru, Dattaka, and several others. The basic texts that concern the quality and aims of life were the *Artha Shastra, Dharma Shastra,* and the *Kama Shastra*. These were the writings that Vatsyayana used as his source material more than 900 years later.

Why republish?

If, today, you were to look back 900 years to the 1100s – well before the time of William Shakespeare – would you be able to make head or tail of a jumble of papers written in a medieval dialect? I think not. So Vatsyayana, understanding the value of his predecessors' penmanship, took the trouble to update the sexual words of wisdom so that his friends and contemporaries might have as much fun with them as possible.

The golden age of Indian history

VATSYAYANA'S TIMES WERE RATHER SIMILAR to our 1960s, a decade when sex was openly and freely discussed. In the Western world, this was a period when people were willing to experiment sexually and generally wanted to know a lot more about sex. In Vatsyayana's day, the climate was similarly liberal and experimental.

Vatsyayana's *Kama Sutra* was compiled during a time of fabulous riches and great economic growth. Farmers grew rice, wheat, ginger, melons, mustard, peaches, apricots, and other tropical fruits. Industrialists were involved in textile manufacturing, copper-smithing, jewel-setting, and woodworking.

All these luxury goods were traded with countries such as China, Arabia, Persia, and beyond.

AN INDIAN COURTING SCENE

In order for sex to be openly regarded, it is vital that there is accepted tolerance of all things liberal. This is exactly what happened in Vatsyayana's day. There was such religious tolerance that Brahmins became highly powerful, and individuals like Vatsyayana were so respected that they could make major cultural decisions. Vatsyayana's own cultural contribution was to compile a sex "bible."

Compiling and publishing the Kama Sutra was a decision of daring and courage on Vatsyayana's part. Even though sexuality was regarded matter-of-factly by the ancient Indians, devoting an entire volume to sex (and how to do it) must have been a challenge.

INTERNET

www.historyofindia.
com/gupta.html

Find out more about the cultural climate in India in Vatsyayana's time – the Gupta era – when literature and learning flourished.

THE MONARCHY — AND ITS SINISTER SIDE

The monarchs of Vatsyayana's time enjoyed a lavish lifestyle. The king was supreme head of state with power of life and death over his subjects. He possessed huge, elegant palaces equipped with fountains, baths, and toilets; he wore many jewels, and perfumed himself with musk and sandalwood. It comes as a surprise therefore to hear about one of the more extraordinary royal customs of the time.

This was a custom that one of the kings during Vatsyayana's lifetime attempted to revive. It was called the *Ashvamedha* which, translated, means "the royal horse

sacrifice." The king's horse was allowed to roam free for a year (dogged by a retinue of priests, soldiers, and grooms) and any land it wandered across was claimed for the king. After a year the horse was killed.

The chief queen was then expected to copulate with the late horse, making coarse and disparaging remarks about the animal's sexual performance. The ladies of the court stood round in a circle, slapping their thighs, and shouting unrepeatable remarks. The Buddhists gathered their courage and objected to this black practice. Unsurprisingly, it was abandoned.

A COURT SCENE

Who was the Kama Sutra written for?

IN THE 21ST CENTURY, *sex manuals are written for men and women who enjoy sex and who want to continue enjoying it. They desire to learn new ideas and new sexual positions; they are happy to discover good psychological reasons for their specific type of sexual behavior and if there is a possibility that all*

this pleasure in the body may lead to a spirituality of the mind, then an ecstatic revelation is particularly welcome. The Kama Sutra would have been written for men and women with very similar ideas about life to ours.

The young male reader was a wealthy, fashionable, educated noble or member of the merchant class known as a *nagaraka*. He would have worn dazzling jewels, fine clothes, and lived in luxurious surroundings in a house likely to have been designed and built by him. His garden would have been full of flowers and exotically colored caged birds, with swings under shady trees, fountains, and pools.

■ The *Kama Sutra* was written primarily for Indian noblemen and wealthy merchants so that they could educate themselves and their women on the art of lovemaking.

The nagaraka was so highly groomed that he would be considered out-of-the-ordinary today: he probably dyed his hair, certainly used cosmetics and toothpicks, and carried parasols and umbrellas for protection against the burning sun and monsoon rains.

The Indian good life

The *nagaraka* had a busy life. In the morning he would take the first of several daily baths. His servants dabbed paste scented with sandalwood or musk on his body, applied black eyeliner, and stained his lips with berry juice. He was then ready for his morning's work, which consisted of inspecting his game fowl, painting a little, and directing the preparation of lunch.

During the afternoon the *nagaraka* visited his friends, with whom he read poetry or engaged in philosophical debate. Or he attended ram, quail, or cock fights. Picnics, garden parties, and country rides were further afternoon activities, as were religious gatherings and meetings of his club.

Today's parallels

Not all the young male readers of the *Kama Sutra* were as indolent as the *nagaraka*. Those of the merchant class worked, yet probably aspired to becoming a *nagaraka*. These days the equivalent is the successful young career man, who earns a comfortable amount of money, drives a luxury sports car, wines and dines at the trendiest restaurants, dates a gorgeous model, and wears Armani suits.

■ **The modern equivalent** *of the Indian nobleman or* nagaraka *would be a successful career man with a wide range of interests and a cosmopolitan lifestyle.*

Where sex fitted in

In the evening the *nagaraka* relaxed by listening to or playing music. Drinking bouts, in the company of lovely courtesans, helped soothe nerves shredded by his exhausting routine. If he enjoyed a special relationship with a *courtesan*, the couple would have made love – busy social life permitting.

Girls who were destined to become courtesans were put on a special diet that was thought to make them beautiful and give them a graceful temperament. The wealthy also ate and drank well. Upper-class women were said to knock back wine in quantities!

The sex profile of the 4th-century AD reader

We know a lot about the background of the eager lover but what do we know about his personal character? Naturally every young man differs from the next but it is possible to guess at some of the characteristics of these wealthy individuals so that we can build up a psychological profile.

As a male child, a boy would have been treasured and probably spoiled. Since a woman's role was to be caring and supportive to her men, the child would have been used to his mother choosing the best food for him, and catering immediately to his physical and emotional needs. If it were not his mother's place to do these things, it would certainly have been his *ayah's*.

 Male children *in the 4th century would have been indulged and cosseted by all members of their household.*

The mother's boy generally grew up to be a macho man. This was perfectly normal for the 4th-century male. The *Kama Sutra* reader expected his women to serve him – including in bed. His women would have been compliant, willing, and agreeable to every experiment he wanted to try. Women were required to be faithful to men, but men would not expect to offer fidelity in return.

A sensitive and skilled lover

Part of being a 4th-century macho man was about being an extremely skilled lover. This involved wooing a young woman with great sensitivity. She would have been taught lovemaking, shown how to be responsive, and given an amazing time in bed. This was the woman's bonus for being subservient.

And what did *he* get out of all this technique and careful instruction? On a physical level he taught his bride how to pleasure him. This meant that he would end up being treated (by her) to just about every favorite touch and sexual position he could imagine. It also meant that as his sexual sensitivity changed over the years, she would be taught how to stimulate him more strongly so that he could continue to get a good erection and enjoy intercourse – even as he began to find this difficult.

As men age, their testosterone levels begin to fall. The outcome of this change is that sexual desire is muted, sexual arousal takes longer, and sensitivity is blunted. When ejaculation arrives – finally – there's less semen and possibly less sensation. (Viagra, of course, is available to modern men and mitigates these problems.)

The women who stood to gain from men's karma

TODAY'S WOMEN gain status from their own achievements. They expect to earn a living and support themselves, find and furnish their own home, and to co-finance their children if they choose to marry. All this fundamental underpinning of money gives women power. Instead of feeling overwhelmed or forced to obey, today's women are strong enough to challenge their men.

In the 4th century AD however, things were rather different. Women acquired an identity only through their association with men. Marriage might be the beginning of forming a more independent character but the woman would always have to put her man first.

Eventually, by running her own household, a woman gained scope to expand her own interests as well as cater for those of others.

■ **Women today** *gain recognition and respect through their own efforts rather than through those of their husband, as was the case in the 4th century AD.*

DEFINITION

Purdah is the separation of the female members of a household from the men. In practical terms, this meant that they occupied separate portions of a house or compound and had little or no contact with males.

Women's freedom

Well-born women in Vatsyayana's day did enjoy an exceptional amount of freedom, compared to their counterparts in more ancient days. Their counterparts were not educated, were expected to live in *purdah*, and had virtually no freedom. In contrast, around the 4th century AD girls were encouraged to read history, legends, and poetry. They also wrote verses, sang and danced, and mastered some of the skills men acquired, such as riding and fencing.

As you will read in Chapter 2, a good sex life was considered to be a component part of a successful lifestyle. The better a woman felt she was able to please her man and the more she could actually see his enjoyment, the more successful she might consider herself. She would be viewed as actually contributing to his riches in life.

The 4th-century recipients of the sexual wisdom imparted by the Kama Sutra must have had wonderful times in bed. By the time they had worked their way through scratching, kissing, biting, and then on to the huge variety of sex positions outlined, they must have fully understood what it was to be greatly aroused.

A simple summary

✔ The *Kama Sutra* was written as a sex manual for young men of leisure and wealth.

✔ The author of the *Kama Sutra*, Vatsyayana, was actually an editor who compiled the ancient *Vedas* on sex and skillfully updated them.

✔ The publication of this unusual book was made possible by the extremely tolerant cultural climate of the time.

✔ The young male reader, although a macho male, was well regarded if he was also a sensitive and skilled lover.

✔ Female recipients of erotic wisdom benefited from much improved sex and a sense that they were emotionally and physically contributing to their family's status.

Chapter 2

The Philosophy Behind the Scripts

THE *KAMA SUTRA* WAS NOT MERELY a sex manual, nor a book solely about social and sexual etiquette. Behind it lay a wider philosophy. The concept of *kama*, on which the book is based, is part of a much greater whole. And this particular whole amounts to "a striving to be a superior person." What's more, although the philosophy had its feet firmly on the ground, what developed from it was a type of spirituality. When, seven centuries later, the notion of Tantra evolved, its teachings were firmly rooted in the great sex manual.

In this chapter...

✓ Sexual spirituality and Tantra

✓ Dharma: Taking moral responsibility

✓ Artha: The acquisition of wealth

✓ Kama: The way to sensual pleasure

THE ACQUISITION OF LOVE WAS ONE OF THREE GOALS TO WHICH THE 4TH-CENTURY CITIZEN ASPIRED

Sexual spirituality and Tantra

TANTRA HOLDS A SPECIAL meaning in the Indian belief system. It embraces just about every part of civilized life. It takes in Tantric art, religion, philosophy, and sex. There are many ways in which Tantra can be experienced, but it's difficult to describe in exact or precise terms because beliefs differ so widely. But there's one central belief that links all these other parts together – the notion of ecstasy.

The meaning of Tantric ecstasy

One of the ideas of the Brahmins (remember Vatsyayana was a Brahmin) was that our real world is an illusion with snares in it that prevent us from experiencing the ultimate Truth. In essence, *Tantra* agrees with this philosophy. But what is the "ultimate Truth?" It is considered to be the experience of Being. If you think of yourself as a teacher, a writer, or even as a human being, you are falling into a trap. Rather you must just *Be*. And you must experience yourself as *Being*.

Try it. It's hard to do. Some might say impossible. But others … and this is where the spirituality comes in … believe you can totally clear the mind and "be flooded with a consuming (yet abstract) version of the Truth." If you are able to achieve this extraordinary mind state, the theory is that your entire mind will be stilled and be at one with the Universe.

In experiencing the "ultimate Truth," your nature ceases to be human and becomes part of an all-inclusive consciousness that is both Being and Bliss.

■ **The point of Tantric sex** *is to aim at merging yourself ecstatically with your partner and, through him or her, with the rest of the world.*

Where Tantra radically diverges from the old Brahmin beliefs, however, is that it encourages the experience of life through its great joys – one of the most potent manifestations of great joy being . . . great sex. In contrast, the Brahmins focused on the horrors of life. They encouraged you to look on the disgusting parts of your own body such as your feces, urine, or even phlegm, and then use these horrors to dissociate yourself from the appalling "real" world. Ugh! What a way to aim at Bliss!

Back to our roots

Although Tantric ideas evolved several centuries after the *Kama Sutra* was compiled, *Tantra* is important because it draws on the notion that if you can do sex really well, you can somehow become a better person. And this idea is the basis of the great sex manual.

So we come to understand that the *Kama Sutra* can be used on several different levels:

 1 You can enjoy good sex for what it is

2 You can take pride and stature from believing you are a good lover

3 And maybe, just maybe, you might be lucky enough to have such an extraordinary sexual experience that you truly feel you are grasping a little bit of heaven

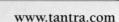

INTERNET

www.tantra.com

Click here for articles and advice on Tantra, details on Tantra workshops, plus a section for beginners.

Today's Tantra

So what's the idea behind *Tantra* today? Put succinctly, it is that you can achieve that ecstatic sense of Being through marvelous sex. When sexuality reaches an almost timeless state, where every movement and every caress feels otherworldly, then you are nearing Heaven. Whether anyone can truly manage to do this through the kind of Tantric regimen recommended for the purpose is debatable. There are some lovers who believe that following *any* kind of prescribed lovemaking is more likely to handicap them than to lead them to nirvana.

Having said that, when you read just what a Tantric routine might consist of, you will probably agree that it certainly couldn't hurt and might, in fact, be a wonderfully pleasurable activity.

■ **Discipline and spirituality** *are important to Tantric sex practices, which when done properly can involve some hard work.*

A TANTRIC SEX ROUTINE

One of the points of the following exercise is to merge your own sense of identity and feelings with those of your partner's so that eventually it is as though you have become one. The first part of the exercise echoes the "touch for pleasure's sake" principle. But the next part moves on to something altogether more profound; something capable of touching the spirit as well as the body.

A much longer explanation of this exercise is to be found in *The Ultimate Sex Guide* by Anne Hooper (listed at the back of the book).

Here's what to do with your partner over a long weekend.

1 Spend Friday going for walks, getting to know each other, and relaxing together.

2 On Saturday, spend the morning lightly stroking and caressing one another's naked bodies (no intercourse). Eat a light lunch, then repeat the stroking in the afternoon – but this time, imagine that every touch you are bestowing on your partner can be felt by you.

3 On Sunday morning, stroke each other all over and continue to feel your partner's strokes as if they were yours. After an hour, move on to inserting the penis into the vagina. Don't launch into fully-fledged intercourse but lie there peacefully until his erection has subsided. In the afternoon, repeat the morning's exercise again for about an hour – but then go for a long, slow intercourse in which the man holds back until his partner reaches orgasm.

■ **The aim of the tantric sex** *routine is to build up the ability to enjoy your partner's sensations so that the man can stay aroused during his partner's pleasure without coming to orgasm himself.*

Dharma: Taking moral responsibility

THE THREE TENETS *by which the right-thinking young man of the 4th century lived were* dharma, artha, *and* kama. *We now know that* kama *is the acquisition of love or sensual pleasure. So what is* dharma? *In Sanskrit,* dharma *means righteousness – and the various* Dharma Sutras *of the time were literally manuals of human conduct with an emphasis on the law.*

■ **Living by the code** *of* dharma *meant that a man had to take moral and material responsibility for his close female relatives.*

Dharma was not only concerned with the dry, dusty aspects of the law, but was (and is) a moral concept that was firmly grounded in daily life and involved taking full responsibility. For example, a man took responsibility for his women – close female relatives – who were perpetually under his guardianship and had to be protected from harm, moral as well as material. At the top of the "male chain of leadership" was the king who, in representing the state, was supposed to take responsibility for everyone. It was through giving out good *dharma* to his household, and in particular to his wife, that a young man could gain both spiritual and worldly status.

A young husband was simply not allowed to be irresponsible. In spite of this, however, many young men never climbed very high on the dharman ladder!

When the British first came to understand *dharma* at the beginning of the 19th century, they were deeply suspicious of what they saw as a religious system of keeping the lower *castes* under control. Eventually, they came to appreciate the written system of *dharma* as being equal to great Roman law or even early English law, both of which they rated highly.

DEFINITION

The Indian class system is made up of castes, *which are indicated by a mark worn on the forehead. You can be of high caste or low caste in this Hindu social order, and to lose caste means to take a step down the social ladder. Traditionally, lower caste people are expected to do the dirty work of a society such as being a street sweeper while those of high castes are the priests and scholars.*

Although the British showed respect for the ideas of *dharma*, in ruling India during the days of the Raj they affected its use by applying it as a very hard and fast system. They found themselves instigating many social changes because *dharma* "law" needed substantial updating. Even as late as 1955, it made no provision for legal divorce nor did it allot equal shares to daughters along with sons in the event of a father's death.

Because there were so many "black holes" in dharma "law," a new legal system had to be invented. It was just too complicated to write additional texts and interweave them with the old. As a result, the Sanskrit language and old Hindu ideas are dying out as they are replaced with modern notions about how life "ought" to be lived.

WHAT IS THE DHARMA OF THE WEST?

Westerners today have a strong concept of responsibility but it is aimed largely towards ourselves. We believe that we should take care of those nearest to us, but this is no longer solely the man's responsibility – it is shared equally between the sexes. The "me"-focused belief system of the past 20 years means that responsibility also takes the shape of getting to know ourselves better. We believe in self-growth; gaining general knowledge and self-knowledge.

But we are also moving back toward the old idea of the state taking responsibility for us. Just as the 4th-century *Kama Sutra* readers would have expected the king to look out for them, today we expect the big organizations in charge of our lives to be responsible for us. The rapid growth of a legal system devoted, for example, to suing the local authority if we trip over broken paving on a sidewalk and hurt a leg, bears witness to this. Perhaps we feel collectively that if we are "nannied", we gain more time for self-growth?

■ **In the West today** *we believe that men and women should take equal responsibility for family members.*

Artha: The acquisition of wealth

IN SANSKRIT, the word artha means wealth or property. The fully rounded 4th-century citizen was expected to acquire riches, and young men and women today hope for much the same. In the 21st century, shopping is a popular way of defining ourselves (as well as giving us a lot of fun). Some 1,600 years ago, an extremely luxurious lifestyle served a similar purpose. If you could afford to be clothed in silk, wear fabulous jewels, and live in splendid houses with the latest conveniences (sumptuous baths, perfumed hot water, and many household servants), you were considered successful.

On this superficial level, it doesn't sound as though *artha* had much to do with a spiritual life. But it had. It was linked to a spiritual system because it was considered to be a necessary ingredient of *moksha*. The 4th-century man believed that material wellbeing was one of the necessities of life – hence his desire to gain wealth. But riches were not by any means a quick fix – just for feeling good in the here and now. They were important because without them, our man couldn't really respect himself: he knew he wouldn't have achieved the all-important *moksha*.

> **DEFINITION**
>
> Moksha *means liberation, or a spiritual release from life.*

In practical terms, the young householder had a spiritual incentive for acquiring a modern home, furniture, and all the trappings. He would have ensured that his wife, parents, and children benefited too, since this would satisfy the rules of dharma.

The link between artha, dharma, and sex

It is, of course, perfectly possible to enjoy wonderful, ecstatic sex while owning no worldly goods at all. But good sex is not just of the body, it is also a creation of the mind. Security of mind plays its part. Most of us need to feel secure about ourselves in at least one major aspect of life in order to relax. And in order to be sensual we need to feel free of stress. Men and women who are subject to major stress (because, for example, they think they are about to lose their job) will testify to going off sex in a big way. A high level of stress and loss of sexual inspiration are linked. So stocking up on *artha* and *dharma* makes sense both sensually and materially. It shores up our sex lives.

Stress is enemy number one. It's important to avoid it as much as possible.

So how is it that many individuals who don't possess much money still manage to have a great love life? Shouldn't this disprove the power of *artha*? If you delve into the background of such people you will find that they have acquired confidence from some other aspect of life. Perhaps they've reaped the benefits of good parenting, or perhaps it's the knowledge that they are loved. Sometimes such confidence even comes from sex itself.

Kama: The way to sensual pleasure

IN ORDER TO SURVIVE *in life you need material goods (artha). In order to survive as a tribe or community of people you need a moral code (dharma). Finally, in order to assure the survival of the species you need eroticism (kama). Eroticism is the inspiration for sexuality. The goal of sex, according to the ancient Indians, was to attain such extended paroxysms of delight that the pleasure became infinite. This is much like the Tantric concept of ecstasy.*

Trivia...
Extraordinary erotic carvings can still be seen on many Indian temples, including some that have now been claimed back by jungle. These images depict heterosexual couples entwined in just about every snake-like pose imaginable. Yet there are some carvings, featuring lesbians, homosexuals, transvestites, and animals that many people consider to have gone a tad too far. Paradoxically, the presence of transvestites at an Indian wedding is still considered to spell good luck – even today.

■ **Achieving heightened** *sensual pleasure was a sought-after goal in 4th-century India.*

The eroticism described in the *Kama Sutra* and depicted in ancient temple carvings and sculptures is a legacy of the freedom and open-mindedness of that time. Modern India has largely rejected this sexual openness and now looks upon its erotic inheritance with shame. Mahatma Gandhi, educated in England, felt so strongly about the temple carvings that he sent troops of his disciples to obliterate them.

This narrow-minded repression doesn't seem to have spread to rural areas of India yet. You can still see sexually explicit paintings on village houses, while erotic drawings are sometimes inscribed on pottery for weddings because these are, by tradition, reckoned to spell good luck!

■ **Erotic carved figures** *can still be seen on temples throughout India and serve as a reminder of the incredibly liberal sexual climate of the time.*

Asians living in North America often give copies of the Kama Sutra to young brides as wedding or engagement presents!

A simple summary

✓ *Tantra* is based on some of the beliefs of the 4th-century Brahmins.

✓ Tantric sex, while ultimately a spiritual sex practice, takes its practical basis from ancient sex writings such as the *Kama Sutra*.

✓ Sex (*kama*) is part of a complete system of beliefs that includes *dharma* (moral responsibility) and *artha* (the acquisition of riches).

✓ If you manage to learn and understand *dharma*, *artha*, and *kama*, you can then aspire to *moksha*, the spiritual release from life, or liberation.

✓ All of these ideas are still valid today.

Chapter 3

The Kama Sutra's Journey West

TODAY WE TAKE IT FOR GRANTED that we should know all about this great erotic Indian classic. Yet there are hundreds of esoteric sex practices and beliefs from the world of the East that we still don't have a clue about. So why should this particular sex manual be the one we get to hear of? How did it reach us from thousands of miles away in the East? And how did it actually travel from East to West?

In this chapter...

✓ The crusaders – medieval sex tourists

✓ Richard Burton – the explorer, not the movie star

✓ Sex and the middle-class Victorians

THE *KAMA SUTRA* INTRODUCED THE IDEA OF EXOTIC SEXUAL BEHAVIOUR TO THE VICTORIANS

The crusaders – medieval sex tourists

IF YOU THOUGHT THAT TOURISM was a 20th-century phenomenon, think again. You might be surprised to learn that from medieval times onward, Europeans were great travelers: trading, fighting, and making the most of the local amenities, including the sexual ones. Thanks to the crusaders (those knights who galloped off to the Holy Land to fight holy wars), strange new ideas about sexual habits began to filter back to the families left behind.

Trivia...

Norman castles were huge, cold, filthy, and drafty. The nobility slept in alcoves curtained off from the great hall (there was no solid wall) while the rest of the household slept on the other side of the curtain. The toilets were crude and the sexual parts of the body none too clean. Women were expected to be virgins when they married and, if discovered in adultery, would be subjected to severe punishment, even death. They were therefore kept sexually naïve. Men, on the other hand, did just about anything they chose, and would have had fairly brutal relationships with social inferiors such as servants. None of this would have been conducive to a life of eroticism.

Who were the crusaders?

The Crusaders were northern European nobles (especially those with restless and ruthless Norman blood) who were motivated (around 1095 AD) to travel far abroad for various reasons. The main reason given, partly as public relations, was that they were fighting holy battles on behalf of Christianity. They were, they let it be known, riding to overcome the *infidels*.

A less well-publicized but significant reason for the nobles to leave their native countries and ride thousands of miles was their desire to grab land and get rich. The Normans of the north were supposed to obey their northern kings and act within an agreed set of laws. But seeing relatives establish themselves in southern kingdoms like Sicily, they too wanted a piece of the action.

DEFINITION

The infidels, in medieval days, were peoples of the Islamic East. These included Arab, Turcoman, Kurdish, Jewish, and other cultures.

Where did they travel?

When the crusaders went east, they encountered two alien cultures, both of which they regarded with the utmost suspicion. The Byzantine empire, encompassing Turkey and much of the land beyond, was ruled by an emperor who was a Christian of sorts, but to the unsophisticated visitors he seemed to live in an unspeakably decadent fashion.

For the first time, the northern Europeans saw upperclass people wearing flowing robes of silk. These potentates perfumed themselves, took baths, and believed in living as comfortably as possible. The emperor lolled on a golden throne with arms shaped like open-jawed lions. What astonished the unsuspecting knights was that the lions were devised so that wind organs made them appear to roar. Worst of all, the Byzantines managed to live fairly peacefully with Islamic neighbors, a highly suspect practice in itself.

The other alien culture was that of the Islamic East. Once settled in their newly conquered kingdoms here, the crusaders were soon living like natives.

■ **The crusaders** *ventured east in the name of religion to battle with the infidels and were eventually captivated by the world of opulence and exoticism they found.*

An introduction to fine living

They learned to avoid wearing thick northern clothing in the sun, to keep clean, and to avoid disease – very new ideas indeed. They developed a taste for fine clothing, spices, music, and even scholarly pursuits. For example, the barons hired scholars to read them stories!

It was in the East that the crusading nobles first began to understand the notion of courtesy – and stirrings of what was later to become a highly elaborate code of chivalry began to develop.

INTERNET

www.islamcity.com/
education/ihame/10.asp

Click here for more information on the history of the crusaders.

What did the crusaders learn about sex?

As far as the crusaders were concerned, sex had been a rapid screwing to beget heirs. Now they began to visit courtesans and dancers for their pleasure and were, for the first time, introduced to erotic techniques. They began to see the appeal of keeping a mistress as well as a wife. They would have seen, or at least heard of, the great harems of the infidels and would have begun to understand the notion that sex might compose the major part of a lifestyle. But their sexual encounters were taking place in physical circumstances a world apart from those rough-and-ready castles back home.

What did the Crusaders bring home?

Many of the crusaders, reluctant to give up their luxurious and exotic comforts, stayed away for many years. When they finally returned, the culture shock was extreme enough to make the travelers intent on improvements. Some very new sex practices were introduced. A notion arose that washing regularly was not wholly unpleasant. Bath houses, both private and public, appeared in France and soon accrued a bad reputation because naked men and women, often strangers, would be in close proximity and were known to stray into one another's areas! The words for "brothel" and "bath-house" were synonymous at one time. There was even a brisk trade in woodcuts, the sought-after pornography of the age, that depicted couples in these baths.

Poetry and music were imported, and troubadours and the idea of courtly love flourished. Western clerics, scholars, and literary men read handbooks on medical matters – including sexual health – penned by the Arabs, who were considered masters of medicine.

New information about sex gained ground in the rough Northern hemisphere. In medieval times, there was an explosion of culture, hygiene, romance, and much better lovemaking.

■ **The northern nobles** *not only brought home plundered riches but a new outlook on sex and the art of lovemaking.*

Richard Burton – the explorer, not the movie star

THE NEXT IMPORTANT CHARACTER *to arrive on the scene was the great Victorian explorer, Sir Richard Burton. Born in 1821, Burton was a member of the English-Irish upper-class. His father was a British army officer who brought up his family in a number of different European countries. As a result Burton learned several languages, the foundation for his subsequent skill as a great linguist.*

SIR RICHARD BURTON

At a very early age, thanks to his itinerant father, he grew used to wandering and felt far happier in the less rigid society of the southern Mediterranean than he did in an overformal, desperately correct England. He became a daring and famous explorer of his time, traveling as far afield as Africa, India, Arabia, and South America. He was an erudite scholar (he had originally studied at Oxford University, but dropped out) and, working for the Foreign Office, was eventually appointed English consul, first in West Africa but eventually, and most famously, in Damascus. His considerable achievements as an explorer brought him into contact with many different cultures and peoples.

What distinguished Sir Richard Burton from his contemporaries was that he noticed the social and sexual customs of the peoples he encountered and was unafraid to write and talk about them. This sounds odd in the sexually liberated 21st century, but in Victorian days it was extraordinary.

INTERNET

www.isidore-of-seville.com/burton/index.html

Visit this site for information about the life and travels of the explorer Sir Richard Burton.

During his travels in the near and far East during the 1850s, Burton became fascinated by all things erotic. It was he who translated the *1001 Tales of Arabian Nights*, which was to become a Victorian bestseller. The book appeared in two editions: one was fit for "nice" consumption, while an unexpurgated version profoundly shocked many of its readers.

Burton's sexual lifestyle

On his early travels as a young man Burton was known to have a beautiful Indian mistress. In her biography of Richard Burton, Mary Lovell quotes one of his poems about the "marriage" that he had enjoyed, like other fellow officers, in Baroda. Here are the first lines:

> I loved – yes, I! Ah, let me tell
> The fatal charms by which I fell!
> Her form the tam'risk's waving shoot,
> Her breast the cocoa's youngling fruit.

When Burton later came to write his notorious sex books, he mischievously described the Indian woman's famous vaginal control, saying it could be so extreme as to hurt the male's feelings!

During Burton's travels in India he was fascinated to hear about the ancient documents that composed the Indian writings on sexuality. Consumed with curiosity to know what such tomes had to say on the subject, and keen to make this esoterica available to interested subscribers, he and a colleague arranged for their translation.

The production of a masterpiece

Burton's younger colleague, Forster Fitzgerald Arbuthnot, worked in the Indian Civil Service. He was only 20 when he met the 30-year-old Burton, and was impressed and fascinated by the older man. Although not as blatantly unconventional as Burton, it was he who initially found two Sanskrit scholars to translate the *Kama Sutra* and then set about rewriting their faulty narrative. Burton, on seeing his young colleague's leaden prose, did a final revision himself to bring life and energy to the pages.

To publish a work about sex in England without being thrown into jail was a difficult hurdle for the pair to overcome. In order to avoid criminal prosecution (such books would have fallen foul of the Obscene Publications Act of 1857), Burton and Arbuthnot were forced to form a society which they named the *Kama Shastra* Society. The declared intention of the *Kama Shastra* Society was the translation of rare and important texts concerned with love and sex. Since such publications could only be sold to Society members, the editors were protected.

DEFINITION

Shastra *means scripture or doctrines.*

Trivia...

The Kama Shastra Society published several of Sir Richard Burton's sex titles. These included the Kama Sutra, *the* Ananga Ranga, *and* The Perfumed Garden. *By the time of Richard Burton's death, there were waiting lists of subscribers to the forthcoming titles.*

THE KAMA SUTRA'S RIVALS

The *Kama Sutra* wasn't the only great Eastern treatise on sex. It had two main rivals, which are still available today. The first, the *Ananga Ranga*, shared common origins with the *Kama Sutra* but wasn't turned into book form until about 1,000 years after the *Kama Sutra*, probably in the late 15th or early 16th century. By this time, society in India had become far more ordered than in Vatsyayana's day when sexuality was freely expressed. So by the time the *Ananga Ranga* was compiled, extramarital sex was censured. The major difference between the two Indian classics was that the *Kama Sutra* was written for lovers, married or otherwise, while the *Ananga Ranga* offered instruction to married men. The author's motive for writing the *Ananga Ranga* was to protect marriage from the sexual tedium that then, as now, can so easily set in.

The *Ananga Ranga* translates as meaning "Stage of the Bodiless One," a reference to the story of how Kama, the Hindu god of love, became a bodiless spirit when his physical body was burned to a pile of ashes by a stare from the third eye of the god Shiva.

Because the *Ananga Ranga* was translated into Arabic, it also exerted a very strong influence on the sexual attitudes of the Islamic world. The book appeared shortly before the start of the crusades and was probably brought back to Europe in the fighting knights' luggage.

■ **The actions of the god Shiva,** *seen bearing gifts (right) in this Indian carving, helped inspire the title of the* Ananga Ranga.

The *Kama Sutra*'s second main rival, *The Perfumed Garden*, was a 16th-century Arabian sex manual, written by Sheik Nefzawi. *The Perfumed Garden* deals with more than just the mechanics of sex: Sheikh Nefzawi also wrote about sensual foods, aphrodisiacs, and the types of men and women he perceived as being sexually desirable.

Although he may not actually have identified the area we now call the G-spot, he had a very good idea of certain sex positions that produced particularly pleasurable sensations in women.

INTERNET

www.parkstpress.com/
titles/kasuilti.htm

Visit this site to order Sir Richard's translation of the three Eastern love texts.

A difficult reception

Burton's books caused a major stir. A Victorian self-appointed "Society for the Suppression of Vice" didn't hesitate to prosecute what it considered to be obscene material. Burton referred to the Society as Mrs. Grundy, and Mrs. Grundy was viewed as a killjoy. However, thanks to their foresight in founding the questionable *Kama Shastra* Society (questionable in that its members consisted only of the two authors), Burton and Arbuthnot managed to avoid prosecution. Unfortunately, this didn't prevent their reputations from suffering.

A sex missionary

Sir Richard Burton might reasonably be described as one of the first sex missionaries. At a time when sex was universally seen as intensely private, something to be kept a dark secret, and when every public expression of sensuality was considered wrong, Burton was a pioneer determined to bring the healthy side of sexuality to the fore.

There have been many sex missionaries since Burton who have risked stigmatization and disapproval in order to educate and enlighten. These include Alfred Kinsey and Masters and Johnson, as well as dozens of perfectly respectable men and women who have chosen to be sex therapists, and even, in a small way, the author of this book.

An unusual marriage

At the age of 40, Richard Burton married Isabel Arundell. Isabel came from an upper-class English family that had temporarily relocated to Boulogne in France in order to save money. It was at social gatherings in this French seaside town that Isabel met and developed a huge crush on Burton. She would witness him entertaining others (usually women) with tales of his daring exploits and exotic travels.

The first time Isabel Arundell set eyes on Richard Burton, she thought him to be the ideal man. Once, after he had danced with her, she kept the sash and gloves she had worn because he had touched them!

Isabel set about reading everything she could about India and, with her considerable intelligence, she very rapidly began to question the role of the conventional Victorian female. It took another six years (of what amounted to a fixation) for Isabel to re-meet Burton, for him to get to like her pretty face and sharp mind, and then for him to propose. The proposal came at a time when Burton had little money and his future was uncertain, but Isabel was prepared to take on absolutely any hardship, so fiercely did she desire him.

BURTON'S WIFE, ISABEL ARUNDELL

It took a special woman to remain married to an extrovert like Burton. His openly declared interest in sex was very unusual for the time, as was his urge to bring sexual esoterica into the open. In addition to Burton's scholarly pursuits, his restlessness, which was channeled into travel and exploration, was also an issue for his wife.

Yet Isabel turned out to be an intrepid character herself; as adventurous as her husband, and whom (letters show) he loved dearly. When separated from one another, they wrote to each other lovingly and it is highly likely that with Burton's passionate interest in sex, he was an inventive and skillful lover.

Although publicly the couple let it be known that Isabel had not read the ancient Indian classics, their private letters reveal that she had. She was not upset by the books, and even laughed at what she considered to be the joke of the *Kama Shastra* Society. What did prove difficult for her was the *opprobrium* that she and her husband ultimately experienced as a result of the *Kama Sutra* publication.

> **DEFINITION**
>
> Opprobrium *means disgrace, reproach, or imputation of shameful conduct, infamy, or anything that brings reproach.*

Burton's close relationships with men spawned debate over his sexual nature, and some people thought him a homosexual. A recently discovered cache of correspondence reveals that he enjoyed a number of heterosexual affairs prior to his marriage. Perhaps he was bisexual. Nevertheless he certainly remained affectionate and appreciative of his wife until he died.

The Scented Garden

The Scented Garden was the title of a proposed new edition of Burton's *The Perfumed Garden*. The original was a translation of a French edition, which had been found in Arabic manuscript by a French army officer in Algiers around the mid-1800s. However, this initial edition was derived from what was believed to be only the first half of the Arabic manuscript. Although Burton tried valiantly to discover the second half of the manuscript, he did not succeed. Nevertheless, by the time of his death, he had virtually completed *The Scented Garden*, which included a highly controversial section on *pederasty*.

> **DEFINITION**
>
> Pederasty *means sexual relations of male with male, often also meaning sex with boys.*

Burton spent many of his last years compiling explicit material on this and other aspects of homosexuality, yet none of it was published. After his death, the original of *The Perfumed Garden* was the edition that was republished and is still on sale today. So what happened to the unfinished revised edition of *The Scented Garden*?

Isabel causes irreparable damage

Burton died in Trieste, Italy, aged 69. Within a few days of his death, his widow, who was her husband's literary executor, went through all his manuscripts. When she came to the controversial *The Scented Garden* manuscript, she burned it, fearing public reaction to a subject matter that was virtually unspeakable in those days (in fact it was illegal and cause for imprisonment).

Not only were subscribers on the waiting list disappointed but several publishers who had stood to gain a lot of money from the book were outraged. No fewer than three publishers subsequently proved untrustworthy, and finally the first book was republished without Isabel's specifically stipulated corrections and alterations. Isabel was enraged but there was little she could do about it. At least the version published did not include the notorious extra section that she had sent up in smoke.

Burton's lasting legacy in the West

Without Sir Richard Burton's courage in bringing sex books to a very stuffy, repressed England, the sexual history of the Western world might have been different. It was partly thanks to Burton 150 years ago that people began to read about and discuss sex, and that others followed his example in publishing erotic reading matter.

It may have taken 150 years to come about, but today's direct conversation about sex derives partly from Richard Burton's courage.

Sex and the middle-class Victorians

OF COURSE BURTON wasn't the only man writing about sex at that time. There were also people like Frank Harris and "Walter." But theirs were personal memoirs rather than nitty-gritty, "how-to" instruction. Not only did the Kama Sutra *introduce the idea of exotic sexual behavior, but even more important, it wrote specifically of doing this with your wife. (Contrary to what many people think about the great Eastern sex manual, little of it actually dwells on specific sex positions and a great deal more on wooing, seducing, and choosing a wife.) For the Victorians, the notion that you might be able to enjoy eroticism with your wife was an eye-opener. Yet this is what the* Kama Sutra *advocated!*

England during the Victorian era was a hotbed of controversy regarding sex, where massive double standards were practiced. These enabled normally hot-blooded Englishmen to appear outwardly respectable. Yet many of these men were privately sexual sometimes to a point of depravity.

■ **The Victorian gentry** *pretended to respectability, even with their wives. Yet outside marriage, they often pursued sexual adventures with lower-class women, such as servants.*

Trivia...

The young Queen Victoria was one woman who didn't conform to the normal sex pattern. She turned out to be exceptionally lucky, being blessed with an easy sexuality and a sensitive husband who actually knew what he was doing in bed. Victoria's enthusiasm for marital sex even became an embarrassment to her prime minister who, poor man, was forced to listen to her enraptured confidences.

At home, well brought-up women were expected to know absolutely nothing about sex. Mothers would have a few words with their daughters prior to their wedding night to let them know that something disgusting would happen when they were left alone with the groom. It was a wife's duty, the young women were told, to submit.

It was during the Victorian era that the immortal line "Lie back and think of England" originated. Not surprisingly, marital sex was often a frightening and even brutal experience. Ignorance was certainly not the best foundation for a loving and passionate marriage, or for sensuality.

The Dickensian prostitutes and brothels

There was also a "depraved" side to Victorian sexuality. In order to fulfill their true sexual desires many Victorian gentlemen visited prostitutes.

INTERNET

www.inform.umd.edu/ ENGL/englfac/WPeters on/VICTORIAN/ weblinks.htm

www.amazon.com/exec/ obidos.ISBN%3D15739 22056/societyforhuman sA/105-7105617- 8333505

To find out more about life in Victorian times, visit William Peterson's site. If you're interested in Victorian erotic literature, click on the Amazon address for details of book sales.

■ **Prostitution** *was rife in Victorian England, and many seemingly respectable gentlemen sought sex with young whores and young male prostitutes.*

Several Victorian sex scandals involved members of the aristocracy and "rent boys" (lower-class boy prostitutes), the case of playwright Oscar Wilde being one of the most notorious. Charles Dickens, the famous novelist, quietly interested in young women himself, wrote euphemistically of these Victorian underclasses.

At one time in Victorian England it was estimated that there were 200,000 female prostitutes (140,000 in London alone). There were thousands of child (girl) prostitutes and London boasted at least one brothel (in Cleveland Street) that provided only boys.

Trivia...

Charles Dickens was a perfect example of the Victorian double standard. In later life, Dickens kept a secret mistress, the young actress Ellen Tiernan. She was forced to live in the strictest privacy because Dickens couldn't afford a whiff of scandal to get out and damage his almost godlike reputation.

A simple summary

✔ The northern Europeans were an uncouth bunch until they met the civilizing influences of the more sophisticated Arabs during the times of the crusades. As a result they cleaned up their castles, washed their bodies, and even began to understand sexual techniques.

✔ The great explorer, Sir Richard Burton, changed the face of sexual history when he brought the ancient *Kama Sutra* from East to West in Victorian times.

✔ Burton had to form a bogus "society" in order to publish material that might otherwise have rendered him open to prosecution.

✔ Even Burton's wife, Isabel, felt distinctly uneasy about his last work on homosexuality and promptly burned his manuscript after her husband died.

✔ Burton's *Kama Sutra* is the forerunner of present-day illustrated sex manuals.

Chapter 4

Modern Times

MODERN TIMES ARE CHANGING TIMES. And attitudes towards sex have changed enormously during the past 40 years. Up until the 1950s, sexual standards were firmly rooted in Victorian customs and beliefs. Men lived by double standards and well-brought-up young women were not expected to be particularly sexual. Thanks to modern contraception, feminism, plus the extraordinary discoveries of sexual pioneers such as Alfred Kinsey and Masters and Johnson, we live in a whole new sexual world. Interestingly, it's a world that still reserves plenty of room for an ancient Indian classic!

In this chapter...

✓ The 1950s and the end of sexual repression

✓ The 1960s and the sexual revolution

✓ The big illustrated sex manuals

✓ A new climate of openness

COUPLES TODAY EXPECT TO ENJOY A FULL AND SATISFYING SEX LIFE

The 1950s and the end of sexual repression

IT SOUNDS STRANGE TODAY, but in the 1950s men and women knew very little about what actually happened during lovemaking. They knew the basics of course, but they were ignorant of what actually happened inside the body. They didn't know that not only might most women experience orgasm but that some were capable of having several in one go; they had no idea that many common sex problems could be overcome; and they understood virtually nothing about homosexuality, transsexualism, or transvestism. The great sex pioneers of the '50s and '60s changed all that.

The shocking Kinsey Report

Biologist Alfred Kinsey specialized in studying the gall wasp. He obsessively recorded statistics about the insect then later applied his detailed methods to studying the sex

lives of humans. You might think his work doesn't sound so unusual. But in the 1940s the study of human sexuality was virtually unheard of. Working in Indiana, Kinsey received thousands of completed sexual questionnaires from large groups of the US population, including prostitutes, and amassed a wealth of previously unrecorded information about the real sex lives of real people.

Kinsey published the results of his studies in two huge volumes: Sexual Behavior of the Human Male (1948) followed by Sexual Behavior of the Human Female (1952).

■ **Alfred Kinsey** *was originally a biologist who eventually became a pioneering figure in the study of human sexuality.*

Kinsey's findings were as follows:

1. Over 96 percent of men masturbated, as did over 85 percent of women

2. Masturbation could help couples adjust to married life. (Previously it had been seen either as a sin or as something intrinsically immature)

3. Women were capable of pleasure and orgasm. (It seems strange to doubt this now, but it was a revelation then. Kinsey was challenging a well-established double standard)

■ **The average 1950s' couple** *possessed little sexual self-knowledge. Kinsey found that some women were married for 20 years until they first experienced orgasm.*

4. At least 37 percent of males would have at least one homosexual experience leading to orgasm, and 28 percent of women would have one or more lesbian experiences by the age of 45

5. At least 14 percent of women enjoyed multiple orgasms. (This fact proved so stupefying that the orgasms were dismissed as the fantasies of hysterical females)

6. Different classes had different sexual behavior: upper and middle classes were more likely to experiment with a variety of sexual activities, whereas the working class favored straightforward sexual intercourse. (Slam, bam, thank you, Mam)

7. Some women didn't reach orgasm until after 20 years of marriage

8. Premarital sex was common for both men and women. More than half of men reported having sex before marriage while just under 50 percent of women had had sex "with their fiancés" prior to marriage

9. At least 26 percent of women and 50 percent of men had had extra-marital sex

The findings of sex therapists Masters and Johnson

Kinsey's controversial work aroused the interest of William Masters, of Washington University, St. Louis, Missouri. He set about methodically recording the sexual responses of men and women under laboratory conditions, wiring up his subjects so that he could record and photograph what happened within their bodies. He was assisted on the project by psychologist Virginia Johnson.

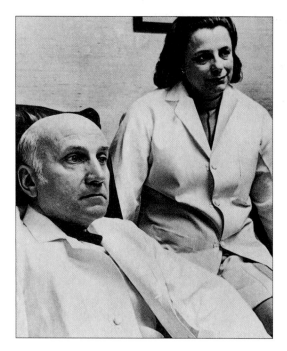

When the eminent researchers came to publish their results, they were so concerned about the impact of their work on the medical profession that they deliberately wrote their books in dense medical terminology. They believed that in doing so, they would preserve their reputation. In spite of this, the books attracted major public attention and the findings detailed were eventually responsible for changing people's lives.

■ **Masters and Johnson** *were instrumental in bringing revolutionary new research on human sexual response to the public's awareness.*

What Masters and Johnson discovered

1. A man's sexual performance is in no way related to the size of his penis

2. There was no evidence to support the Freudian theory about the vaginal versus clitoral orgasm

3. Women are capable of multiple orgasms

4. There is a distinct pattern to human sexual response, consisting of excitement, plateau, orgasm, and resolution

5. Even though the postmenopausal woman loses some of her hormone output, the psyche is equally important in determining sex drive and she is therefore able to continue her enjoyment of sex into old age

6. In the aging male, although the ejaculatory response is reduced, the erectile response remains unaffected

7 About 82 percent of pregnant women in the middle three months of pregnancy reported a marked increase in eroticism and satisfactory lovemaking

8 In the last few weeks before term, pregnant women are markedly less sexually "relieved" by orgasm, with their genitals remaining extremely sexually "congested" after orgasm – resulting sometimes in requiring stimulation to achieve further climax

9 The sexual response cycle is remarkably similar for men and women

10 The belief that uncircumcised men have more ejaculatory control than circumcised men was untrue

11 A rare orgasmic pattern, dubbed "status orgasmus" by Masters and Johnson, is experienced by some women." It consists either of an extremely long orgasm or possibly so many rapidly recurrent orgasms that it isn't possible to distinguish among them

> ### Trivia...
> Based on Masters' and Johnson's work, sex therapy can be used for couples with problems of impotence, premature ejaculation, inability to experience orgasm, retarded ejaculation, and vaginismus.

The start of sex therapy

As part of their work, Masters and Johnson devised the concept of sex therapy. Their methods form the basis of most sex therapy work practiced today. It is due to them that men and women all over the world grew to understand and communicate more about what actually goes on between the sheets. Their books also paved the way for the first popular illustrated books about sexuality, books that non-medical individuals would find easy to understand.

■ **Sex therapy** *today helps many couples to overcome their sexual and relationship problems. It is thanks to Masters and Johnson that the profession began to be taken seriously.*

Change your clothes, change your sex

Throughout history there have been men and women who have chosen to dress in the clothes of the opposite sex. They are called transvestites. But for unhappy individuals who feel they were born into the wrong body (transsexuals), there was little to be done. Little that is, until the late 1950s and the 1960s. It was at around this time that an assortment of sexological pioneers developed transgender surgery, or surgery that adapts the human body so that it appears to change sex.

Today, breasts can be removed or added, genitals can be reshaped, and facial hair can be removed by electrolysis. Hormones can induce either masculinity or femininity and cosmetic surgery can further enhance your chosen gender. The result is that in the 21st century people of cross-gender are more accepted than at any other time in history. Pop stars and other celebrities who openly display cross-gender characteristics are completely acknowledged and *androgyny* is no longer seen as unusual. Such acceptance exemplifies how much more sexually tolerant people have become.

> **DEFINITION**
>
> Androgyny *is the state of possessing both male and female characteristics. Pop stars, such as Freddie Mercury, k.d. lang, Alice Cooper, Marilyn Manson, and David Bowie, are considered androgynous because they wear (or have worn) the clothes and hairstyles of the opposite sex.*

The acceptance of an erotic classic

So where does the *Kama Sutra* figure against this background of increasing sexual tolerance? After having been bought through private subscription by the Victorians in the mid- to late-1800s, it gradually faded out of the picture. For the first 60 years of the 20th century, the *Kama Sutra* was unpublishable in the English language because it was considered obscene. The *Kama Sutra* didn't hit the bookshops again until the 1960s.

■ **After a long absence,** *the love positions of the* Kama Sutra *finally came to light again in the 1960s.*

With world wars being fought, basic issues like survival took precedence over the improvement of people's sex lives.

A major breakthrough in sex publishing came with the establishment of Luxor Press in the UK. In the 1960s Luxor printed a series of sex books, all bound in a readily identifiable bright yellow cover. It was Luxor who dared to republish the *Kama Sutra*. Strictly words only, the immortal sex positions were clearly described. It was this yellow-bound volume that proved a valuable sourcebook for many ambitious publishers later.

The 1960s and the sexual revolution

THE SEXUAL DISCOVERIES *of the '50s and early '60s began to filter through to ordinary, everyday relationships by the late '60s and '70s. In addition to new information on sex, the contraceptive pill was invented, abortion was legalized in several countries, and laws concerning homosexuality were liberalized. The result of these major changes was a rapid alteration in sexual lifestyle. It was the start of the Sexual Revolution.*

The centerfold

During the '60s and '70s, sex magazines came into their own. *Playboy* started the trend, then *Penthouse* overtook it. *Penthouse Forum*, the journal of human relations, published real people's real accounts of sex, and spawned many offshoots. The traditional magazines didn't wait long before catching up. In the mid-1970s *Penthouse Forum* rejected an article on cunnilingus on the grounds that it was too explicit. Imagine the editor's surprise when the same article appeared unabridged in the new edition of *Cosmopolitan*. It was the beginning of a massive sexualization of the popular media.

Books also broke new ground. Works of literature that appeared in the 1960s (and in some cases disappeared again thanks to court proceedings) included *Lady Chatterley's Lover*, the print version of the *Kama Sutra*, and *Last Exit to Brooklyn*. The 1970s saw the publication of *The Secret of O*, *Emmanuelle*, and *The Hite Report*.

The outrageous years

In California, sex churches were established as legal charities, homosexuals went openly to gay bathhouses where public sex was the norm, and huge supermarkets sold domination and bondage equipment. S-and-M houses offered the ultimate experience in pain and pleasure. Sandstone, a sexually liberated community in Topanga Canyon, attracted increasing numbers of people, and couples swung all over the States and Europe.

In the 1970s, books and magazines acted as a backdrop for what was going on sexually. Betty Dodson ran Bodysex workshops for women in New York City, conducted in the nude. Preorgasmic groups sprang up in the US and UK where women experimented with masturbation and used speculums in order to determine the state of their sexual health.

The sexual university

A sign that sex had become deadly serious was the US government's licensing of the first bona fide institution to award a degree in sexology: the Institute for the Advanced Study of Human Sexuality in San Francisco. It remains the only college to award such a degree today. The unique training scheme for sex educators and counselors is the brainchild of Methodist minister Reverend Ted McIlvenna who, appalled by the amount of sexual prejudice he encountered through his ministry, decided to combat it.

Extraordinary sex establishments, such as Platos, opened in New York. Such premises were a mixture of nightclub and leisure club, where couples could enjoy public swinging either as voyeurs or as participants. They simply paid a fee and walked in.

The big illustrated sex manuals

LARGE, ILLUSTRATED BOOKS *with clear and accessible information about sex were marketed in a major way towards the end of the 1960s. The best sex manuals were put together by talented authors who knew their subject well, illustrators who produced tasteful explicit drawings or photographs, and expert design teams. As a result of this group approach the books looked gorgeous, were extremely easy to read, and were both practical and educational.*

The first major bestseller to hit the bookshops was Alex Comfort's *The Joy of Sex*. Comfort was a medical man with a special interest in sex. He was a founder member of Sandstone, the American sexual community, and was very comfortable with aspects of sexuality that most other medics were not.

A stroke of genius on the part of *The Joy of Sex* art director, Peter Kindersley, was to commission very beautiful line drawings of couples with flowing locks and lovely bodies to illustrate Comfort's words of wisdom. The combination of large illustrations, dozens of pictures and very controversial text ensured that the book went straight to the top of the bestseller lists. Today it has been published in many different versions, including the earliest version of multimedia.

Liberating Masturbation was a small illustrated sex book which, unlike others listed here, started off in a small way. Written by artist and sex educator Betty Dodson, it is illustrated with Dodson's line drawings of women's genitals. These are devised to make the genitals look like exotic flowers and showed perfectly how beautiful and extraordinarily varied women's labia can appear.

For many years Dodson couldn't get her book published since mainstream publishers considered it too extreme. Undeterred, she sold it herself. Slowly but surely, the book's fame grew and a decade later, an established publisher decided to take the risk. Over the years the book has sold thousands of copies, and is still available under the title *Sex for One*.

INTERNET

www.amazon.com

Click on this site and find the sex or erotica sections to order copies of all the sex books mentioned on these pages.

INTERNET

www.bettydodson.com

Visit Betty Dodson's site to see her collection of sex books, videos, and vibrators.

The sex therapists' bible

While Masters and Johnson wrote a popular laymen's edition of their seminal work, the resulting book expounded their sex training techniques in words rather than pictures.

This left a gap that Helen Singer Kaplan, a respected sex therapist and educator from Chicago, decided to fill. Kaplan had written a sex textbook called *The New Sex Therapy*, which for many years was regarded as a "bible" for therapists. In 1974 she had the idea to produce a sex book that described sex therapy along with pictures.

The Illustrated Sex Manual duly appeared with explicit drawings. It sold extremely well but then disappeared from the bookshelves. It was only many years later that the book was reissued.

■ **Helen Singer Kaplan** *was the first author to produce a sex manual with pictures. It was thanks to her that behavioral sex therapy was first illustrated.*

A new climate of openness

BY THE 1980S, the discussion and practice of sex had opened up considerably. In the last 20 years, if it hadn't been for the advent of AIDS we might have gone a lot further. Perhaps we would have got used to the idea of more public sex. Or maybe the pendulum of public opinion would have swung so far in the opposite direction that we would have returned to the days of keeping sex strictly secret.

At the start of the 21st century, we are left with an odd mixture of sexual openness in conversation, grief for those friends who have died of AIDS, hesitation about the wisdom of going for full intercourse early in a relationship, and massively increased sales of condoms.

Fears about sexual safety mean that sex today is a much more stressed ball game. Having sex with a new lover without a condom is now a complete no-no.

■ **Couples today can talk frankly** *about sexual issues. Women in particular are far more knowledgeable about both their own and their partner's needs and have far more confidence in the sexual arena.*

Trivia...

One of the great transformations of the 20th century was the massive change in women's experience of sex. One hundred years ago, women were expected to lie back and think of their mother country. But the spread of reliable birth control, the fact that women were given the vote, and a growing understanding of women's sexual natures brought about great developments. A century later, women now expect to enjoy a sex life, are learning to be unafraid of asking a man for a date, and are becoming more confident about asking for what they want in bed. Of course, in order to know what you want sexually, you have to know quite a lot about your own sexuality. This is all a far cry from living in complete ignorance as our own grandmothers did 100 years earlier.

In the 1980s there were a number of illustrated sex manuals published, but none of them had the same kind of visual impact as the earlier books, nor did the written material prove so compelling. In 1992, the former art director of *The Joy of Sex*, Peter Kindersley, by then a managing director of his own publishing company, decided to go for a follow-up to his former sex success. He commissioned Anne Hooper's *Ultimate Sex Guide*.

The *Ultimate Sex Guide* combined knowledge of sex therapy with writing skills. It had a softer approach to describing sexual relationships, combined with experience from the author's clinical practice in the UK and American training, which helped create a book that offered not so much sex therapy but sexual enhancement.

INTERNET

www.dk.com

For details of Anne Hooper's books, visit Dorling Kindersley's web site. Click on the health then sex sections.

Readers were "coming of age" and therefore no longer needed the excuse of therapy in order to buy sex books. Breaking new ground with tasteful photographic illustration, the book was extremely successful.

A simple summary

✓ The sex researchers and therapists of the '50s and '60s laid the groundwork for free discussion about sex.

✓ Following the pioneering work of William Masters and Virginia Johnson, sex therapy was developed during the '60s and '70s. Over these two decades, layers of sexual repression were gradually lifted and sexual experimentation reached a peak.

✓ Against this backdrop, the *Kama Sutra* was republished after an absence of 50 years. Since then it has been in print continuously.

✓ The big illustrated sex manuals were methods of demonstrating, visually as well as in words, the newly successful sex techniques. As a result, the '80s were a time of far freer discussion and openness about sex in general.

Chapter 5

Sex Today

So what is the state of sexual play in the brave new 21st century? We've seen that sex pioneers of the last century opened up the field of sexual knowledge. Thanks to them we understand our most intimate behavior, in contrast to 50 years ago when there was plenty of speculation but little scientific fact. We have moved ahead. In the new millennium we have at our command drug therapy and counseling for couples; the media is soaked in sexual reportage; new sex toys are being invented for the first time since the vibrator. Yet the *Kama Sutra* continues to hold its popularity. Let's look at sex today in order to work out why.

In this chapter...

✓ Remedies old and new

✓ The new sex industry

✓ The new sex books

✓ The enduring appeal of the Kama Sutra

BY THE END OF THE 1980s, MANY TABOOS ABOUT SEX HAD BEEN BROKEN DOWN

Remedies old and new

REMEDIES FOR SEXUAL DIFFICULTIES *are not a new idea: lesser known chapters of the* Kama Sutra *focus on "Success in Love" and "Arousing a Weakened Power," offering primitive sex therapy and herbal solutions, complete with recipes. So let's look at what the* Kama Sutra *advocated for its readers, and what's on offer in terms of medical help today, now that prescription drugs can be used to aid many sex problems that received little or no help in the past.*

Virility and fertility

Here's the *Kama Sutra's* recipe for giving extra power to your sperm:

- Crush sweet potatoes in cow's milk and mix with sugar, honey, and ghee (fat)
- Combine this with wheat flour in flat shapes and bake. Crush the resulting biscuits in cow's milk

According to the Kama Sutra, if you continually eat the special recipe cookies it prescribes, your sperm will acquire such force that you will be able to sleep with thousands of women.

Recipes for love

Here are some *aphrodisiac* recipes from the *Kama Sutra:*

- Mix garlic root with white pepper and licorice, then stir into sugared water to improve virility
- Boil ram's or he-goat's testicles in sugared milk to feel horny
- Mix crushed camel bone with antimony and use as mascara to enable you to bewitch any person at first glance. Crushed bones from a peacock, falcon, or vulture will achieve a similar effect

■ **Crushed peacock bones** *were used as a component of mascara, believed to have bewitching properties.*

Some of the recipes in the back of the original Kama Sutra can be extremely dangerous. Whatever you do, do not ingest mercury, arsenic, lead, or datura through the mouth or through the skin. These are all poisonous substances.

Boosting arousal

Today, our carefully tested medicines, taken in correct dosages, are likely to do a great deal of good.

1. If you are depressed, antidepressants lift the mood and once you are off anti-depressant pills, your libido returns

2. If you can no longer have an erection, Viagra gives you the mechanism for arousal, although you must still actually desire your partner for erection to happen

3. If you're a woman who wants to get aroused more easily and experience orgasm more intensely, phentolamine (prescription-only) can help lower your inhibitions and make it easier to respond, or testosterone in gel or patch form can give you extra sex drive and sexual sensitivity

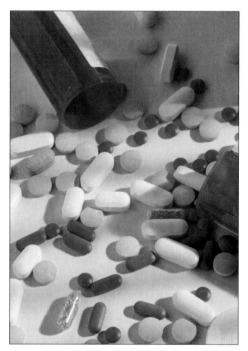

■ **Modern drugs can help** *with many sexual problems, including anxiety and a loss of interest in sex.*

Turning off

A common sex problem, especially for men, is not becoming aroused but wanting to turn off. This is the case for men who suffer from premature ejaculation or who want far more sex than their partner does.

A type of anxiety is known to trigger instant needs and reactions in some of these men, which can be treated with beta-blocker drugs. Beta-blockers help lower anxiety levels and slow down sexual response.

It may reassure you to know that most men grow out of premature ejaculation as they get older and their sexual response naturally slows down.

The new sex industry

ANCIENT EROTIC PAINTINGS *reveal that sex toys, such as* dildos, *were invented thousands of years ago. Many old Indian and Chinese illustrations show them being cunningly introduced – no prizes for guessing where. Until recently, the newest sexual toy was an improved version of the dildo, the vibrator. But suddenly there are all sorts of novelties on the market, and thanks to the Internet, these toys are more accessible than ever.*

DEFINITION

A dildo *is the name given to an artificial penis. Early versions were made from bone, later they were made from china or thick glass, and today they're plastic.*

The latest sex toys

Among the newest inventions are some genuinely novel creations. One example is a "black box" that produces a galvanic electrical force. Its computerized clips are attached to extrasensitive parts of the anatomy and operated by remote control. Other recent fun products include edible lubes, which are capsules that you pop into your mouth prior to oral sex and bite on as you approach your partner. Your mouth is then flooded with fruit-flavored massage gels so that you can dine off your partner in style. Vibrators have improved, too: the latest whispering models don't make the irritating buzzing noise that their predecessors made, so the in-laws in the next room won't be able to hear you when you're using one!

■ **At one stage** *it was reckoned that so many vibrators had been sold in the UK and North America that every adult must own at least four!*

INTERNET

www.goodvibes.com

Click on Antique Vibrator Museum to see examples of vibrators from 1869, through to the 1970s, and learn about their different uses over the past 150 years.

There is any number of variations of the multiple moving dildo. You can now get models that penetrate just about every orifice simultaneously and send you completely wild because each dildo pumps to a different action. Feisty women swear by the corkscrew version!

Sex workshops

The latest in a long line of training and vacation workshops is the Tantric workshop. Subscribers spend the weekend in a beautiful countryside location and attend classes where they learn "a practical and playful way of experiencing their sexuality as a flowing together of physical, erotic, and cosmic energies." Beats painting holidays into a cocked hat!

For those interested in the S-and-M experience, there's the opportunity to subscribe to lessons in domination and bondage. Encouraged to take things at their own pace, students are introduced to a variety of "torture" rooms and can participate in games for beginners. And don't worry – once you have "graduated" there are advanced classes, too.

■ **Workshops** *in S-and-M reveal the world of bondage and domination to students. There are classes for novices and for the more experienced.*

Sex on the Web and on TV

The Internet has more sites dedicated to sex than to any other subject – and these sites attract vast numbers of fascinated surfers. As well as sex-aid stores and sexually oriented chat rooms there are sites selling exclusive sex books, sites featuring erotic art and fiction, and serious sexological research sites, such as the Kinsey Institute.

INTERNET

www.indiana. edu/~kinsey

www.iashs.edu

www.basrt.org.uk

Click on the above addresses to access the web sites of the Kinsey Institute, the Institute for the Advanced Study of Human Sexuality, and the British Association of Sexual and Relationship Therapists.

In the US, an upcoming Web project is to provide access to a sexual art collection featuring hundreds of art objects willed to the Institute for the Advanced Study of Human Sexuality. In the UK, the British Association of Sexual and Relationship Therapists is compiling a "Check out your sex problem" site that will also list therapists.

INTERNET

www.fetishhotel.com

See this site for an extreme adult experience (no juveniles).

Type the words Kama Sutra into your search engine and hundreds of references will blitz the screen.

As well as being easy to download on our computer screens, increasingly sexualized entertainment is now being transmitted on late-night TV shows. Cable and satellite subscription channels have been around for years but today, sex is regarded as just another regular variety show.

In North America, many explicit sex shows regularly break the boundaries of cable TV by showing full-frontals of naked males and introducing fetishes explicitly and with humor. Explicit sexual commentary is more and more common on mainstream television as well, usually in the guise of scantilly-dressed women and sexual jokes by talk show hosts.

This seems to mean we can get away with viewing strong stuff, which for decades was not allowed. Where will it all end?

■ **Watching late-night** *television is fast becoming an X-rated pastime as more channels broadcast sexually explicit material.*

INTERNET

www.exn.ca/sexfiles/ home.cfm

Canadian TV show The Sex Files takes a down-to-earth approach to sex, blending serious science with vibrant visuals and cheeky humor.

PROOF THAT SEX CAN STILL SHOCK

Even in the current climate of sexual openness, sex can still cause controversy. US sex instructors Steve and Vera Bodansky are among an exceptional group of teachers who believe so strongly in getting their sexual message across that they actually demonstrate what they are talking about. When a video of their teaching was recently reviewed, the Bodanskys were lambasted by journalists who recoiled from the open display of sex techniques.

The new sex books

WHEN VIDEOS FIRST WENT ON SALE, *the end of the film industry was predicted. Why should anyone bother to go out to a movie if they could watch it in their living room? Fortunately, not only were the doom merchants proved wrong but the opposite happened. The film industry received a shot in the arm because people became so addicted to feature films on the small screen that they rushed to the big one to see the very latest. They craved more instant gratification – not less. The same thing is now happening to books.*

Virtually any kind of book with sex as its central theme sells. There's nothing new in this except that rather than becoming bored by a flood of sex books, it seems that the more people get, the more they want.

Sex books are attracting new consumers: In an era of sexual openness in the media, even the conservative middle classes feel comfortable with giving sex books as gifts. Admittedly, these are upmarket types of sex book: beautifully laid out volumes with tasteful photography and design.

Quality publications are convincing people who, not long ago, would not have dreamed of buying or giving sex books, that it is acceptable to show a healthy interest.

The *Joy of Sex* paved the way for sex books to become mainstream. Later on, Andrew Stanway's *Lovers' Guide* series and Anne Hooper's *The Ultimate Sex Guide* manuals sold millions of copies worldwide. Anne Hooper's latest title, the *K.I.S.S. Guide to Sex*, is set to be yet another big seller.

Specialist titles

Books that concentrate on specific aspects of sex for a niche market also promise to be a growth area. This has been made possible by the advent of Internet selling.

Already, small publishers are rushing to print their own titles that put forward unusual or controversial ideas and can only be bought on the Internet. The advantage of Internet selling is that publishers can reach a wider audience and so can afford to print material that might not otherwise be expected to achieve good sales.

INTERNET

www.bettydodson.com

Click on the above address to see what this small publishing company has to offer.

■ **Erotic literature** *can heighten a woman's libido and improve her sexual enjoyment in and out of the bedroom.*

Sexual fiction

It's no secret that many women are suckers for romantic fiction – preferably with a whiff of passion. Romantic passion is the female aphrodisiac and what better place to imbibe it than from a good novel, preferably accompanied by a box of chocolates. Or you can read aloud in bed and entertain your partner between your black satin sheets.

Of course, men too are turned on by erotic fiction, so why not both pep up your bedtime reading by looking at Anne Hooper's *The Great Sex Guide* or *Sex Games*. You'll find some useful stories tucked away at the end of these volumes.

Sex in soaps

Soap opera is now taken so seriously that you can study it at university. This is because storytelling is recognized as one of the best ways to learn. From stories, you discover what may be available to you in your own life and you also glean new information on subjects you might otherwise have known nothing about.

INTERNET

www.eroticprints.org/
bedside.htm

If you're interested in reading some erotic fiction, check out this site.

INTERNET

www.soapcentral.com

www.unmissabletv.
com/tx/soaps

Visit Soap Opera Central for the latest news on the top American soaps. For features, star profiles, and updates on British and Australian soaps, including Coronation Street, EastEnders, Brookside, and Neighbours, click on to the unmissable TV site.

Abortion, safe sex, AIDS, and contraception are all topics that have been tackled on television and radio. These days you can log onto daily soap operas on the Internet and follow the amazing exploits of men and women who fearlessly open themselves up to a variety of sexual experiences.

The enduring appeal of the Kama Sutra

IT'S NO ACCIDENT that the portion of the Kama Sutra most people remember is the section on sexual positions. The book caters for the great need that all humans possess – the need to reassure ourselves we can be skillful lovers. It is a need that is revisited through the generations. Sex is a major driving force and an obvious way in which to learn about sex is to see other people do it. In our society voyeurism is not acceptable but reading the Kama Sutra allows us to actually view a demonstration of the sex act. In a

A LOVE POSITION

sense, therefore, the Kama Sutra is not only one of the greatest sex manuals – it is probably the oldest.

A gentle wooing

The *Kama Sutra* teaches young males how to go about wooing and seducing their lovers with the utmost sensitivity. Today there are many men who would benefit from reading these sections.

But women also gain from reading the *Kama Sutra*. Slow and tactful overtures mean that women are able to gain the trust and confidence they need in order to relax enough to be able to enjoy sex.

Work in contemporary preorgasmic workshops shows that a sense of confidence is often linked to women's ability to enjoy sexual stimulation and to experience orgasm. The more confident women feel, the more able they are to experiment with self-stimulation and learn how to climax.

TODAY'S BELIEFS ABOUT SEX

The most recent surveys about sex and sexuality show that men and women expect:

1 To be sexually satisfied by their partner

2 Each to take the initiative sexually

3 To learn about sex together

4 Fidelity from each other

5 To tolerate the very occasional lapse from fidelity

6 To avoid paid-for-sex (although many don't)

7 To go in for some of the sex variations such as mutual masturbation, oral sex, sexual massage, and some sex games (but not hard-core games)

Much of this is in direct contrast to what 4th-century men and women expected. When the *Kama Sutra* was compiled, men were expected to take the initiative and women were expected to be responsive. As for learning about sex, few women were given writings such as the *Kama Sutra* since the book was written specifically for men. In general it was the man's responsibility to teach his bride. Yet though our beliefs today may be very different, the *Kama Sutra*'s wisdom is just as relevant now, as then.

■ **Modern women** *are as sexually knowledgeable as men and are just as likely to take the initiative when it comes to lovemaking.*

Retelling the tale

Since the 1960s there have been literally dozens of versions of the great Indian classic. That the book continues to be produced in ever-varying editions says a great deal for the timeless fascination it holds.

Out of dozens of editions of the Kama Sutra, one of the most important is by Alain Danielou, who retranslated the Sanskrit text. Equally important are my contemporary illustrated versions, in which I have reinterpreted the ancient texts to make them more relevant to today's readers. Millions of copies of these versions have been sold around the world.

What was different about my editions of the *Kama Sutra* was that they were the first to feature photography instead of drawing or painting. They were also the first to present the ancient sexual information in a contemporary light, relating the famous sex positions of the 4th century to our own behavior 16 centuries later.

The combination of old-fashioned description next to modern interpretation seems to have fulfilled some atavistic need. The *Kama Sutra* has fed, and still is feeding, a general hunger for sexual information. And it doesn't seem to matter at what time in history we are born, we always appear to possess this hunger.

A simple summary

✔ There's nothing new about the idea that certain drugs and foods can help make you feel sexier. However, today's medications are better researched, safer, and work efficiently.

✔ Developments in the field of sex are becoming truly space age. The Internet, television, books, and the media in general have become increasingly sexualized.

✔ Perhaps the very existence of the *Kama Sutra* encourages us to feel safe in reading about and learning more about sex. It may also act as the basis on which all new sex books are founded.

✔ The *Kama Sutra* continues to fit into our modern culture. Its sex positions as described and illustrated seem to fulfil an atavistic need for information.

PART TWO

A SLOW, SENSUAL BUILD-UP LEADS TO GREAT SEX

BUILDING UP TO DIVINE SEX

A PHYSICAL BUILD-UP is essential for good loving. The preliminaries of sexual play – hugging, embracing, even shampooing each other's hair – are tenderly described, and with good reason. These are the small activities that allow men and women to become *intimate*, long before anything overtly sexual happens.

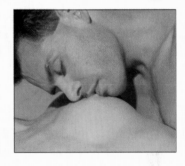

Although the original *Kama Sutra* did not offer massage strokes, they are included here because today we know how wonderful *sensual massage* can be for pleasuring the body and teasing the erogenous zones. Vatsyayana's touch-teaching goes instead into scratching, pounding, even offering your partner blows! And last but definitely not least is the sensual mouth. Every possible nuance of kissing and biting is described in almost fetishistic detail.

Chapter 6

Sex Is More Than Intercourse

GENTLE FOREPLAY is the most wonderful way to begin your lovemaking. Physically and emotionally working your way up to sex prolongs the experience and intensifies it when you get there. The *Kama Sutra* stresses the importance of preparing the environment, relaxing the mind, and cleansing the body as a prelude to sex. The following pages reveal how to best to embark on a sensual erotic journey to hedonistic pleasure.

In this chapter...

✓ Setting the scene

✓ Preparing the body

✓ The erogenous zones

A BATH AND GENTLE BACK SCRUB WITH YOUR PARTNER IS AN IDEAL PRELUDE TO SENSUAL LOVEMAKING

Setting the scene

THE ENVIRONMENT IN WHICH *you make love should be conducive to focused and undistracted sex. Give some thought to preparing your room so it becomes a haven for unadulterated passion. Vatsyayana is clear on the importance of comfort and aesthetics in your room of love:*
" . . . balmy with rich perfumes . . . a bed, soft, agreeable to the sight, covered with a clean white cloth, low in the middle part, having garlands and bunches of flowers upon it . . . "

Your first step towards great lovemaking is to ensure you won't be disturbed. Choose a comfortable room (it doesn't have to be the bedroom) where you can take your time without fear of interruption. Unplug the telephone, hang up a "do not disturb" sign (if necessary), and allow the fun to begin. You may want to shout out with lustful pleasure during your lovemaking, so make sure you're far enough away from any other members of your household.

■ **Choose a suitably exotic** *essential oil and place a few drops in a burner so that it fragrances the room.*

Fragrance and flowers

Create a seductively fragrant atmosphere in your boudoir by lighting some sweetly perfumed joss-sticks or placing a few scented candles around the room. Alternatively,

you could burn a few drops of essential oil and allow its mood-enhancing vapors to pervade the air. Choose an oil that has properties in keeping with the hedonistic and passionate atmosphere you want to create, such as stimulating cedarwood or lavender or confidence-boosting mandarin, which will help you lose your inhibitions.

Don't go too overboard on the love scents — you don't want to choke on them!

■ **The sight and scent** *of fresh flowers help create a seductive atmosphere for lovemaking.*

Place some colorful cut flowers in a vase or, for a special sexy touch, sprinkle some single petals around the room and on the bed. Not only do flowers look beautiful but they also smell fresh and fragrant.

As flowers of love, roses are a natural choice, but a couple of elegant, well-placed orchids might suit your personality better. Choose whichever flowers most appeal to you. Vatsyayana's perfumed petals of choice would be "a garland of the yellow amaranth flowers."

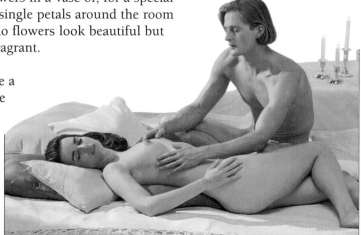

■ **Soft materials** *like chiffon and silk, fluffy pillows, and cushions can transform an ordinary room into a temple of love.*

Using soft fabrics

To enhance the sensual effect, surround yourself with carefully chosen textures and materials. Swathe your bed with soft silk or cotton sheets and plenty of fluffy pillows.

An assignation on scratchy sheets won't bring you a great deal of pleasure and your discomfort will detract from your ultimate sexual enjoyment.

Dim the lights, cue the music

Harsh lighting can be a real turn-off when it comes to relaxed lovemaking. Often bright electric bulbs are unforgiving and make people feel self-conscious about their bodies.

Many women feel overexposed and unattractive under harsh light. However, being plunged into complete darkness is a passion-killer, too. To fully appreciate one another's bodies, you need to be able to see what you're doing.

Try opting for soft lamp lighting that will give your skin a sexy glow, or perhaps a few well-placed candles might help you feel amorous.

Select some music that reflects the way you would like to feel. Go for a mellow, sensual sound rather than anything too loud and fast. You and your partner may even have a special song that's guaranteed to put you both in the mood. Play your chosen music at a low volume – it's for background effect only.

For many couples, enjoying dinner is an integral part of a romantic evening. Eat early and choose light, fragrant food as part of a small but satisfying meal. You could finish dinner by feeding one another pieces of fresh fruit or spoonfuls of sorbet to cleanse your palates and make you feel fresh.

> *Trivia...*
> *Vatsyayana recommends that men imbibe various hearty milk concoctions to increase sexual vigor before lovemaking. One such "cocktail" is made from milk, sugar, and licorice, while another is a less appetizing mix of milk and ram's testicles.*

Relax your mind

As you build up toward sex, take time to communicate and flirt. Seductive conversation can be wonderful foreplay in itself. Keep it relaxed and comfortable. If a glass of wine – or better still, champagne – helps you relax, then enjoy a glass or two.

Take care not to overindulge in alcohol – you want to keep your mind clear and focused for later.

■ **Take time to** *flirt with each other over a light meal and a glass or two of wine. Some suggestive conversation will help put you both in the mood for lovemaking.*

Preparing the body

VATSYAYANA STRESSES THE IMPORTANCE of scrupulous cleanliness when it comes to lovemaking. The body should be treated with respect and cleansed and cared for with reverence. This will help you to feel relaxed about your body, which is vital if you are to enjoy truly satisfying and liberating sex.

Breathe easy

Bad breath is a real no-no in the arena of passionate lovemaking. You'll find it difficult to be swept away by desire if your partner's breath makes you nauseous.

Most problems can be easily combated with flossing, gum massage, or breath-freshening mouthwashes and handy sprays. Fortunately, oral hygiene has moved on from Vatsyayana's day, when the antidote to an unattractive-smelling mouth was to chew on betel leaves. But even if you don't have breath problems, it can't hurt to freshen up a little before lovemaking.

Bad breath is difficult to diagnose yourself. If you suspect you might suffer from halitosis, ask a good friend for an honest opinion.

INTERNET

www.beautycare.com

Visit this site for information on oral cosmetics and dental care. Simply type "dentistry" into the search section.

Soap it up

Relaxing together in a warm bath, scrubbing each other's backs, and shampooing one another's hair are great ways to prepare yourself for love – physically and emotionally.

You can enjoy taking charge of your partner's personal hygiene; while fragrant soapy suds cleanse your bodies, you can use your hands to indulge in gentle and loving caresses as a prelude to sex. If you have a bath large enough for both of you, one partner can sit snugly behind the other, with your legs wrapped around. Wash your backs all over by taking a soapy sponge up and down each other's spine.

■ **Soaping up** *and washing your partner's back is an intimate and sensual activity.*

Then use your hands to rinse off the suds with warm water, caressing with caring fingers as you do so. Your partner can then return the favor.

After your bath, be sure to moisturize and soften your skin. A gorgeously perfumed, non-greasy body moisturizer will make you feel special all over. Pay particular attention to any dry areas, such as the elbows, knees, and buttocks. For extra sexy foreplay, you and your partner can have great fun moisturizing one another's bodies. A little perfume can also work wonders – use a scent that you know will drive your lover crazy with desire.

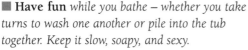

■ **Have fun** *while you bathe – whether you take turns to wash one another or pile into the tub together. Keep it slow, soapy, and sexy.*

INTERNET

www.lush.co.uk

Visit this site for some of the most extraordinary soap you have ever seen. Click on products, then soap.

Sexy grooming

Bristly faces, legs, or armpits will not only feel uncomfortable against your partner's skin but they can also leave a nasty rash after a night of passion. If you shave, make it as close as possible. This will help you feel fresh, soft, and desirable as well as giving your partner a smooth ride.

Women can have great fun soaping and shaving their partner's face before lovemaking. Lathering and giving him a close shave fosters closeness and intimacy as well as giving you peace of mind – after all, it's in your power to prevent yourself from being scratched by bristly stubble later.

Men: Allow your partner to take charge when shaving you – this is a superb exercise in trust!

■ **Give your man** *a close shave – it's a great way of building up trust and a feeling of intimacy.*

Shampooing the hair

The head is a significant nerve center and you can drive your mate to distraction by massaging and stroking as you shampoo their hair.

With the ends of your fingers and the palms of your hands, use slow, controlled movements as you gently work the shampoo into the scalp.

Be careful to avoid getting any lather into your partner's eyes as you rinse off the shampoo.

Drying off

When the two of you are squeaky clean, it's fun to sensually rub each other down with soft bath towels.

Wrap your partner in a huge, warm, fluffy towel and dry them off all over, stroking their body through the towel, and making sure you get into all the curves and contours!

■ **Treat your partner** *to a head massage while shampooing his hair, and by the time you rinse out the soap he'll feel pampered and relaxed.*

NECK RUB

A gentle massage of the neck and shoulders while you groom each other is a wonderfully relaxing and erotic interlude. Keep your movements soft and gentle – you don't need to use structured massage strokes – just casually stroke your partner into a state of tingling tranquillity. Using your thumbs, knead the taut areas at the back of the neck leading down to the shoulders.

The erogenous zones

DOES A BREATHY KISS *on the neck drive you insane with lust? Or maybe a gentle stroke of the calf sends you into paroxysms of desire. It can be fun finding out which areas of your partner's body are most responsive to loving caresses. Take time to discover what makes your partner's erotic clock tick.*

The *Kama Sutra* recommends kissing and stroking a number of areas up and down the body, such as the lips, forehead, and breasts, for maximum tantalizing sensation.

The lips and neck

The mouth is undoubtedly an erotic center: Most lovemaking begins with a simple kiss. Touch your partner's lips gently with soft fingers and kiss and lick their mouth with loving movements. Don't neglect the rest of your partner's face, though, and be sure to concentrate on the sensitive throat.

Kissing, or merely breathing on, your partner's neck – particularly just below the ears – could be enough to make your lover moan out loud.

■ **The lips and neck** *are particularly sensitive areas – the lightest touch, or even breath, here will make your partner's skin tingle.*

The breasts and nipples

Kissing and stroking the breasts can be highly arousing. Tease your partner by caressing the *areolae* before you move on to kissing or stroking your lover's receptive nipples.

> **DEFINITION**
>
> The areolae *are the brown, slightly bumpy areas surrounding the nipples.*

Many men like their nipples to be caressed too, so there's no reason why women should have all the fun. You might go on to lick and suck the nipples gently, provided your partner finds it erotic. Please remember that not everyone does, so take careful note of his or her reactions before making this move.

■ **Kissing a woman's breasts** *and nipples can be highly arousing – and men often enjoy the same kind of attention, too.*

Sexy legs

Travel up your partner's legs from ankle to thigh, stroking, kissing, and licking as you go. The inner ankle, the back of the knee, and the inner thigh are particular hot spots, the latter of which will leave your partner begging you to continue your little journey.

The buttocks are visually and sensually stimulating for both men and women, so don't forget to pay them some attention, too.

■ **Pay particular attention** *to your partner's feet and you could find that she'll be like putty in your hands.*

Trivia...

The feet contain reflex points that connect them with key areas all over the body. A gentle rub and massage all over the base of your partner's foot will relax him or her. Concentrate your fingers on individual areas, such as the toes, the ball of the foot, the in-step and the heel, to tap into your partner's body bit by bit. This will leave your lover gloriously relaxed yet stimulated.

Sensitive feet

Kissing and licking a partner's toes can be highly erotic for some people, though very ticklish, too. Cup your partner's heel in your hand and gently kiss or lick the instep (the curve of the foot) to make your partner squeal. Then work your way down to the toes, kissing and licking them individually.

INTERNET

www.dkonline.com/
dkcom/dk/massage.html

Visit this web page for a step-by-step account of how to give a relaxing foot massage with scented oils. For more ideas go to www.google.com and type in "foot massage."

Sensual skin

Sensitive nerve endings all over the skin make it the largest pleasure zone of the body. Stroked, rubbed, kissed, and licked, it's a wonderful source of sexual excitement.

By touching the skin in an erotic way, and in the most sensitive places, you can impart waves of intense erotic sensation to your partner.

A combination of soft fingertips and ticklish nails will give your partner glorious goose bumps, and a gentle flick of the tongue or a light lick in the right area can be agonizingly sexy.

Be cheeky

The skin on the buttocks is highly sensitive to a light touch. Plus there's the bonus that the sight of your partner's delicious *derrière* may turn you on. So spend a little time caressing this part of the body to show how aroused it makes you feel and, of course, to turn your lover on. Stroke and swirl your fingertips across your partner's buttocks, paying particular attention to the skin on the underside of the curve. This can be electrifying.

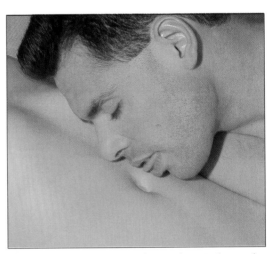

■ **Be soft and gentle** *with your lover's skin and you'll spark off tantalizing sensations. Intersperse a firm touch with lighter, teasing ones.*

A simple summary

✔ The comfort and tranquillity of your lovemaking environment is vital for the success of your sexual interlude.

✔ It's important to feel good about lovemaking (i.e. to really want to go ahead with it before you embark on touching and stroking).

✔ Vatsyayana stresses the significance of a sweetly cleansed and well-groomed body as a precursor to sex.

✔ Take a journey around your partner's body to find the power points of pleasure that will really get him or her going.

✔ The skin is an enormous erotic area, so play on it with wonderfully tender fingers and lips.

Chapter 7

The Art of Caressing

CARESSING AND EMBRACING are the glorious first stages of physical contact between lovers. Everyone knows that such touching leads to satisfying lovemaking. But did you know that it also constitutes a major part of the intimacy of sexual congress? Vatsyayana, who was well aware of tactile temptations, breaks down the types of embrace between lovers and divides them into groups. Maybe you and your partner already enjoy such close behavior, or perhaps you'll learn something new that will bring you dynamically closer.

In this chapter...

✓ Early embraces

✓ Intertwining of bodies

✓ The arousal of male desire

✓ Embrace of the whole body

GENTLE PHYSICAL CONTACT IS A WAY OF EXPRESSING DESIRE

Early embraces

THESE INITIAL EMBRACES *are coyly playful ways of expressing attraction and desire through gentle physical contact. The* Kama Sutra *says that they "indicate the mutual love of a man and a woman who have come together." If you haven't yet found yourself embracing spontaneously, there are some brilliant ideas to get you started. And if you are already glued to each other's bodies, perhaps you'll find something here to offer added interest!*

The Touching Embrace

The *Kama Sutra* describes this embrace as follows: "When a man, under some pretext or other, goes in front of or alongside a woman and touches her body with his own, it is called 'the touching embrace'."

Vatsyayana describes the Touching Embrace as occurring between "persons who do not, as yet, speak freely with each other." This is all well and good, but you should be sure that the object of your desire reciprocates your attraction, otherwise you could be accused of invading their personal space.

Between lovers, this is an affectionate action, to be made perhaps when you are in company as a way of communicating current desire and the promise of fulfilling it later when you are alone.

THE TOUCHING EMBRACE

The Piercing Embrace

The *Kama Sutra* says of this embrace, "When a woman in a lonely place bends down, as if to pick up something, and pierces as it were a man, sitting or standing, with her breasts, and the man in return takes hold of them, it is called a 'piercing embrace'."

Like the Touching Embrace, Vatsyayana describes this contact as occurring between a couple who are not yet lovers. It is, he believes, an indicator of attraction. This should not be interpreted literally: The terms "piercing" and "taking hold" are somewhat crude in today's sexual arena. The movement is more likely, nowadays, to refer to a man gently brushing his chest against his lover's body as she moves around him. But if she responds by taking things further, he might also brush his fingers across her breasts.

THE PIERCING EMBRACE

THE RUBBING EMBRACE

The Rubbing Embrace

"When two lovers are walking slowly together, either in the dark or in a place of public resort, or in a lonely place, and rub their bodies against each other, it is called a 'rubbing embrace'."

The *Kama Sutra* recognizes this as a movement between more established lovers or "peculiar to those who know the intentions of each other." Many lovers, particularly young ones, like to snuggle together or put their arms around each other as they walk along. Such physical closeness can foster a sense of unity and warmth as a couple step out together.

The Pressing Embrace

"When on the above occasion [the rubbing embrace] one of them presses the other's body forcibly against a wall or pillar, it is called a 'pressing embrace'." The Pressing Embrace is more common among young lovers, but can be enjoyed by any spirited couple.

The next time you are walking in a quiet part of town or in the country with your partner and are overcome by a spark of lustful emotion, make it happen! Most people find it exciting when their partners behave in such a spontaneous manner.

THE PRESSING EMBRACE

97

Intertwining of bodies

THESE MORE INTIMATE EMBRACES *take place "at the times of meeting," according to Vatsyayana. They begin with physical entwining while standing and later move on to closer contact during sexual congress.*

The Twining of a Creeper

This spiralling embrace is described in the *Kama Sutra* as follows: "When a woman, clinging to a man as a creeper twines round a tree, bends his head down to hers with the desire of kissing him and slightly makes the sound of *sut sut*, embraces him, and looks lovingly towards him, it is called an embrace like 'the twining of a creeper'."

By coiling her body around her partner's in this way, a woman is expressing her desire and initiating sexual union. Vatsyayana's description assumes that the female is shorter than her partner because she coaxes his head down toward her with a kissing sound, but you and your partner can enjoy wrapping yourselves around one another no matter what the difference in height!

THE TWINING OF A CREEPER

Climbing a Tree

"When a woman, having placed one of her feet on the foot of her lover, and the other on one of his thighs, passes one of her arms round his back, and the other on his shoulders, makes slightly the sounds of singing and cooing, and wishes, as it were, to climb up him in order to have a kiss, it is called an embrace like the 'climbing of a tree'."

This is taking the Twining of a Creeper embrace a step further in that the woman literally begins to "mount" her lover in a more forceful and erotic way. Most men would probably adore this kind of proactive show of desire from their partner.

CLIMBING A TREE

THE MIXTURE OF SESAME SEED WITH RICE

Gently express desire audibly with inarticulate noises, like the "sut sut" kissing sound or the "singing" and "cooing" described above. Why? Because it can be a cute way of teasing and arousing your partner. You may wish to voice your feelings this way purely to illustrate your affection.

The Mixture of Sesame Seed with Rice

"When lovers lie on a bed, and embrace each other so closely that the arms and thighs of one are encircled by the arms and thighs of the other, and are, as it were, rubbing up against them, this is called an embrace like 'the mixture of sesame seed with rice'." Isn't this a great title for a love position? The name poetically evokes the complete intermingling of bodies and limbs in order to maximize skin-to-skin contact.

The Milk and Water Embrace

"When a man and woman are very much in love with each other, and, not thinking of any pain or hurt, embrace each other as if they were entering into each other's bodies either while the woman is sitting on the lap of the man or in front of him, or on a bed, then it is called an embrace like a 'mixture of milk and water'."

This is a strong and firm embrace in which lovers can experience the sensation of fusing and of union. You and your partner feel as if you are really merging and disappearing into one another, just as water disappears into milk.

THE MILK AND WATER EMBRACE

The arousal of male desire

VATSYAYANA EXPOUNDS *the role of embraces in the stimulation of the male libido: "The whole subject of embracing is of such a nature that men who ask questions about it, or who hear about it, or who talk about it, acquire thereby a desire for enjoyment. Even those embraces that are not mentioned on the Kama Shastra should be practiced at the time of sexual enjoyment, if they are in any way conducive to the increase of love or passion . . ."*

Remember to keep these embraces low-key and controlled early on so that your man stays at a comfortable level of arousal. As Vatsyayana warns: "The rules of the Shastra apply so long as the passion of the man is middling, but when the wheel of love is set in motion, then there is no Shastra and no order."

Visual stimulation

Men are turned on visually, so as you embrace him and move your body gracefully and sexily around his, make sure he can see your naked body in all its glory.

Eye contact is important and adds to the intimacy of the poses, so gaze into your partner's eyes with passion as you drape yourself around him.

Close contact

While the feeling of your skin against his is enough to light your lover's candle, the closer and more intimate your embraces become, the brighter his flame (of desire) will burn. To send his temperature soaring, use tantalizingly soft touches at first and then gradually work up toward pressing your body against his.

■ **Drape your body** *around his and move sensuously down his naked torso, kissing and stroking him as you go.*

The way you move your body while embracing can heighten the eroticism. A stroke of the hand or a rub with the thigh as you hold your partner is erotically suggestive. The trick is to get his mind transmitting wild messages to his genitals, so move your body slowly and gently to find out what really turns him on.

Be creative

As Vatsyayana points out, the embraces that you and your partner can enjoy are not confined to those in the *Kama Sutra*. If you know a way to hold your lover that makes him feel really special and sexy, go for it! And if you're not certain about the kind of embraces that excite him, experiment – there's a realm of passionate possibilities for you to discover.

Embrace of the whole body

THE KAMA SUTRA goes on to explore "four ways of embracing simple members of the body." This takes different parts of the body one by one and shows how, by concentrating on physical contact in these areas, you can heighten desire.

The Embrace of the Thighs

"When one of two lovers presses forcibly one or both of the thighs of the other between his or her own, it is called the 'embrace of the thighs'."

Pressing the thighs together in this way produces a sensation of physical pressure between you. The position also brings your genitals into contact, adding to the sensations of excitement and anticipation.

EMBRACE OF THE THIGHS

The Embrace of the Jaghana

"When the man presses the *jaghana*, or middle part, of the woman's body against his own, and mounts upon her to practice, either scratching with the nail or finger, or biting or striking or kissing, the hair of the woman being loose and flowing, it is called the 'embrace of the *jaghana*'."

DEFINITION

According to Vatsyayana, the jaghana is "the part of the body from the navel downward to the thighs."

The *Jaghana* is a close embrace in which the centers of the lovers' bodies are pressed together. Some couples may find the scratching, biting, and striking during this embrace a little too much, but performed with gentleness and humor, such game-playing can add to the eroticism of the embrace.

THE EMBRACE OF THE JAGHANA

The Embrace of the Forehead

"When either of the lovers touches the mouth, the eyes, and the forehead of the other with his or her own, it is called the 'embrace of the forehead'."

An intimate and seemingly innocent embrace, the closeness of lovers' faces adds to the intensity of sexual desire. This is a wonderfully affectionate and loving posture whose strength is in its very gentleness.

THE EMBRACE OF THE FOREHEAD

The Embrace of the Breasts

"When a man places his breast between the breasts of a woman and presses her with it, it is called 'the embrace of the breasts'."

Allow your nipples to brush against one another as you enjoy this upper body embrace. You needn't interpret Vatsyayana's instructions literally – the man's breast doesn't have to be placed "between" the woman's breasts entirely. But by skimming your chest across the tips of her nipples you could provoke an immediate erotic reaction.

THE EMBRACE OF THE BREASTS

A simple summary

✓ Vatsyayana breaks down early embraces into four – two of which are shared between people who are not yet lovers, the other two between people who are already sexual partners.

✓ A further group of embraces become more physical and intimate, enjoyed by lovers as a build-up to lovemaking.

✓ Vatsyayana is clear on the importance of male arousal and on the prudence of keeping it within its limits at this stage of sexual encounter.

✓ Vatsyayana lists "four ways of embracing simple members of the body" with varying degrees of physical contact to stimulate erotic sensations.

✓ Although not part of Vatsyayana's categories of embrace, mutual grooming can be a great way of enhancing closeness.

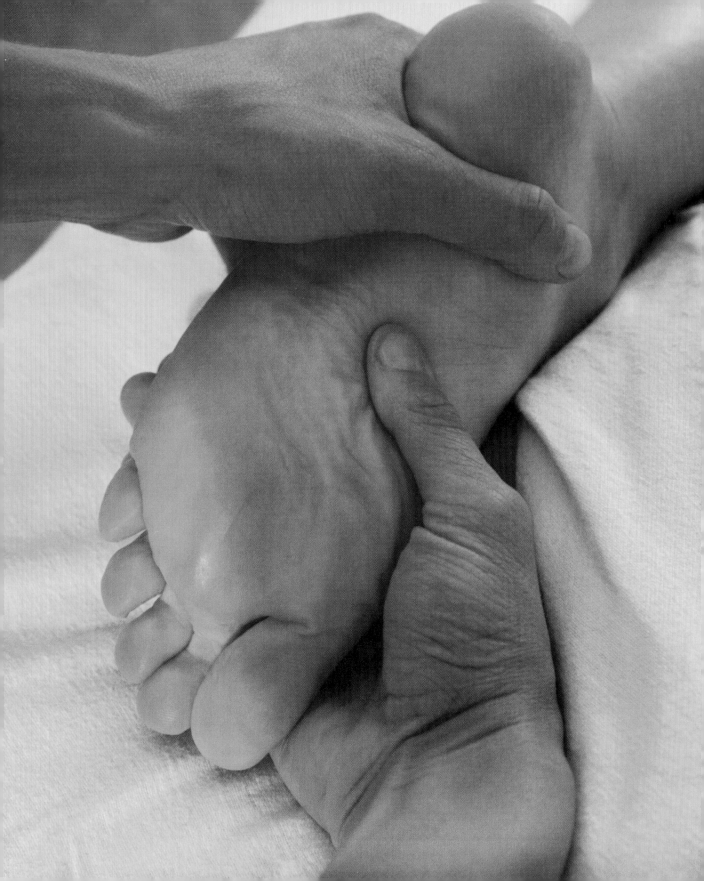

Chapter 8

The Skills of Touch

THE *KAMA SUTRA* is clear on the importance of a loving touch – using your hands to give comfort and pleasure to your partner is an important skill to master. Your touch can impart a range of sensations to your lover, depending on how you use it – you can refresh, revitalize, arouse, and excite. So let your fingers do the talking!

In this chapter...

✓ Sensual massage

✓ Oiling up

✓ A sensational massage experience

✓ I'll scratch your back

✓ Hair play

FEET ARE PARTICULARLY SENSITIVE TO TOUCH, AND CAN BE HIGHLY EROGENOUS ZONES

Sensual massage

MASSAGE IS NOT DESCRIBED in the Kama Sutra, *but for thousands of years it has been valued as a means of soothing away tiredness and tension. And yet, because we link touch with sex, we tend to steer clear of touching each other for fear of being misunderstood. This habit can extend, inappropriately, to our partners. This means that many lovers miss out on the pure delight of stimulating the body all over via the huge tactile area of the skin. So read this chapter to make sure you give your lover the all-over fingertip treatment.*

INTERNET

www.amazon.co.uk

Anne Hooper's The Ultimate Sexual Touch, *which contains many more details on how to pleasure the body, can be ordered through Amazon's web site.*

Massage doesn't have to lead to sex. It can be simply a wonderful way of relaxing the muscles and the mind. You can treat your partner to a massage and cuddle up on the sofa feeling blissfully restful, or use massage to rub each other up the right way in preparation for a steamy night of passion. Before you set off across your lover's skin, it's important to create a peaceful, comfortable, and romantic setting. Here's how to create the right environment:

- Ensure the room is warm and there are no drafts
- Make sure both the massage oil and your hands are warm
- Lock the door if you fear interruption
- Use low lighting, perfume the room, and decorate it with some flowers so that it looks visually appealing

■ **A really good** *massage session can be like a really good lovemaking session, but without the sex. And whether you're giving or receiving the massage, you'll feel wonderful afterward.*

THE BASIC MASSAGE STROKES

The basic massage strokes are easy to master with a little practice, and can be used to produce a range of sensations. You don't have to remember them all – the important stroke is circling, which is so versatile that you can use it on any part of the body.

1 **Circling:** Place both hands, palms down, on the back and move them in opposing circles outward and away from the spine. The circles can be small or large, firm or soft, or you can use only your fingertips – just remember to synchronize the movements of your hands

2 **Gliding:** Also known as *effleurage*, this involves using your palms to make sweeping movements over your partner's body. Put your body weight behind the movement as you spread your hands over your partner's skin, relieving tension and tightness in the muscles

3 **Kneading:** This is a stronger movement in which you curve the palms of your hands and place them on your partner's body. Lightly squeeze and then release the flesh, drawing out tension. Use the kneading stroke on fleshy areas of your partner's body, such as the buttocks and thighs

4 **Using fingers:** Use the pads of your fingers and thumbs to apply gentle pressure to your partner's back. Move your fingers in a circular motion, so that the muscles are softened and stroked evenly. This technique is known as *petrissage* and is very effective when used either side of the spine, to loosen muscular tension. Don't apply pressure directly onto the spine, however

5 **Percussion:** There are three main types of percussive massage stroke, in which your hands leave the body between strokes. Use all of them during your massage session to give your partner a range of sensations:

Hacking: Use the sides of your hands to give your partner a few quick "chops" – much like a karate chop but softer – on the top of the back and shoulders. Remember to keep your movements rhythmic

Tapotement: Put your fingers together and, using the tips of your fingers, drum on your partner's body lightly and quickly

Cupping: Curve your hands, tuck your thumbs in, and pound your partner's body with your hands, keeping the "cup" shape rigid for maximum effect

Oiling up

MASSAGE OILS OR LOTIONS *will help your hands to glide over the skin more smoothly, making your strokes more effective. There is a wide variety of suitable oils and lotions to choose from, or you might prefer to make your own personalized version.*

Which is best, an oil or a lotion? You can opt for plain oils, such as almond, olive, or sunflower, which are absorbed by the skin, but can leave a greasy residue. Oil-free creams and lotions are just as effective, although they're not quite as lubricating and long-lasting, so you may need to reapply them more frequently during your massage session.

Some people use baby oil as a massage lotion, but I don't find the smell of babies too sexy!

DEFINITION

An essential oil is a volatile oil that is derived from a plant. These oils evaporate easily and have a distinctive fragrance.

It's essential

Why not add a few drops of an *essential oil* to your base oil to give your partner both physical and psychological therapy while you massage? Essential oils permeate the skin, transferring their wonderful enriching properties into the bloodstream. Select an essential oil to suit your partner and the occasion.

Try the following:
- Frankincense – for spiritual liberation
- Patchouli – for arousal
- Geranium – for intimacy
- Ginger – for hot passion
- Jasmine – for love and joy
- Sandalwood – for unity
- Ylang ylang – for sensual desire

■ **Essential oils** *are absorbed through the pores of the skin during massage and eventually reach the nervous system, which influences our emotional and physical wellbeing.*

Not only do these essential oils transfer their properties through the skin, but they are also beautifully aromatic – allowing both you and your partner to breathe in and absorb their benefits.

To make up enough scented oil for one massage session, use about 1 fl oz (30 ml) of a base oil, such as almond, and add up to 12 drops of your chosen essential oil, depending on the potency required.

Warm it up

Slapping cold oil or lotion on to the skin is more likely to induce shock than pleasure. This is because the skin reacts to defend itself against cold, so that subsequent touches may be painful rather than enjoyable. For this reason, it's important to warm the oil or lotion by rubbing it between your palms before you apply it to your partner's skin. If you are using an essential oil, this will also help to release its aroma, preparing your lover for a wonderfully scented sensual session.

MASSAGE OIL

Rub it in

Rub the oil or lotion into the area of your partner's body that you will be massaging, working it into the skin, and keeping your strokes fluid so that the oil is absorbed. Replenish if you need to – your hands should glide effortlessly over your partner's body and the caressing should feel great to both of you.

INTERNET

www.annsummers.co.uk

www.goodvibes.com/fyi
/ingredients.html

These sites offer a good range of massage oils to buy online.

■ **Aim to keep** *your massage strokes rhythmic, even, and symmetrical. Make sure that your partner is lying comfortably and is happy with the amount of pressure you are applying. Ask for feedback.*

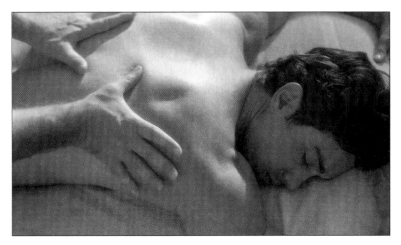

A sensational massage experience

FOR A TRULY SENSUAL MASSAGE, *it's important to tune into your partner's reactions so that you, too, feel some of them. Hands are packed with sensitive nerve endings and erogenous zones, so massage can make you – as well as your lover – feel fantastic.*

The head and shoulders

Begin by stroking your lover's shoulders and neck, then build up to stronger strokes on the shoulders to ease tension in the muscles. You should actually feel any knots of tension disappearing beneath your fingers as you knead.

Many people enjoy having their foreheads massaged gently at the temples to release tightness. Take your fingers to the top of your partner's head and knead the scalp as though you are shampooing the hair – this will give your partner a tingling release.

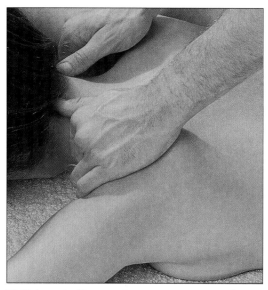

■ **Using circling strokes,** *massage across the shoulders to the neck, letting your thumbs circle into the hairline.*

Gently brush your partner's jaw, chin, mouth, and eyelids with your fingertips. This will help to relax all your partner's facial muscles.

The back

You can use some real pressure and the full palms of your hands to stroke and knead the back. Work your hands up from the buttocks to the very top of the spine, moving your fingers gently and (if you like) erotically, to relax and excite.

Warning: Never massage directly on to the spine.

The feet and legs

Begin by massaging your partner's toes, kneading them individually and stretching them out gently. Then, move on to the soles of the feet, using firm strokes with a deliberate action. Now bend your the legs gently from the knee as your partner lies on their stomach and use smooth upward and downward strokes with your hands – from knee to ankle and ankle to knee. You can then move up to the backs of the thighs, drawing your hands up and down rhythmically and lovingly.

■ **Don't forget to caress** *and knead each foot in turn, gently manipulating the toes and soles.*

I'll scratch your back

WHEN PASSIONATE INTENSITY HEIGHTENS, *try using your nails to scratch your partner's skin. For example, you could hold your partner close and scratch their back, or claw at their chest with animal passion.*

SCRATCHING DURING LOVEMAKING

As Vatsyayana says: " . . . nothing tends to increase love so much as the effects of marking with the nails, and biting." However, he recognizes that this practice is not for everyone: " . . . pressing with the nails is not a usual thing except with those who are intensely passionate. It is employed . . . by those to whom the practice is agreeable."

According to Vatsyayana, pressing, marking, or scratching the body with the nails takes place between lovers at the following times: "On the first visit; at the time of setting out on a journey; on the return from a journey; at the time when an angry lover is reconciled; and, lastly, when the woman is intoxicated."

You can use such strokes whenever you feel incredibly passionate and compelled to leave your marks of love.

Leaving your mark

As Vatsyayana says: "The places that are to be pressed with the nails are: the armpit, the throat, the breasts, the lips, the *jaghana* or middle parts of the body and the thighs." But you can leave your mark anywhere that suits you and your partner.

You may wish to leave a scratch mark of passion where everyone can see it or in a secret place known only to the two of you "for the remembrance and increase of love."

Do use your hands and nails to leave their impression on your partner's body, but don't break the skin. Keep your scratching erotic to intensify physical passion, but stop short of administering pain or injury.

■ **Using the fingernails** *to mark each other's skin during foreplay and lovemaking is deemed a very pleasurable activity by the* Kama Sutra.

Trivia...

Vatsyayana says there are circumstances when visible marking is appropriate and those when it should be kept under wraps. A young female lover may openly display these signs of passion: "When a stranger sees at a distance a young woman with the marks of nails on her breast, he is filled with love and respect for her." For a married woman, however, such a display is deemed inappropriate. Her scratches of love should be kept well out of sight!

The blows of love

Striking with the hand is an extension of scratching. The *Kama Sutra* describes it as a harmless ritualized activity that serves to heighten excitement and passionate intensity during lovemaking. These blows of love take place in the following areas of the body: "The shoulders, the head, the space between the breasts, the back, the *jaghana* or middle part of the body, and the sides." Strike gently, using the following parts of your hand to give your partner a range of feelings:

- Back of the hand
- Fingers
- Fist
- Palm of the hand

Be controlled with these blows — they are not meant to cause pain to your partner but are a physical expression of heightened emotion during lovemaking.

Hair play

THE KAMA SUTRA ACKNOWLEDGES *the eternal fascination that a woman's hair holds for a man, stating that "dressing the hair with unguents and perfumes and braiding it" is one of the arts that a woman should learn. Pubic hair can also feature in the preliminaries to lovemaking and for lovers, the sight and feel of each other's pubic hair heralds the erotic anticipation of intercourse.*

Remember that hair should be touched gently – that is, stroked rather than pulled!

A light touch

A woman with long hair can use it to caress her partner's naked body. Sit astride your man as he lies on his back and bend your head forward so that your soft tresses brush over his chest and shoulders. Sweep your hair all over his skin, giving him a tingling sensation. Shorter hair needn't stop you from enjoying this sexy game – you'll simply need to move your head down further towards your lover's body as you tickle him with your locks!

■ **Hold your body** *clear of your partner's so that only your hair is touching his skin. Sweep your tresses over his whole body, including his penis, to heighten desire.*

Running your fingers through your partner's clean, soft hair gives you both pleasurable sensations. Allowing your fingers to become loosely entangled in your partner's silky strands and giving a little playful tug as you enjoy a passionate encounter can arouse and excite.

Revealing the neck

Clean lustrous hair can be a powerful aphrodisiac, inviting lovers to toy with it and bury their hands in it. Its texture and sheen are attractive in themselves, but when the hair is lifted to reveal a soft, delicate neck, the joy is even greater.

Touch your partner's hair as you approach from behind, and make their neck tingle.

Trivia...

Necking is the old-fashioned term for making out, for kissing, and winding your heads around each other. But did you know that some women possess such sensitive necks, especially just behind the ears, that if you kiss, nibble, and lick them there for long enough they can actually climax? Try it one day.

■ **Stroking your partner's hair** *to one side and gently touching the nape of the neck with tentative fingers will make the hairs on the back of the neck stand on end with pleasure!*

Hair below

What about the other body hair? The curly variety that adorns the Mound of Venus? Take things a step further. Caress your partner's pubic hairs softly with your fingers, stopping short of actually touching the genitals.

Your secret weapon here? Hold little tufts of hair between your fingers and gently tug on them. By doing this rhythmically up and down the pubic area, your partner will experience a sensual prickling that will drive them wild.

■ **Caressing your partner's pubic hair** *can be a highly erotic experience for both of you.*

A simple summary

✔ Although the *Kama Sutra* does not discuss massage, the physical and emotional benefits that the practice imparts are directly in keeping with its teachings.

✔ A knowledge of massage strokes will allow you to give your partner a fabulous touch experience. You don't have to be an expert – just keep moving your hands very slowly.

✔ Oils and lotions enhance the massage experience.

✔ Using your nails to leave your mark on your partner in the height of passion, or as a playful exercise, can give an unexpected kick to lovemaking.

✔ Hair can be used as an erotic aid – and pubic hair massage is a secret erotic weapon.

Chapter 9

The Pure Delight of Kissing

THE *KAMA SUTRA* devotes a chapter to kissing, recognizing its significance as a tender expression of affection and a highly erotic exercise. The lips are among the most sensitive areas of the body and have a powerful role to play in exciting and satisfying lovemaking. Why should we concentrate so hard on this relatively innocent-sounding occupation? Because done well, kissing can propel men and women into a passionate experience of sexuality.

In this chapter...

✓ Innocent kisses

✓ A young girl's kiss

✓ Passionate kissing

✓ Playing kissing games

✓ Kissing all over

TENDER, NON-PENETRATIVE KISSES ARE A WAY OF EXPRESSING AFFECTION AND CLOSENESS

Innocent kisses

SO WHAT SORT OF KISSES are we talking about here? Can there really be so many different sorts? And is one kiss really any different from another? Read on for the answers. Even if a kiss is fleeting and non-penetrating, it can still be highly sensual and even erotic. As a starting point, the Kama Sutra describes four kinds of sweet, innocent kiss.

The Bent Kiss

Vatsyayana describes this as a kiss in which "the heads of two lovers are bent toward each other, and when so bent, kissing takes place."

For this kiss you could place your hand behind your partner's neck to guide their head toward yours. This is a natural and gentle experiment in which the lovers' faces are angled easily and comfortably towards each other. Turning your head slightly to the side also aids this natural delight.

THE BENT KISS

The Turned Kiss

THE TURNED KISS

"When one of them turns up the face of the other by holding the head and chin, and then kissing, it is called a 'turned kiss'."

This is often a kiss of emotion, when one lover is perhaps caught by a moment of passion and draws their partner's face toward them to express this feeling. Using your hands to guide your lover's face toward your own adds to its intensity and ardor.

According to Vatsyayana, "on the occasion of first congress, kissing . . . should be done moderately; . . . and should not be continued for a long time." Once a sexual relationship has been established, however, the reverse is the case.

The Pressed Kiss

This kiss involves pressing the lower lip with the fingers with "much force." Vatsyayana also describes "the greatly pressed kiss," in which one lover holds the other's lower lip in their fingers, then touches the lip with their tongue before kissing the lip with "great force." This is a highly erotic and intense exercise which can be seen as a prelude to kissing – a kind of "playing with the lips" before embracing. Look into your lover's eyes as you press the lower lip to increase sexual tension.

THE PRESSED KISS

The Straight Kiss

This is a kiss in which "the lips of two lovers are brought into direct contact with each other."

In this kiss, the faces of the two lovers are level rather than angled to one side. As such, this must be a very tender and affectionate kiss rather than an intensely passionate one – noses would collide if the lovers' mouths were to open!

This is a kiss that could be repeated several times to build up to a more passionate embrace.

If it feels natural to take the innocent kisses further into a more erotic and raunchy exchange, then go for it!

THE STRAIGHT KISS

A young girl's kiss

ACCORDING TO THE KAMA SUTRA, *there are three types of kisses that a young girl may give to her partner. These are truly innocent kisses and are performed with a wonderful shyness that can be enjoyed by all couples.*

■ **A young girl's kiss** *as described in the* Kama Sutra *is flirtatious and full of promise rather than overtly sexual.*

The Nominal Kiss

"When a girl touches only the mouth of her lover with her own, but does not herself do anything, it is called the 'nominal kiss'."

This kiss could be used with tantalizing effect to exhibit controlled desire between lovers. Because of the lack of movement, it is loaded with sexual tension.

Brushing your lips against your partner's in this way makes for a beautifully modest exchange, but with a promise of something more.

The Throbbing Kiss

"When a girl, setting aside her bashfulness a little, wishes to touch the lip that is pressed into her mouth, and with that object moves her lower lip, but not the upper one, it is called the 'throbbing kiss'." This is a step on from the Nominal Kiss and can be used in tandem with it. Just a slight movement, almost a trembling of the lower lip, can be enough to excite your lover, following the stillness of the previous exchange.

Be aware of how the sensitivity of your lips is heightened as you enjoy these slow and focused kisses.

The Touching Kiss

"When a girl touches her lover's lip with her tongue, and having shut her eyes, places her hands on those of her lover, it is called the 'touching kiss'."

Here touch is introduced very gently with the tongue and hands simultaneously. The strength of this kiss is in its softness and tenderness.

Playing the young girl

The sexiness of the young girl's three-fold kiss lies in its tantalizing cumulative nature. Taking your time over kissing, as described here, is a great habit to get into.

When enjoying these kisses with your partner, keep them gentle and measured — building up the intensity but without self-consciousness. Try not to think about it too much or worry about the order because then it won't feel natural.

INTERNET

www.virtualkiss.com

Click here to find out more about magic moments of momentous kissing.

Passionate kissing

WHEN A KISS BECOMES *increasingly passionate and erotic, sensuality and anticipation are also heightened. These kisses, as described in the* Kama Sutra, *have a more overtly sexual tone – the mouth is more open as lovers begin to drink one another in.*

The Kiss of the Upper Lip

This kiss is described by Vatsyayana as follows: "When a man kisses the upper lip of a woman, while she in return kisses his lower lip, it is called the 'kiss of the upper lip'."

This is a highly erotic exchange, in which each lover is almost feasting with animal passion on the mouth of the other. You can really bond as you eat your way into this delicious kiss.

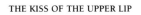

THE KISS OF THE UPPER LIP

Although the Kiss of the Upper Lip describes the man as initiating the embrace, Vatsyayana makes it clear that kisses can be initiated by either lover – so no woman should feel uncomfortable about making the first move. Most men are delighted when their women make the advances!

121

The Clasping Kiss

"When one of them [the lovers] takes both the lips of the other between his or her own, it is called "a clasping kiss'."

This is an enveloping kiss in which one lover's lips are drawn into those of the other. A truly consuming and abandoned kiss, this can be repeated several times as tension rises.

THE CLASPING KISS

Don't try the Clasping Kiss if you happen to possess a moustache. Vatsyayana points that a woman can only take this kiss from a man who is clean-shaven, otherwise she will get a mouthful of coarse bristle instead of soft lips!

The Fighting of the Tongue

This leads on from the Clasping Kiss and is described as follows: " . . . if one of them [the lovers] touches the teeth, the tongue, and the palate of the other with his or her tongue, it is called 'the fighting of the tongue'."

The Fighting of the Tongue is what we would now probably call "French kissing," in which the tongue moves around the mouth, tenderly (or sometimes fervently) exploring the inside.

Playing kissing games

PLAYFULNESS AND PHYSICAL FOOLING *around can spice up your kissing. Flirtatious horseplay is common among younger lovers, but many couples lose this element of fun as their relationship matures. If you and your partner would enjoy a little game-playing, get going – you may find it wonderfully refreshing. You could make up your own games if you prefer – perhaps taking a few pointers from the* Kama Sutra's *kissing game below.*

"Getting hold of the lower lip," as described in the *Kama Sutra* kissing game (opposite), can add a gloriously erotic edge to your kissing. Don't bite the lip hard, however – simply take it firmly between your teeth with playful pressure.

(Biting is an important part of the *Kama Sutra* and is described in more detail in Chapter 10.) A valuable part of the *Kama Sutra's* kissing game is the element of assuming and acting out a role. If you want to get the most from playing the game, why not take on the roles of the dominant male lover and the naive young girl, as described?

Role-playing is enjoyed by many couples in all aspects of lovemaking and can be a very liberating and rewarding experience.

The most pleasurable element of this mock fight is, of course, the making-up afterwards. Nothing is more unifying than melting back into a lover's arms after a disagreement (fictional or otherwise!). Cash in on the tongue-in-cheek "quarreling" aspect of the game and have fun "kissing each other better!"

THE KAMA SUTRA'S KISSING GAME

The *Kama Sutra* describes the following game that can be enjoyed by two lovers to add an element of fun to their kissing.

A KISSING GAME BASED ON A WAGER

"As regards kissing, a wager may be laid as to which (of the lovers) will get hold of the lips of the other first. If the woman loses, she should pretend to cry, should keep her lover off by shaking her hands, and turn away from him and dispute with him, saying, 'Let another wager be laid.'

If she loses this a second time, she should appear doubly distressed, and when her lover is off his guard or asleep, she should get hold of his lower lip, and hold it in her teeth, so that it should not slip away; and then she should laugh, make a loud noise, deride him, dance about, and say whatever she likes in a joking way, moving her eyebrows and rolling her eyes. Such are the wagers and quarrels as far as kissing is concerned, but the same may be applied with regard to the pressing or scratching with the nails and fingers, biting and striking."

Kissing all over

KISSES NEEDN'T JUST BE MOUTH TO MOUTH, *of course – pay a little lip service to the whole of your lover's body. Some areas are more sensitive to the softness of a kiss than others. According to Vatsyayana, "Kissing is of four kinds: Moderate, contracted, pressed, and soft, according to the different parts of the body which are kissed, for different kinds of kisses are appropriate for different parts of the body." Unfortunately there are no explanations as to which type of kiss should be pressed where, but you can use your imagination.*

Moderate kisses

These seem to be quite general, measured kisses, without too much intensity. A tender kiss like this on the back can be highly arousing. Surprise your partner as he or she lies on his or her front with some affectionate smooches along the length of the spine.

Contracted kisses

These could be interpreted as little staccato kisses, in which the lips are applied to the skin and quickly pulled away in a playful, affectionate way. You could perhaps lavish such kisses on your partner's thighs and buttocks, to drive them crazy with desire.

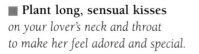
■ **Plant long, sensual kisses**
*on your lover's neck and throat
to make her feel adored and special.*

Remember that the inside of the thigh is a particularly sensitive and erotic area, so concentrate kisses here for the greatest effect.

Pressed kisses

This type of kiss would involve placing your lips on your partner's body and applying gentle pressure while holding your mouth there for a moment. This kind of kiss is a truly loving and emotional kiss, in which you are almost reluctant to draw your lips away from your lover's body.

Soft kisses

These would be the most tender and gentle of kisses, in which you just brush your partner's skin with your lips. You could perhaps lavish these on such sensitive areas as your partner's neck and throat, or, perhaps, move down to the chest. A woman's breasts are, of course, particularly sensitive to loving lips, but many men also enjoy having their chests and nipples kissed softly.

While treating your partner to an all-over kissing session, don't forget to use your tongue and hands from time to time to increase their pleasure. A little licking and stroking will intensify the passion of your kiss.

A simple summary

✔ Start your kissing with tender, non-penetrative exchanges as an expression of affection and closeness.

✔ Vatsyayana describes three kisses that a "young girl" may give to her partner, with advancing intensity.

✔ Build up the level of passion in your kisses, allowing desire to take hold as you lead up to lovemaking.

✔ You can take elements of the *Kama Sutra's* kissing game to add some spice to your kissing.

✔ Don't neglect the rest of the body as you enjoy your kissing – you and your lover can both have fun bestowing kisses all over each other.

Chapter 10

Making Mouth Music

THE ANCIENT INDIANS CARRIED KISSING much further than we do in the West. They did not stop at passionate kissing. When passion heated up, they reckoned that kisses turned into something harder and sharper: The embrace of the teeth. I guess many of us have felt like biting and eating up a partner, so profoundly have we desired them. Some instinct makes us want to draw this lover deep inside and, since we are kissing, the mouth tends to be the easiest point of entry. But most of us haven't realized that the teeth could be used with quite the skill depicted by the *Kama Sutra*. Sexual biting is, it seems, an art form.

In this chapter...

✓ **The bites of love**

✓ **Cunnilingus**

✓ **Fellatio**

✓ **The Congress of a Crow**

THE *KAMA SUTRA* DESCRIBES HOW THE MOUTH CAN BE LOVINGLY USED TO EXCITE GREAT PASSION

The bites of love

IN THE INDIAN EROTIC TRADITION, *biting is an integral part of the lover's repertoire. The Kama Sutra catalogs different kinds of tooth titillation in detail. The bites described can be given almost anywhere on the body and range from playful, teasing nips to sustained sucking that leaves a pronounced mark (better known as a lovebite today) to more forceful biting at the height of passion.*

If forceful biting constitutes part of your lovemaking, take care not to injure your lover.

A PASSIONATE BITE

Using the lips

Some bites simply involve using the lips with varying degrees of force, resulting in a slight reddening of the skin. These are:

● **The Hidden Bite:** "The biting that is shown only by the excessive redness of the skin that is bitten"
● **The Swollen Bite:** "When the skin is pressed down on both sides"

These bites are expressions of passion, where the skin is rubbed and pressed by the mouth with ardor, leaving tell-tale traces of a passionate encounter.

Making a Point

Vatsyayana then describes bites of love in which the teeth are introduced:

● **The Point:** "When a small portion of the skin is bitten with two teeth only." A tentative and subtle bite, this can then lead to:
● **The Line of Points:** "When such small portions of the skin are bitten with all the teeth." This is a fuller, more carnal bite, in which nibbling the skin progresses to feasting on it

Trivia...

The ancient Indians intended bites of love to be seen by others. Love marks were visible signs of passion and a passionate lover was a sought-after one.

The Jewels

The following types of bite are concerned with using the teeth – or "jewels," as the *Kama Sutra* describes them:

- **The Coral and the Jewel:** "The biting that is done by bringing together the teeth (jewel) and lips (coral)"
- **The Line of Jewels:** "When biting is done with all the teeth." Using the lips, or "coral," in this bite probably softens the contact with your lover's skin, creating a kind of half-bite

The Broken Cloud

"The biting that consists of unequal risings in a circle, and that comes from the space between the teeth, is called the 'broken cloud.' This is impressed on the breasts."

In pressing the skin with the teeth, the aim of this bite is to raise the skin into the spaces between the teeth rather than to pierce the skin, leaving marks in the form of raised areas of flesh.

An appropriate bite for the very sensitive breast area, Vatsyayana describes it as loaded with "intense passion."

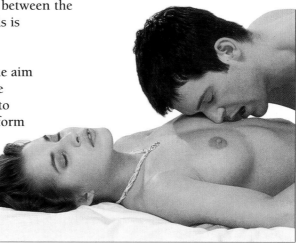

THE BROKEN CLOUD

THE PLACES FOR DIFFERENT BITES

According to Vatsyayana, there are specific areas of the body where the different bites of love should be used:

- **Lower lip:** Hidden Bite, Swollen Bite, and Point
- **Cheek:** Swollen Bite, Coral, and Jewel
- **Throat, armpit, joints of the thighs:** Line of Points and Line of Jewels
- **Forehead, thighs:** Line of Points

The Biting of a Boar

Like the Broken Cloud, Vatsyayana describes this bite as being employed by "persons of intense passion." "The biting that consists of many broad rows of marks near to one another, and with red intervals, is called the 'biting of a boar.' This is impressed on the breasts and the shoulders."

Marking the shoulders

This kind of bite could be left on the shoulders during lovemaking in the "spoons" position, in which the man enters the woman from behind, curling his body into hers. The woman can also perform the bite, curled up behind the man. This is an erotic way of expressing passion and desire with the mouth in a position in which kissing is often impractical. The tops of the shoulders and the lower part of the neck are exceptionally sensual areas.

THE BITING OF A BOAR

Keep it clean

When delivering the Bite of a Boar, or indeed any bite, oral hygiene is very important. Vatsyayana describes the qualities of good teeth as follows: "They should be equal, possessed of a pleasing brightness, capable of being colored, of proper proportions, unbroken, and with sharp ends." It sounds as though he's advocating acquiring a set of vampire-like fangs!

No one wants to be devoured by a mouth full of dirty, neglected teeth. Brush your pearly whites thoroughly before you start chewing on your partner.

Trivia...

Research has revealed that women are more enthusiastic than men about biting during lovemaking. It has been suggested that this is because men are generally more muscular than women, and so it feels more natural for them to express passion through forceful bodily gestures rather than through biting. By the same token, it might also mean that when a man is bitten it hurts more!

Cunnilingus

THE KAMA SUTRA *touches only fleetingly on the subject of cunnilingus in comparison to its coverage of fellatio. "Some women of the harem, when they are amorous, do the acts of the mouth on the yonis (genitals) of one another, and some men do the same thing with women." Nowadays, however, cunnilingus is enjoyed by many heterosexual couples and constitutes a valuable – or possibly essential – part of satisfying lovemaking.*

INTERNET

www.halcyon.com/elf/
altsex/cunni.html

Visit this site for more information on cunnilingus.

The sexiest and most erotic way of stimulating a woman is by using cunnilingus. When a woman is sexually stimulated, her vagina produces a natural lubricating fluid which, as well as allowing the vagina to receive a fully erect penis without discomfort, alters the way in which genital touch is experienced, making it pleasurable and full of sensuality. Stimulation doesn't have to be focussed exclusively on the vagina, although it is usually more effective when it is.

Clitoral stimulation

The clitoris is the most sensitive nerve center of a woman's body. Position yourself so that you can stroke your tongue upward over the shaft and head of her clitoris. Stimulate each side of the clitoris in turn, always from underneath. Use featherlike strokes on the head of the clitoris. Try flicking the underside of the shaft from side to side with the tip of the tongue.

Your lover can be sitting, standing, or lying down to receive oral stimulation, but the longer you do it, the more likely she is to turn weak at the knees, so if you're hoping to bring her to orgasm, she might be safer if she's horizontal!

The vagina

Once your lover is moist with desire, you can take the melting movements of your tongue and lips down to the vagina. Flick your tongue around the outside of the vagina and include the *labia* in some of your loving licks and strokes. Run your tongue over the lips and kiss them softly.

DEFINITION

The labia are the fleshy outer lips surrounding the vagina.

■ **The man** *should lie comfortably on his side with his head between his partner's legs, while the woman should simply relax and enjoy the erotic pleasure he is giving her.*

The perineum

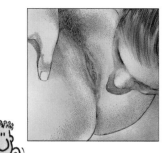

This is the area of skin between the vagina and the anus. It's rich in nerve endings and so very responsive to being touched, stroked, or licked.

Lick the perineum with featherlike strokes – but take your cues from your lover's moans of pleasure.

Women who do not produce much natural lubricant can use one of the many water-soluble creams and jellies specially formulated for use as vaginal lubricants. These are inexpensive and available from any pharmacy.

Tongue insertion

When your lover is gasping with desire you might insert your tongue into her vagina. Mimic the penis with your tongue by first flicking just the tip into the moist vagina and then strengthening your strokes and darting your tongue in further. Vary the level of penetration to give her a series of tantalizing sensations, entering and withdrawing both slowly and quickly.

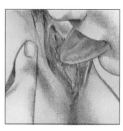

Fellatio

ACCORDING TO THE KAMA SUTRA, "mouth congress," or fellatio, is practiced by eunuchs and by "unchaste and wanton women, female attendants,

and serving maids" and is not deemed an activity that should be part of the sexual relationship of two loving partners. Nowadays, however, fellatio forms part of most loving relationships.

■ **Fellatio was often a duty** *for female attendants and serving women.*

Licking the penis

Start fellatio by licking the shaft of the penis with your tongue, holding the base of it in your hand as you do so. Treat it as a delicious ice cream cone, savoring it with every stroke of your tongue.

The butterfly flick

Varying the strokes of your tongue will give your partner the most pleasurable sensations. Use the end of your tongue to flick lightly along the ridge and the underside of the penis. You can also employ this technique on the very sensitive head of the penis, keeping your strokes gentle but quick.

Sucking the penis

As your partner's excitement increases, take his penis in your hand and place the very tip between your lips. First move it around gently between your lips – Vatsyayana describes this as the "nominal congress" – then begin to suck it, moving the head

THE BUTTERFLY FLICK

in and out of your mouth very slightly. By doing this you are mimicking the sensation provided by the vaginal lips. Your lover may begin to thrust with his hips as the sexual intensity mounts.

You can use a kind of kissing action with your lips while drawing the penis in and out of your mouth. Take the end of the penis into your mouth and press it with your lips, then withdraw your lips completely. You can then press your lips against the very end of the penis, without putting it into your mouth, and draw away again. This is a kind of teasing action. You could then take the whole penis in your mouth and suck – with a kind of swallowing action.

Don't take the whole penis in your mouth if you don't feel comfortable with it, or if you fear choking on it. Instead, you could simultaneously stimulate part of the shaft with your hands while sucking on the tip.

INTERNET

www.halcyon.com/elf/ altsex/fella.html

Visit this site for more information on fellatio. Find the answers to many of the most frequently asked questions about oral sex and pick up some fascinating tips. For example, men who consume certain foods and drinks can sweeten the taste of their semen!

■ **While performing fellatio,** *increase his pleasure by varying your lip and tongue movements. You don't have to suck the whole penis – the head is the most sensitive part.*

THE EIGHT KINDS OF FELLATIO

Vatsyayana itemizes the kinds of fellatio with which a eunuch can pleasure his master – in the pretense of shampooing him. You can use all of these techniques as you pleasure your partner – without any pretense whatsoever!

1 The nominal congress

Place the penis between your lips and move it about.

2 Biting the sides

Gently nibble the shaft of the penis.

3 Pressing outside

Press the end of the penis with your lips and draw it out.

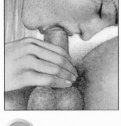

4 Pressing inside

Put the end of the penis into your mouth before pressing it with your lips and withdrawing.

5 Pressing the penis

Kiss the penis while holding it in your hand.

6 Rubbing the penis

Touch the penis all over with your tongue.

7 Sucking a mango fruit

Insert half of the penis into your mouth and suck it.

8 Swallowing up the penis

Put the whole of the penis into your mouth as though swallowing.

The Congress of a Crow

VATSYAYANA DESCRIBES THIS AS FOLLOWS: *"When a man and woman lie down in an inverted order, with the head of the one toward the feet of the other and carry on in this congress, it is called the 'congress of a crow'."* This is what we would nowadays refer to as the "69" position in which lovers give each other oral pleasure simultaneously.

To experience the Congress of a Crow successfully, both you and your partner should be lying comfortably so you can concentrate on what you are doing and feeling. Aching elbows and hips will distract you from pleasure. Lie on your sides and settle into a relaxed position.

From this position, your usual approach to your partner's genital area will be inverted, but keep your technique soft and varied at first. Take advantage of your improved access to areas such as the perineum and give your lover waves of pleasure. Tongue insertion can also be much easier from this position as you bury your face into your partner's genitals.

The deeper techniques, such as sucking the penis and swallowing, can be challenging from this angle. You may need to let the end of your tongue do most of the work here, licking the head of the penis lightly and rubbing your tongue over the end with a flicking action.

THE CONGRESS OF A CROW

Working together

It can be difficult to concentrate on what you are doing during the Congress of a Crow because your own pleasure can be distracting. A little give-and-take is what's required. Let your partner pleasure you while you withdraw for a few movements and then you can return the favor. You can enjoy periods of mutual oral stimulation, punctuated with erotic episodes in which one of you does the work – whatever feels natural and good.

You don't have to achieve orgasm in this position – many couples don't – but if you do, the experience can be pretty overwhelming.

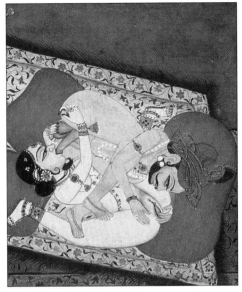

LOVERS WORKING IN HARMONY

A simple summary

✓ The *Kama Sutra* expounds biting as a key part of lovemaking, but care needs to be taken to prevent it from becoming savage.

✓ Biting can be arousing, a mark of conquest, a power trip, and a means of artistry.

✓ Although the art of cunnilingus is not explored fully in the original *Kama Sutra*, nowadays it is an integral part of most couples' sexual repetoires.

✓ Like cunnilingus, fellatio has a key role in sex these days. It is no longer a kind of "master and servant" service as described by Vatsyayana.

✓ In the Congress of a Crow position, couples can both give and receive oral stimulation simultaneously as cunnilingus and fellatio are enjoyed in unison. It's the ancient equivalent of our present-day "69" position.

PART THREE

KAMA SUTRA LOVE POSITIONS ARE MANY AND VARIED

THE SEX POSITIONS

IN SECTION THREE WE GRADUATE to the more "advanced" love positions. The original *Kama Sutra* text referred to *35 positions* that every woman should learn (from her man) in order to be a good sex partner. I also bring in other *ancient Indian sex postures* from the *Ananga Ranga*, and from *The Perfumed Garden*, both of which were published by Richard Burton's *Kama Shastra* Society.

The huge variety of sex positions makes it very clear that sex was used for recreation (that is, fun), overcoming sexual difficulties (such as partial impotence), and even for physical fitness (a kind of ancient aerobics). The idea of sex as a fitness regime may sound strange but in ancient India sex was also part of the pathway to being a *better person*. Sex was perceived as a duty – a way of getting closer to nirvana.

Chapter 11

Man-on-top Positions

BEFORE EMBARKING ON HIS DESCRIPTIONS OF THE SEX POSITIONS, Vatsyayana points out that some sexual partners are better suited than others because of the size and shape of their genitals. In this chapter, we learn that men were categorized as either horses, bulls, or hares, while women were classed as deer, mares, or elephants – then we discover which partnerships were considered most and least compatible. And if the words "Kama Sutra" conjure up visions of impractical, bizarre, or even impossible lovemaking positions, this section should dispel them. Most of the sexual positions that follow are relatively easy to accomplish and involve the woman lying on her back with her legs in a variety of postures.

In this chapter...

✓ Are you a hare or an elephant?

✓ When the woman lies on her back

✓ A man's duty to his partner

THE MISSIONARY POSITION AND ITS VARIATIONS WERE FAVORED SEXUAL POSTURES IN THE *KAMA SUTRA*

Are you a hare or an elephant?

VATSYAYANA BEGINS HIS TREATISE on sex positions with common sense by pointing out that men and women have different-sized and shaped genitals. The 4th-century monk's cutting edge observation is that size and shape alter how you experience sex. What's right for a man of large proportions won't necessarily be right for a large woman. So before you think about intercourse you need to take into account the kind of fit you are about to experience!

Are you a male hare?

According to the original *Kama Sutra*, man is divided into three categories, "according to the size of his lingam [penis]." These categories are:

(1) Hare

(2) Bull

(3) Horse (or stallion)

Not only do these descriptions denote size (horses being the largest), they also indicate temperament, an interesting psychological idea that predates the thinking of famous psychologist, Alfred Adler, by about 1,700 years. A hare might be timid, a bull bullish, and a stallion supersexual and rampant.

■ **A man described as a hare** *would have had a small penis and a timid temperament.*

Are you a female elephant?

Women were also divided into three classes, according to the size of her yoni. These classes were:

(1) Deer

(2) Mare

(3) Elephant

> **DEFINITION**
>
> *The Sanskrit word yoni is a symbol of the female genitals venerated by the Hindus. In this context it means the female vulva.*

Ironically, whereas men of biggest girth were considered superior, it was women of smallest girth who were most highly rated. Women in each category were also attributed different characteristics. A deer was considered fleet of foot, graceful, and compact, a mare handsome, dependable, maternal, and sturdy, while an elephant was said to be big, jolly, unrestrained in showing emotion, humorous, powerful, and slightly clumsy.

The best combinations of male and female

The equal unions (for obvious reasons) were considered to be:

 1 Hare and deer

2 Bull and mare

3 Horse and elephant

But these were not necessarily rated as the best unions. For maximum sensuality and combination of temperament, resulting (hopefully) in reaching a high plane of sensuality, the most highly rated combinations were, in descending order:

 1 Horse and deer

2 Horse and mare

3 Bull and deer

■ **A woman in the elephant category,** *as well as having a large-sized vulva, was considered to be jolly, powerful, and rather clumsy.*

The *Kama Sutra* was literally talking about penile/vaginal fit, advocating the biggest penis and the smallest vagina as the ideal.

 *The Kama Sutra is biased toward the male in advocating its largest penis/smallest vagina philosophy. Women today, while certainly enjoying a wide penis, do not necessarily want a very long one since it can seriously hurt. Many women also choose skilful hands and tongue over a large penis.*

ORGAN INFERIORITY

In 1907 Alfred Adler published his study of "organ inferiority." The gist of the theory is that people are influenced by their particular shape or size and grow up to develop feelings of confidence correspondingly. As a result, individuals might change their entire life pattern in order to overcome a perceived inferiority and feel "accepted" by society. For example, if you had a weak leg as a child, you may strive to compensate by becoming a runner or an athlete in later life. Although this might be admirable, Adler pointed out that sometimes such compensation could be overdone. For example, an overweight child, instead of slimming sensibly, might go to extremes and become anorexic. He also felt that the cause of sexual problems could be found in these same congenital weaknesses in that if an individual feels somehow lacking, they strive overly to compensate sexually.

Combinations least likely to succeed

Male-female combinations that are likely to be sexually and emotionally unsatisfactory are, in descending order:

1. Elephant and bull

2. Mare and hare

3. Elephant and hare

However, although there may be physical reasons why the *Kama Sutra*'s recommended male and female combinations add up to good sense, we really don't think the same any longer.

There's only one problem with all this assessment of genital size. By the time you get familiar with your partner's shape and appearance, isn't it just a little too late? Don't take this advice too seriously!

Trivia...

People in Vatsyayana's day believed in learning all they could about the workings of the body, including the sexual parts, since sexual knowledge was all part of the divine plan. It was thought then that the more you studied and practiced sexuality, the closer you came to God. Today we think it's an excellent idea to know your body and how your own sexual response functions. Unfortunately, we don't all believe it brings us closer to God, but we do feel that it brings us nearer to bliss with our partners.

When the woman lies on her back

ONCE YOU HAVE FIGURED OUT (somehow) whether your partner is a stallion or an elephant, it makes sense to start thinking about sexual intercourse. The missionary position (and its variations) was practiced thousands of years before it ever got its name. It's what Vatsyayana moves on to next. Although women are told to occasionally take some of the pressure off their man, nearly all the sex positions described place the woman firmly on her back with the man on top. However, there are many different varieties of these woman-underneath postures. These are what Vatsyayana starts off with.

The Yawning Position

Lovemaking begins with a straightforward man-on-top position, in which both partners' legs are outstretched. From this starting point, the Yawning Position often develops quite naturally. The woman raises her thighs and parts them widely, raising her legs high on either side of her partner as he kneels up and thrusts forward.

The barrier presented by the woman's thighs in this position does not allow for deep penetration, and it is unlikely that her clitoris will receive much stimulation. Offsetting this, though, is the undeniable eroticism of the position. With her genitals displayed, there is also a feeling of helplessness that, for the woman, can be a powerful turn-on.

YAWNING POSITION

The Yawning Position – a variation

The deepest possible penetration, giving intense pleasure to both partners, is achieved with this variation of the Yawning Position. The man leans forward and over his partner while her legs are raised so high that they rest on his arms and shoulders. Because of the extreme depth of penetration, the woman should be fully aroused, with her vagina completely dilated, before her partner enters her.

This is the position you are most likely to slip into after playing with the Yawning Position. It is far more satisfactory because it combines the ease of the missionary position with greater penetration and a greater erotic element derived from the woman's legs being held so high.

YAWNING POSITION – A VARIATION

The Widely Opened Position

The woman may find herself moving into this position quite naturally, pushing her own pelvis up from the ground to meet her man's pelvis, simply through her eagerness to be extra close. Alternatively you may find this is a natural position to slip into immediately after the Yawning Position.

With your head thrown back, arch your back and raise your pelvis to meet your partner, opening your legs wide and giving an angle of entry that ensures deep penetration. Once your body has moved up to meet his, look your lover in the eyes to increase your sense of poignant intimacy.

WIDELY OPENED POSITION

The genital contact offered by this position is likely to bring more satisfaction to the woman than to the man. This is because it gives her clitoris full exposure to the friction of intercourse. He, however, may miss the feeling of tight containment he gets, such as when she closes her legs underneath his to clasp his penis.

Beware of keeping up the Widely Opened Position for too long. It can be pretty tough on the lower part of the spine. So take care – don't let your enthusiasm run away with you!

A man's duty to his partner

THE KAMA SUTRA puts the obligation on the man to satisfy his partner. To help him achieve this aim, the text offers hints on sensual movements he can use during lovemaking to provoke the utmost sensuality around her clitoris and the opening of the vagina.

The man's duty is very penis-oriented by today's standards. It includes, however, some good ideas for stimulating the female genitals. Using the penis as a kind of vibrator can be immensely arousing for women. The recommended sensual movements are:

- Moving forward: straightforward penetration
- Churning: holding and moving the penis in the vagina
- Piercing: penetrating the vagina from above and pushing against the clitoris
- Pressing: pushing forcefully against the vagina
- Giving a blow: removing the penis and striking the vagina with it
- Blow of the Bull: rubbing one side of the vagina with the penis
- Blow of the Boar: rubbing both sides of the vagina with the penis
- Sporting of the Sparrow: moving the penis rapidly and lightly in and out of the vagina

■ **The *Kama Sutra*** outlines a number of sensual ways in which the man can move his penis to deeply satisfy his partner.

The Position of the Wife of Indra

Achievable by only the loosest of limb, this position is recommended by the *Kama Sutra* as suitable for the "highest congress" – lovemaking in which the vagina is fully open, ensuring maximum penetration. Most couples who try it, however, will probably use it simply as a brief interlude between less demanding positions.

It's a strange, tight love position where the woman finds herself bundled up into a kind of package. A woman might experience a sense of deep sexual tension from such a cramped position. She could also achieve considerable arousal by tensing her vaginal muscles, which happens when the legs are drawn up as close as possible to the body. However the truth is she may feel just rather silly.

Trivia...

An interesting extract from the poetry of the Kama Sutra reads as follows: "Such passionate actions and amorous gesticulations or movements, which arise on the spur of the moment, and during sexual intercourse, cannot be defined, and are as irregular as dreams."

INTERNET

www.krsnabook.com/ch24.html

Click here to learn more about Indra, the Hindu god, and his adventures with Krishna who lived in India 5,000 years ago.

POSITION OF THE WIFE OF INDRA

The Position of the Wife of Indra is named after the beautiful and seductive wife of a Hindu deity. In early Vedic writings, Indra was both king of the gods and god of rain and thunder.

WHY IS TENSION IMPORTANT?

In the build-up of sexual excitement, tension is vital. Orgasm is the relief of sexual tension, and without enough tension orgasm is very difficult and sometimes impossible to achieve.

The areas around the pelvis, in particular the thighs and buttocks, fill with sexual tension and it is possible to aid and enhance a climax by deliberately building up physical stress. Bioenergetic exercises such as flexing the thighs and buttocks, or practicing the Kegel exercises (see Chapter 12), all assist in building up sexual tension.

A simple summary

✓ It's a good idea to explore each other before going on to intercourse so that you assess whether you will be a good emotional and penile/vaginal fit. The *Kama Sutra* believed that by understanding your sex fit, you could also gauge the success or failure of a relationship.

✓ Most of the famous sex positions in the *Kama Sutra* were based on the belief that sex works best with the man on top.

✓ However, men are also instructed to use their penis as a kind of sex toy. Use it to rub, beat, press, and churn.

✓ It is important to practice many sex positions, even when some of them do little for your sensuality. Perhaps this is because seeing the body in a variety of positions can be visually, even if not physically, stimulating.

Chapter 12

Positions for Ultimate Touch

Touch is an important and enhancing aspect not only of sexual relationships but also of many other forms of human contact. For example, patients in a coma respond positively to routine touch by nurses, and research shows that babies who are touched frequently are more easily soothed and more likely to show better emotional and physical development than those who are not. Consider, therefore, the hidden power of clasping, pressing, and moving naked skin against skin. In addition to arousing sexual feelings, you are also likely to feel loved and cared for.

In this chapter...

✓ Clasping and caressing

✓ Understanding the chakras

✓ Using the PC muscles

THE FEEL OF A LOVER'S SKIN IS AN IMPORTANT STIMULUS TO SEXUAL AROUSAL

Clasping and caressing

HOWEVER NERVOUS YOU or your lover may feel at the beginning of lovemaking, being held and caressed with no great hurry and no particular agenda is one of the most reassuring of all sensual activities. Skin on skin is the first and most primitive experience that any of us enjoy as tiny babies when we are placed onto our mother's body after birth. Cuddling, touching, and stroking are at the root of parent/child love and also of child development. There is something about touch that quite literally rouses us into life.

Did you know that a mother bear actually licks her newborn cub into life? And that if she doesn't lick the cub, it doesn't breathe?

The looks of love

As you nestle your body against another's you confirm feelings of security, affirmation, and pleasure as well as the more dramatic sensations of eroticism. When infants first snuggle close and open their eyes, even though they cannot yet see properly, they perceive the shape of their mother's face. They recognize it rapidly and that loving look, not to mention her scent and touch, help the child to feel calm and secure.

The great bonus of being held as you snuggle side by side facing one another, is that you can look into your lover's eyes and mirror the love and appreciation that they are showing.

SIDE-BY-SIDE CLASPING

Trivia...

When two people are attracted to each other the pupils of their eyes dilate. Even though they are unaware of such ocular changes, their dilated pupils actually influence the other person's feelings. There's a well-known psychological test in which a man is shown two apparently identical sets of photographs of a woman and is asked which one he finds most attractive. In one of the pictures, the woman's eyes have been altered so that they appear dilated – and this is the one that the majority of men opt for, without knowing exactly why. It's as though such eye changes cause bonding.

Slipping into intercourse

It's easy to slip from clasping and gazing to intercourse. From having wrapped yourselves around each other and allayed anxieties, you can then comfortably and unhurriedly slide together so that his penis penetrates her vagina or so that her vagina encloses his penis. If she wraps her legs around his and holds him around the neck, while he pulls her close by a warm hand on her buttocks, you can start a very gentle moving toward each other and then letting go. Of course movement is restricted when side-by-side and penetration is unlikely to be deep. But it's a slow, sensual start.

Clasping with the man on top

You may roll from your side into this man-on-top position while still embracing, or the man may just rest over the woman as you hold each other close. For added intimacy you might like to twine your legs together. This is more a loving embrace than a practical position from which to move in the rhythm of intercourse. It's about holding, loving, and caressing rather than the thrust of penetration.

CLASPING WITH THE MAN ON TOP

MUTUAL CARESSES

Today sex therapists for couples who feel their sex lives are not working too well, often advocate a program of simple caresses. In the 1990s, sex therapist Irene Kassorlas promoted a multi-faceted program that included:

- **Lying in the spoons position:** Lying with the woman's back tucked into her partner's front and synchronizing their breathing
- **Hand play:** Stroking, clasping, rubbing, and caressing each other's hands for 10 minutes
- **Cuddling:** Spending 15 minutes simply cuddling one another
- **Fingertipping:** Spending 15 minutes running your fingertips over one another's backs

Good sensuality is built upon unhurried times together when couples can establish trust through trust. These games return us to our early steps of learning.

Toward the end of the 20th century, as a result of easy access to birth control, Western lovers began to lose sight of many of the pleasures of foreplay and focused instead on intercourse. The sad fact that we tend to rush things today is all the more reason to use the Clasping Position. Prolonging holding and cuddling feels great and promotes trust.

The Pressing Position

In the most fulfilling lovemaking, as the *Kama Sutra* tells us, a sequence of positions unfolds in which lovers slip effortlessly, like dancers, from one embrace and one rhythm to another. In this way the Clasping Position leads naturally to the Pressing Position.

This is a version of the missionary position where the man, having penetrated his partner, presses hard and close up against her genitals. Variations on the Pressing Position include the man moving very slightly over the woman's genitals as if churning his penis in her vagina. The aim is for the man to grind softly over and around her clitoris.

The pressure of this grinding can be enough to bring some women to climax almost immediately. Other women find that the pressure from the penis on the inside wall of the vagina also makes them come.

THE PRESSING POSITION

Women can vary the sensation of the Pressing Position by raising their thighs and squeezing their partner between them. Pushing with your feet against the insides of his legs will help you to grip him tighter.

■ **Spontaneous lovemaking** *can be likened to a flowing erotic dance.*

The beautiful dance

What is wonderful about spontaneous lovemaking is that it can flow like a beautiful dance, where every inch of the body feels as if it is coming to life. Looked at in terms of arousal, that is, of course, exactly what happens. When the body reacts to intimate touch, the skin itself "erects" as tissues beneath it fill with fluid and muscular tension mounts. The more you roll around and press your limbs together, the greater the sexual charge.

UNDERSTANDING SEXUAL RESPONSE

The three stages of the sexual response cycle are:

1 Desire – you want it

2 Arousal – you have to have it

3 Orgasm – you can relax now

Desire is a hard-to-quantify emotion. In men, some say that it's an attitude of mind while others think it the product of hormone activity. It often blends with the next stage, arousal. Some men become aroused with little or no physical stimulation while others may need a great deal. As stimulation continues, by hand or during the thrusting of intercourse, a man's arousal and excitement intensify, leading to the final stage of orgasm and ejaculation. Excitement then subsides as he enters the refractory period during which his body slowly returns to normal.

■ **The two stages** *of desire and arousal often blend.*

The cycle of a woman's sexual response also begins with desire. The second stage is arousal and, while some women are very rapidly aroused and ready for orgasm almost immediately, others take far longer. Some women need up to 45 minutes of stimulation before orgasm becomes possible. During orgasm, the orgasmic contractions are very similar to those of a man. The majority of women then experience a loss of sexual and muscular tension as their bodies return to their normal physiological condition – the exception being the minority who go on to have multiple orgasms.

Orgasm begins with muscular contractions that take on a rhythmic quality as sexual tension is released. Women usually have between 3 and 15 contractions, and sometimes the uterus and anus contract, too.

The Twining Position

Giving powerful expression to her desire to weave herself about her partner, the woman uses this variation of the Pressing Position. She places one leg across her lover's thigh, as if twining it around him, and draws him close.

As the choreography of the dance progresses, the breast tissues swell, the nipples become erect, the muscles begin to tense, and the labia, clitoris, and penis become erect. As both partners become more excited, their chests may display a sex flush, which is a reddening of the skin on the face and chest that appears during extreme sexual excitement and fades after orgasm.

THE TWINING POSITION

Understanding the chakras

THE THEORY OF THE CHAKRAS *was already in existence at the time the Kama Sutra was written and is still very much alive today. The chakras are thought to be the energy by which all the functions of the individual – spiritual as well as physical – are carried out. This means that when people talk about the* chakras *they are describing not only physical but also psychological behavior.*

The seven chakras

The chakras are related to the health and well-being of different parts of the body. The seven chakras and their corresponding functions, starting with the lower body and moving upward, are illustrated opposite.

DEFINITION

The chakras *are centers of energy that occur at seven points in the astral body, which the yogis believe surrounds and permeates the physical body. Six chakras are located along the equivalent of the spine in the physical body, while the seventh crowns the head.*

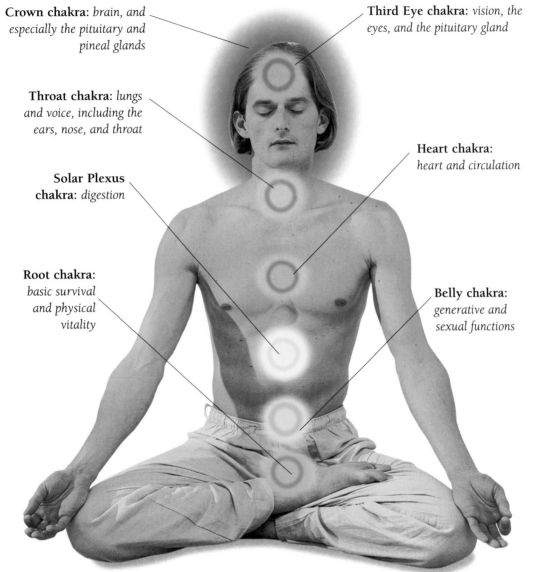

Crown chakra: *brain, and especially the pituitary and pineal glands*

Third Eye chakra: *vision, the eyes, and the pituitary gland*

Throat chakra: *lungs and voice, including the ears, nose, and throat*

Heart chakra: *heart and circulation*

Solar Plexus chakra: *digestion*

Root chakra: *basic survival and physical vitality*

Belly chakra: *generative and sexual functions*

THE SEVEN CHAKRAS AND THEIR FUNCTIONS

The three lower chakras (the Root, Belly, and Solar Plexus) correlate to basic primary needs – those of survival, procreation, and will – and have a larger physiological component to their functioning. The four higher chakras are associated with our psychological make-up.

The Heart, Throat, and Third Eye chakras are more advanced and mature, defining love, communication, and knowledge. The Crown chakra is purely spiritual, providing the connection to the universe beyond.

The awakening of the chakras

So what's the connection between the chakras and sexuality? The lowest chakra (the Root chakra) has a special function: it houses an energy called *kundalini*. It is through the use of the *kundalini* energy that the activity of the chakras is spiritually enhanced. This enhancement is known as the "awakening" of that chakra, in which its color supposedly becomes brighter and its speed and energy-processing capabilities are greatly increased. Awakening a chakra confers psychic abilities or *siddhis*.

There are many people who say when they have experienced a particularly extraordinary sexual experience that they have reached a different heightened place where their consciousness clocks out to an ecstatic sense of pure being. Remember the idea of achieving *moksha* in the *Kama Sutra*? There's also the idea of a heightened ecstasy through Tantric sex practice, and which is explained in more detail in Chapter 2.

INTERNET

www.calmness.com/ chakras.htm

Click here for detailed information on the chakras.

In order to get to this heightened place a special energy is utilized – *kundalini* energy – which itself is generated from intercourse.

So if you want to better yourself spiritually and give yourself the chance of moving on to an ecstatic plane of consciousness, it is the Root chakra, via lovemaking, that will help you do so.

■ **When *kundalini* energy** *is aroused by sexual activity via the Root chakra, it travels up through, and energizes, all the chakras, revitalizing body and spirit.*

Using the PC muscles

THIS TECHNIQUE, *in which the woman employs her pubo-coccygeal (PC), or vaginal, muscles (those that contract at orgasm) to squeeze the penis as if milking it, can be applied in several different positions. It produces highly pleasurable sensations in both the vagina and the penis.*

The Mare's Position

Although in theory you can do this internal penis massage in any position, it's most effective in the Mare's Position, or when the woman sits astride the man, either facing him or with her back to him.

He can support himself with one hand and use the other to fondle her. She can use one of her own hands to stimulate her clitoris while focusing on squeezing her partner.

Please note: The Mare's Position is not in any way related to the Mare woman.

Trivia...

The Kama Sutra's reference to the internal squeezing technique shows there's nothing new about it. Since the 1960s we have been teaching young women to exercise and use their pubo-coccygeal (PC) muscles by using the Kegel exercises (see page 160). This helps to improve vaginal tone after childbirth, improves orgasmic response (stronger vaginal muscles lead to more powerful orgasms), and gives male partners extra stimulation.

THE MARE'S POSITION

159

PRACTICING THE KEGEL EXERCISES

Named after US gynecologist Dr A.H. Kegel, who popularized their use, these exercises help women strengthen their vaginal muscles, or their "inner snake." You can do these simple, effective exercises anywhere, any time – in the office, at home, or in the garden. And men, there's a version for you, too! Improving the muscle tone of your penis will also enhance the quality of your penile contractions and therefore the force of orgasm. Some guys feel they have succeeded with the Kegel exercise when they can hold up a towel on their erection!

For women

1. Next time you go the toilet, stop the flow of urine. The muscles you use to do this are the PC muscles. Practice controlling the muscles by stopping the flow several times. Then lie down, slip a finger into the vagina, and contract the PC muscles again. See if you can feel the contractions around your finger

2. Try the Kegel exercise: Contract the PC muscles for 3 seconds, relax them for 3 seconds, then repeat. Try doing this 10 times, on three separate occasions every day

3. Flutter your vagina. Do the main Kegel exercise, but much faster so that your vagina feels as if it is "fluttering." Do this 10 times, three times a day

4. Finally, pretend that the inside of your vagina is an elevator. Your job is to move the elevator to the top of your vagina, making three stops on the way. When it reaches the fourth and highest stop, hold it there for a while before letting it descend to the "ground floor," again pausing at each stop on the way. Try this exercise twice a day

For men

1. Tweak the muscles between the base of the penis and the anus. See if you can twitch the head of the penis

2. Squeeze the penile muscles for 3 seconds, and relax them for 3 seconds, then repeat. Try doing this 10 times, three times a day. When you can twitch rhythmically, actually keeping a tempo, you will know you have strengthened your penile muscles

THE RISING POSITION

The Rising Position

Not every woman can use her vaginal muscles as forcefully as she might like. If your attempts at fluttering your vagina around your man's penis don't work out too well, you might like to move on to another *Kama Sutra* position – the Rising Position.

In this posture, the woman lies on her back and raises her legs straight up, above the shoulders of the man, who kneels in front of her and introduces his penis into her vagina. By pressing her thighs together, she squeezes him and increases the friction as he moves inside her, producing exquisite sensations.

A simple summary

✓ Begin lovemaking by clasping each other side by side so that you can gaze into each other's eyes. This is because your naked bodies reassure each other by the simple expedience of touch.

✓ This simple touch is important because it takes us right back to the nurturing days of childhood and makes us feel secure.

✓ We want to feel secure when we make ourselves most vulnerable when we first have sex.

✓ Lovemaking can be a natural progression and can flow so easily that it seems like a sinuous dance.

✓ The chakras are centers of energy that are integral to our physical and spiritual enjoyment.

✓ Toning up the vaginal and penile muscles using the Kegel exercises can help us carry out some of the more esoteric *Kama Sutra* love positions.

Chapter 13

Acrobatic Positions

THE *KAMA SUTRA* is probably most famous for its depiction of some incredibly athletic, if not downright acrobatic, sex positions. We don't know for sure whether the original script meant its readers to take the more extreme postures seriously or whether they were supposed to be satirical. One thing is for certain: The men and women of the 4th century AD would have needed to be supremely supple and fit to follow the more ambitious positions! But I'm not sure any of this matters. What is important is how you choose to interpret them.

In this chapter...

✓ Yogic sex

✓ The Turning Position

✓ Standing positions

✓ Woman-on-top poses

✓ Taking inspiration from nature

ADAPT SOME OF THE MORE ACROBATIC POSES IN THE *KAMA SUTRA* TO SUIT YOU AND YOUR PARTNER

Yogic sex

THE FOLLOWING LOVE POSITIONS owe *much of their invention to yoga. In the following sequence of rather acrobatic moves, the woman diligently folds and unfolds her legs during the liaison. These should not be taken too seriously: most women would struggle to assume the Lotus position in normal circumstances, let alone during sexual intercourse.*

■ **Classic yoga** *positions inspired many of the more challenging sex poses.*

The Splitting of a Bamboo

This aptly named position calls for a simple evolution from the basic man-on-top posture, yet requires considerable suppleness in the woman. She raises one leg and puts it on her partner's shoulder for a time, then brings that leg down and raises the other. This sequence can be repeated over and again. "Splitting the bamboo" in this way makes the vagina squeeze the penis and, whatever the rate at which the woman changes the position of her legs, it is a stimulating cycle of movements for both partners. The man thrusts while kneeling but leaning forward. Common consensus is that this position is actually impossible!

Positions like the Splitting of a Bamboo remind me of the way young couples use their bodies and have fun inventing crazy sex poses during the early days of their physical relationship.

SPLITTING OF A BAMBOO

Fixing of a Nail

Rather than place her leg on her partner's shoulder as above, in this position the woman places her heel on his forehead. Her leg and foot then resemble a hammer knocking in a nail, represented by his head. Again, the man kneels while he thrusts.

FIXING OF A NAIL

The yogic positions are meant to be enjoyed in a lighthearted manner. In other words, have fun while you are making love. No one has decreed that sex ought to be a solemn business!

The Crab's Position

In this highly pleasurable position, which constricts the vagina around the penis, the woman bends and draws in both legs and rests her thighs on her stomach, rather like a crab retracting its claws. The man, kneeling up, holds her knees tight against him so that he can keep her close.

INTERNET

www.yogasite.com

www.ivillage.com

www.yogauk.com

These sites are good sources of information on yoga, whether you want to find a yoga teacher or class in your area, or enjoy some yoga instruction online.

THE CRAB'S POSITION

The Lotus-like position

Imitating the familiar Lotus position in yoga, the woman draws in her legs and folds one over the other as far as possible. Again her vagina is pulled up to meet the man's penis. Most women who try this challenging sex position find that they cannot hold it for long if, indeed, they can achieve it at all.

THE LOTUS-LIKE POSITION

The Turning Position

THE FIVE STAGES OF MOVES that constitute the Turning Position are purely for fun. There's simply no way that this slow-motion spinning-like-a-top position could do anything for erotic sensation, though it might prompt a couple to double up with laughter. But what's wrong with that?

The five stages

While the man is on top he can (with practice) lift one leg, and then another, and move right around his partner's body in a full circle without losing the penis-vagina connection. During lovemaking, varying a position can often be used to increase the feeling of closeness. In this case, when the man turns around, his partner can demonstrate her tenderness by embracing or caressing his back, shoulders, and sides.

1 The first stage of the Turning Position is to begin lovemaking with the basic man-on-top position where the man lies with both legs between those of his partner.

2 Supporting himself on his arms, the man begins the tricky maneuver of moving around and above his partner like a compass needle. Here he lifts first his left leg and then his right leg over her right leg, without withdrawing his penis. His partner, meanwhile, might be wise to support him by placing her hands under his chest to help him balance.

(3) By this time, the man should have maneuvered himself so that he is at a right angle to his partner's body, with his legs sticking out to one side of her abdomen. His abdomen is covering hers from the side, and his chest, arms, and head are supported by his hands on the opposite side of her abdomen from his legs. Yes, it does sound complicated! She needs to keep her legs slightly parted so that his penis remains inside her vagina instead of being forced out.

(4) At this stage, the man ends up with his head and chest between her legs and one leg on either side of her shoulders. Whether or not he manages to reach this stage, he will certainly agree with Vatsyayana's comment that this position is learned only through practice! Penetration is certainly going to feel very different for both partners now since the angle of the penis is pressing on totally different areas of the vagina. Some people like to finish the Turning Position here; others like to take it one stage further . . .

(5) The final stage of the Turning Position is known as the Twizzle. All this means is that you keep on going until you have completed a full circle while remaining firmly in situ!

The outer third of the vagina, especially the lower part of the perineum, is equipped with some particularly sensitive nerves. During the slow encircling of the Turning Position, the vagina is stretched at several unusual angles, giving the woman a chance to experience some rare sensations that couldn't be produced any other way. Unfortunately, it's just as likely that she won't feel much at all!

Standing positions

THE KAMA SUTRA, *the* Ananga Ranga, *and other classic Eastern love texts placed great emphasis on standing positions. Evidence of their special status can be seen in the erotic carvings and sculptures that adorn old temple walls – most of which depict couples in standing rather than sitting or lying positions.*

■ **Indian erotic** *art favoured standing poses when depicting lovemaking.*

The Suspended Congress

In this position, which calls for a fair amount of strength in the man, he leans against a wall, while the woman puts her arms around his neck. He then lifts her by holding her thighs, or by locking his hands beneath her bottom.

If the woman is light, the man may be able to support her with one arm around her waist, using the other hand to caress her. The woman needs to grip his hips with her thighs and push off from him with her feet against the wall. In this case, she is the one who must do the thrusting.

The Suspended Congress is not a position for men to try if they have even the inkling of a bad back! Women need to beware of wrenching their arms out of their sockets.

THE SUSPENDED CONGRESS

The Supported Congress

Lovers achieve the support referred to either by bracing themselves against each other or by leaning against a wall. Sometimes when sudden passion overwhelms you, you may prefer to dispense with the preliminaries and make love standing up. The advantage of leaning against a wall is that, with the woman firmly supported, the man finds it easier to thrust vigorously.

To give him deeper penetration, the woman can spread her thighs by wrapping one of her legs around his. This widens the entrance to her vagina and brings her closer up against his body. He can hold her thigh up, which helps to take some of the strain from her and also gives him something to hang onto as he thrusts.

INTERNET

www.kamat.com

For text and photographs of erotic Indian temple carvings go to this address, scroll down the page and click on Erotic Arts of India under the heading "What's Popular."

Trivia...

Making love while standing face to face can be difficult if the man is much taller than the woman (or vice versa). The problem can often be alleviated by him standing with his feet apart and bending his knees slightly, or by her standing on tiptoe. But most people find it impossible to maintain these postures for long.

THE SUPPORTED CONGRESS

169

Woman-on-top poses

THE KAMA SUTRA RECOMMENDS *three movements to be used when the woman adopts a position on top of her partner ("acting the part of a man") during lovemaking. She can do this either as a variation for its own sake or when her partner is tired but she is still not satisfied.*

The Top

According to Vatsyayana, this movement requires considerable dexterity and is achieved only through practice.

While sitting astride her partner, who is lying flat on his back, the woman raises her legs to clear his body and swivels carefully around on his penis so that she faces his feet and then eventually his head again.

STAGE 1

While perfecting this maneuver, the woman should take care not to lose her balance or she might end up inadvertently "Bobbiting" her unfortunate man!

STAGE 2

STAGE 3

Although possible to achieve, I'm convinced that this position and its variant, the Swing, are the ancient Indians' idea of a joke. If an accident were to happen, most of the damage would be inflicted on the man. So be warned: Men should hold their partner while she's moving.

The Swing

In a variation of the Top, the man sits
up but leans back on his hands. This safe,
21st-century version of the *Kama Sutra*'s
Swing (which has the man still lying
down, but with his back arched)
has been reinvented because
the original can be
dangerous.

THE SWING

The original Swing would
only be feasible if the man
had a strong back – and even then it is unlikely he would be able to sustain the posture
for very long. He could be in real danger of hurting himself.

It is more practical for him to lie flat, or as in our picture, to prop himself up on his
arms. His seated position might make the swinging maneuver more difficult for his
partner but it is also safer in that she is far less likely to topple over as she swivels!

The Pair of Tongs

This is perhaps the most practical of the three women-on-top positions suggested by the
Kama Sutra. The man lies flat on his back while the woman sits astride, facing him, with
her legs bent at the knee. She draws his penis into her and holds it tight for a long time,
repeatedly squeezing it with the muscles of her
vagina. Penetration is deep.

By using her vaginal muscles (see Chapter
12 for exercises to improve these muscles)
the woman may stimulate her man while
also arousing herself. Some women use
vaginal fluttering to give pleasure and,
combining this with a little
movement, find it a gentle method
of sexual enjoyment.

THE PAIR OF TONGS

Taking inspiration from nature

VATSYAYANA BELIEVED, LIKE ALL MEN *of his time, that the human race had much to learn from the animal kingdom. He makes it clear that it is the association in the imagination with mating animals that gives entry-from-the-rear positions a special eroticism.*

■ **The mating** *habits of animals were worthy of study in 4th-century India.*

In his chapter on sexual congress, Vatsyayana acknowledges the impossibility of listing every known lovemaking position. Instead he suggests that lovers can greatly extend their repertoires by studying the mating habits of animals. After his description of the Congress of a Cow (see opposite), Vatsyayana says that "in the same way can be carried on the congress of a dog, the congress of a goat, the congress of a deer, the forcible mounting of an ass, the congress of a cat, the jump of a tiger, the pressing of an elephant, the rubbing of a boar and the mounting of a horse. And in all these cases the characteristics of these different animals should be manifested by acting like them."

The Elephant Posture

This is such a popular sex position that it is listed in the *Ananga Ranga* as well as the *Kama Sutra*. The woman lies face down with her breasts, stomach, thighs, and feet all touching the bed, and the man lies over her with the small of his back arched inward.

Once he is inside her, the woman can intensify the sensations for both partners by pressing her thighs close together. Rear-entry positions, such as this one, allow for deep penetration.

THE ELEPHANT POSTURE

According to Vatsyayana, "A man should gather from the actions of the woman of what disposition she is, and in what way she likes to be enjoyed."

The Congress of the Cow

The powerful symbolism of mating animals can serve to heighten passion for many couples. In this challenging version of the more common rear-entry postures in which the woman kneels, she supports herself on her hands and feet and her partner mounts her like a bull. It makes deep penetration possible, and allows the man to control the depth and power of his thrusts.

Although it is much harder for a woman to enjoy orgasm in rear-entry positions, the additional stimulation provided by the man's fingers reaching around the front of her thigh to stroke her clitoris (perhaps in the same rhythm as his thrusting) can be highly erotic. So too, can the sensation of his front pounding against her buttocks, close to her sensitive perineum and anus.

THE CONGRESS OF THE COW

A simple summary

✔ Acrobatic love positions are for fun and most of them were probably intended as jokes. However, it's great to laugh and not see intercourse as being deadly serious!

✔ A few of the swivelling positions are positively dangerous and not to be encouraged.

✔ A good time for the woman to be on top during sex is when she remains unsatisfied yet her partner is tired.

✔ Imagination plays a great part in sex and adopting the characteristics of certain animals is a way of adding extra eroticism to the sex act.

Chapter 14

Ananga Ranga Positions

THE *ANANGA RANGA* shares common origins with the *Kama Sutra* but was written up to 1,500 years later, probably in the late 15th or early 16th centuries. Therefore, it is much closer in time to the Arabian classic *The Perfumed Garden*, although it is culturally very different. The *Ananga Ranga* was translated into Arabic; as a result it exerted a strong influence on the sexual attitudes of the Islamic world.

In this chapter...

✓ Kneeling and lying positions

✓ Therapeutic positions

✓ Positions for reaching a higher awareness

✓ Sitting positions

✓ Positions to please her

VARIATIONS ON SITTING POSITIONS ARE A FEATURE OF THE *ANANGA RANGA*

Kneeling and lying positions

KALYANA MALLA, THE AUTHOR of the *Ananga Ranga*, reflected a rigid society that censured extramarital sex. The major practical difference between the two classics is that the *Kama Sutra* was written for lovers while the *Ananga Ranga* does not question the sanctity of marriage and explicitly offers instruction to the married man. Equally clear is the author's motive for writing the Ananga Ranga in the first place – to protect marriage from sexual tedium.

■ **This 17th-century** *Indian painting illustrates two lovers using a variation of the Kneeling Position.*

Level Feet Posture

In this first *uttana-bandha* position, the man lifts his partner's body, bracing himself against her, and places her outstretched legs over his shoulders. If the partner is just the right size, she can rest her buttocks on the bed but, although this is not as demanding, it is less mutually satisfying.

The *uttana-bandha* positions are good for couples who like deep penetration. The man has a sense of control because he can move the woman into the most comfortable pose to suit his need to penetrate, while she experiences a sense of helplessness that can be powerfully erotic.

> **DEFINITION**
>
> Uttana-bandha *are positions in which the woman lies on her back and the man enters her while kneeling between her legs. They are also termed supine postures.*

LEVEL FEET POSTURE

DEFINITION

The G-spot is a super-sensitive area on the vagina's front wall, about a half to two-thirds of the way in. If pressed firmly (by the penis or a finger) a powerfully erotic sensation is created. Research indicates that not all women possess a G-spot, but many of those who have one know that it can trigger orgasm.

Raised Feet Posture

Lying on her back, the woman bends her legs at the knees and draws them back, in the words of the *Ananga Ranga*, "as far as her hair." Her partner enters her from the kneeling position. Because the man is kneeling, he does not need to use his hands to support himself or to maintain his balance, so he can comfortably use them to caress his partner and fondle her breasts.

RAISED FEET POSTURE

By raising her hips with both hands, he can penetrate her at an angle that allows his penis to stimulate the front wall of her vagina, along which is located the highly sensitive G-spot.

The Refined Posture

Instead of resting on her partner's shoulders, as in the Level Feet posture, the woman's legs pass on either side of his waist, which allows for deep penetration.

Greater stimulation is possible if the man raises the woman by using his hands to support her buttocks. When he is lifting her and supporting her buttocks, he can apply a little gentle pressure to draw the buttocks away from the anus and perineum. This gives her extra erotic sensation.

THE REFINED POSTURE

INTERNET

www.thriveonline. oxygen.com/sex/ gspot.html

Find out more about the G-spot and how it functions at this site, which analyzes the facts and fictions about this sensitive hot spot.

Therapeutic positions

MOST PEOPLE THINK *that sex therapy is a recent phenomenon that has developed in the West. But certain moves and love positions were used centuries ago to help overcome physical weakness and failing libido. It's useful to have this kind of specialist knowledge to fall back on should you ever discover yourself going through a difficult time with your partner.*

The Gaping Position

The woman lies on her back and pillows and cushions are used to raise her bottom up towards the man. The opening of the vagina receives strong stimulation and, for this reason, some women value the position as a prelude to deeper penetration.

■ **A supporting** *cushion is a well-tried aid for enhancing sexual feeling.*

THE GAPING POSITION

Raising the pelvis with cushions, so that the genitals are more open than when lying flat, was a favourite sex therapy technique in the 1950s for women who didn't reach orgasm. The theory is that if the clitoris is exposed to the thrust of intercourse, it is more likely to be stimulated. However stimulation is usually achieved more efficiently by nimble finger work.

The Splitting Position

The woman lies on her back and the man enters her from a kneeling position. He then lifts her legs straight up, resting them on his shoulder. Such positions are excellent for older men who need a more robust sensation during intercourse. The penis is snugly contained by the woman's vagina and being gripped by her thighs provides the extra friction he needs to bring him to orgasm.

To enhance the Splitting Position, the woman should try to keep her knees and thighs pressed close together as he thrusts — this increases the friction on his penis.

THE SPLITTING POSITION

The Crab Embrace

Positions where the woman lies on her side with her partner facing her are called the *tiryak-bandha* or transverse positions. In this warm and inviting variation of the basic side-by-side position, the man enters the woman and lies between her thighs. One of her legs remains beneath his and she passes the other over his body, just below his chest.

The Crab Embrace is a useful position when either partner is tired but still feeling passionate. Penetration is deep and although the man's movements may be restricted, the woman's are not.

THE CRAB EMBRACE

Side-by-side positions are excellent for men who need more friction during intercourse. Women, too, are more likely to become aroused and reach orgasm in these poses because the penis is pressed against the insides of the labia by the legs, so the man's thrusts can be felt more strongly.

The Transverse Lute

The lovers lie side by side with their legs outstretched. After the woman has raised one leg slightly to allow her partner to enter her, he raises one leg and rests it on her thigh. By pulling himself up a little higher in relation to the woman's body (that is, toward her head), the man can ensure that his penis brushes against her clitoris.

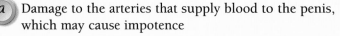

THE TRANSVERSE LUTE

THE EFFECTS OF AGING ON MEN

It is now believed that as many as two out of three cases of male sexual dysfunction are caused by physical changes, often as a result of the aging process. We know that the effects of aging can include:

a Damage to the arteries that supply blood to the penis, which may cause impotence

b Weakness of the "locking system" at the base of the penis that holds in blood when it is erect. This can cause loss of erection

c Hormonal changes (part of the natural aging process) can result in a lower sex drive and less genital sensation

There are many readily available treatments for these conditions. Men who have experienced any of the above problems should always seek medical advice.

INTERNET

www.worldhealth.net/index.shtml

The World Health Network site is dedicated to slowing the aging process and promoting longevity research. It provides information on specialist anti-aging medicines and lists practitioners from 60 countries.

Positions for reaching a higher awareness

THE KAMA'S WHEEL and its associated positions illustrate a dimension of sexuality that likens good sex to meditation. It's a dimension where sex brings us to a high level of awareness, a sharpness of appetite, and an increased sense of wellbeing. The object of Kama's Wheel is not to build erotic feeling or to achieve orgasm. It is rather to obtain a balance of mind that feels clear, calm, and happy.

■ **Certain sexual** *poses were thought to bring lovers to a higher consciousness.*

The Kama's Wheel

The man sits with his legs outstretched and parted, and his partner lowers herself on to his penis, extending her legs over his. He then passes his arms on either side of her body, keeping them straight. In this way he completes the spoke-like pattern of limbs that gives the position its name. The position allows each of the lovers to kiss with ease and to enjoy looking at each other.

Remember that the 4th-century Indians believed sex might bring you to a higher consciousness. So contemplation, while practicing penetration, was important.

THE KAMA'S WHEEL

The Placid Embrace

This position is associated with great tenderness. It encompasses pure feelings of love in that she twines both her arms and her legs around her lover as an expression of closeness and trust. It is another aspect of nearing ecstasy as well as a natural progression from Kama's Wheel.

The woman lies on her back while the man, kneeling, lifts her buttocks and enters her. By crossing her ankles behind his back, she can draw him closer to her and increase the feeling of intimacy.

THE PLACID EMBRACE

If the man then shifts his hand up to the small of her back and helps her arch toward him, her head will fall back and allow her to feel "otherworldly," all adding to a sense of transgressing ordinary consciousness.

TAKING IT SLOWLY

American sex researchers Dr William Hartman and Dr Marilyn Fithian recommend that a couple aiming for multiple orgasm should take intercourse slowly. They advocate letting desire and response develop gradually and advise against a great deal of vigorous thrusting. This is because to enjoy multiple orgasm, men and women need a far greater build-up of sexual tension than for a single climax.

To achieve that increased build-up, you need time to tease and tantalize the senses, so it is unwise to tire yourself out by treating lovemaking as a gymnastics session. The various sitting positions suggested by the *Ananga Ranga* can be useful in this context since they do not involve any vigorous thrusting, are not too tiring, and they allow couples more control over the build-up of sexual tension.

The Intact Posture

The third of these special embraces works particularly well as a follow-up to the Placid Embrace. Slip into the Intact Posture while she is still reeling from having been held half upside down.

The woman does this by raising her legs, bending them at the knee and pulling them back toward the man's body. Her knees then rest against his chest as he kneels between her thighs. Before he enters her, he puts his hand below her buttocks and lifts her up slightly.

With the Intact Posture, the woman is treated much like a package. If control and helplessness are important aspects of your relationship, then this position could be extremely stimulating mentally, although in sexual terms it is not particularly satisfactory for the woman.

Trivia...

According to the Ananga Ranga, the Placid Embrace, which was first named by poets who lived some 1,300 years earlier, was "a form of congress much in vogue."

THE INTACT POSTURE

Sitting positions

THE FOLLOWING FOUR POSITIONS are *forms of what the* Ananga Ranga *terms* upavishta, *or sitting postures, in which the woman effectively sits across the man. The postures can be friendly, charged with eroticism, youthful, comic, acrobatic, or fun, depending on your frame of mind. Since the woman tends to do all the work in these positions, they are a bit of a treat for the man! But the ancient love texts can't really be faulted for their fairness – although written from a male point of view, they do pay equal attention to the sexual needs of both partners.*

■ **The pleasures** *of seated positions were appreciated by the author of the* Ananga Ranga.

The Lotus Position

Author Kallyana Malla described the Lotus as a favorite. Are we hearing something of his own personal preference? The Lotus is certainly a very friendly move to make: The man sits cross-legged and the woman sits on his lap, facing him, and lowers herself on to his penis.

The *Ananga Ranga* suggests that the man place his hands on his partner's shoulders, but he can just as comfortably, and perhaps more affectionately, put his arms around her body or about her neck. It also gives him the perfect platform from which to kiss and nuzzle her face and throat.

THE LOTUS POSITION

The Accomplishing Position

This variation on the Lotus Position requires the woman to raise one leg slightly, perhaps using her hand to help keep her balance. Raising one leg changes the tension between her vagina and his penis. Like the other face-to-face positions, it allows the couple to kiss and the man to fondle the woman's breasts. However, the man's thrusting movements are restricted.

THE ACCOMPLISHING POSITION

The Position of Equals

Sitting astride the man and facing him, the woman stretches out her legs alongside his body, passing them under his arms at about elbow height. To help her lift and lower herself on his penis he might hold her under the armpits and assist her rise and fall by lifting her slightly.

According to Kalyana Malla, the man should lift the woman's legs into position when she is seated astride his lap, but at the height of passion either partner may make the adjustment.

Another suggestion is that the man should clasp his hands about his partner's neck – but since the hands can play a more active role in this position, you may find better things to do with them!

THE POSITION OF EQUALS

The Snake Trap

In this position, the woman sits astride the man, facing him, and each partner holds the other's feet. This arrangement allows the couple to rock themselves back and forth in a stimulating seesaw-like movement but, since it restricts thrusting, is best adopted when the man is either tired or satisfied, and is making love again for his partner's pleasure.

THE SNAKE TRAP

Neither the Position of Equals nor the Snake Trap serve any real purpose with regard to sexual stimulation. They are just for play, yet can be really enjoyable as such.

Positions to please her

■ **Indian love** *artworks suggested various poses that gave women more control.*

THE ANANGA RANGA *details three woman-on-top positions to be used when the man is tired or when he has not satisfied his partner. Termed* purushayita-bandha, *or role-reversal positions, they are fascinating because they show that a woman's sexual needs were deemed as important as those of a man. The following postures demonstrate an informed awareness of the differences between male and female sexual response. They are the forerunners of techniques advocated by modern sex therapists.*

The Orgasmic Role Reversal

Because of the freedom of movement this position gives to the woman, she can control the speed, angle, and degree to which she moves her pelvis in circles and from side to side. She can also add extra variety to the sensations she feels by varying the depth of penetration.

Kalyana Malla likens the woman's posture in this position to that of a "large bee" and asserts that she "thoroughly satisfies herself." She squats on the man's thighs, inserts his penis, closes her legs firmly and adopts a churning motion.

THE ORGASMIC ROLE REVERSAL

The Ascending Position

For the woman whose "passion has not been gratified by previous copulation," the *Ananga Ranga* recommends the Ascending Position.

Sitting cross-legged on the man's thighs, she should "seize" his penis and insert it into her vagina, then move herself up and down

THE ASCENDING POSITION

The Inverted Embrace

The man lies on his back, then the woman lies on top of him and inserts his penis. Pressing her breast to his and steadying herself by gripping his waist, she moves her hips in every direction. Like the other woman-on-top positions

THE INVERTED EMBRACE

shown here, the inverted embrace puts her in control of the movements of lovemaking. The feeling of power that it gives can increase her excitement – just as the man's pleasure can be increased, provided he is not afraid of relinquishing control.

The woman can alter the angle of her partner's penis to give herself the kind of stimulation she wants, and ensure that her G-spot receives attention. She can also stimulate her clitoris herself, and this, with her movements on the penis, may be enough to bring her to orgasm.

A simple summary

✔ There are certain sex positions, kneeling and lying positions in particular, that are especially helpful to men who are experiencing difficulties with lovemaking.

✔ Sex therapy, far from being an invention of the 20th century, was used in an early form way back in the 4th century AD.

✔ A sex position such as The Kama's Wheel makes it very clear that sex can be a form of wonderful contemplation as well as an erotic activity.

✔ Far from expecting the man to do all the work in bed, the woman is actively encouraged to play her part by shifting over to become the partner-on-top!

✔ The *Ananga Ranga* recognizes women's sexual needs and proposes three special positions by which she can actively seek a climax while her man lies passive.

Chapter 15

Perfumed Garden Positions

I N THE MALE-DOMINATED NORTH AFRICAN culture of the late 15th century, in which *The Perfumed Garden* was written, such a book would have been kept strictly hidden from the womenfolk. It was compiled as a manual of practical sex advice for men, and concerned what a man could do with his wife or mistress. However, although the manual was not aimed at women, its author, Sheikh Nefzawi, was clearly exceptionally knowledgeable about sex. As a result, some of the first-class advice he gave was of particular benefit to women.

In this chapter...

✓ Concerning praiseworthy men and women

✓ Positions for men who are long – and short

✓ Techniques for deep penetration

✓ Poses for artistic lovers

THE PERFUMED GARDEN STRESSES THE IMPORTANCE OF THE MAN GIVING HIS PARTNER PLEASURE

Concerning praiseworthy men and women

THE PERFUMED GARDEN *contains many pearls of wisdom on the merits of men and women. Its author, Sheikh Nefzawi, believed that men who deserved to succeed with women were those who were "anxious to please them." In describing the woman to be admired, he stipulates a long list of characteristics – some of which we would regard as distinctly unattractive. The Sheikh may have been extremely picky, but his descriptions of wonderful sex moves designed to give great pleasure to the woman imply that he also had a very generous disposition.*

Sheikh Nefzawi on men ...

The Sheikh writes the following about a man's physical attributes when he gets close to a woman: "His member grows, gets strong, vigorous, and hard; he is not quick to discharge, and after the trembling caused by the emission of the sperm, he is soon stiff again. Such a man is relished and appreciated by women; this is because the woman loves the man only for sake of coition."

He goes on to say that: "His member should, therefore, be of ample dimensions and length; he should know how to regulate his emission and be ready as to erection; his member should reach to the end of the canal of the female and completely fill it in all its parts." So there you have it. The Sheikh is convinced that women's love is all about penis size. And this is still a hotly debated issue in the 21st century!

■ **Black hair,** *a wide forehead, and an elegant nose were all features that Sheikh Nefzawi deemed important in a woman.*

... and on women

The Sheikh described his ideal woman as follows: "In order that a woman may be relished by men, she must have a perfect waist, and must be plump and lusty. Her hair will be black, her forehead wide, she will have eyebrows of Ethiopian blackness, large black eyes, with the whites in them very limpid. With cheek of perfect oval, she will have an elegant nose and a graceful mouth; lips and tongue vermilion; her breath will be of pleasant odor, her throat long, her neck strong; her breasts must be full and firm."

The Sheikh's sexual requirements!

"The lower part of the belly is to be large, the vulva projecting and fleshy, from the point where the hairs grow, to the buttocks; the conduit must be narrow and not moist, soft to the touch, and emitting a strong heat and no bad smell."

"She must have the thighs and buttocks hard, the hips large and full, a waist of fine shape, hands and feet of striking elegance, plump arms, and well-developed shoulders. If one looks at a woman with those qualities in front, one is fascinated; if from behind, one dies with pleasure." Dream on, O Sheikh!

THE MOVEMENTS OF LOVE

The author of *The Perfumed Garden* lists a number of movements for use during intercourse. It is with these kinds of love techniques that the book comes into its own. The idea that you can use special techniques to prolong or extend some of the heart-stopping excitement of penetration is practical as well as thrilling. Among the techniques suggested are:

1 **The Bucket in the Well:** "The man and woman join in close embrace after the introduction. Then he gives a push, and withdraws a little; the woman follows him with a push, and also retires. So they continue their alternate movement, keeping proper time. Placing foot against foot, and hand against hand, they keep up the motion of a bucket in a well."

2 **The Mutual Shock:** "After the introduction, they each draw back, but without dislodging the member completely. Then they both push tightly together, and thus go on keeping time."

3 **The Approach:** "The man moves as usual, and then stops. Then the woman, with the member in her receptacle, begins to move like the man, and then stops. And they continue this way until ejaculation comes."

Positions for men who are long – and short

RATHER THAN GIVE the sex positions he advocated fancy names, Sheikh Nefzawi often merely labeled them in numbered order – but each position was chosen for a special reason.

First Posture

The straightforward man-on-top position is said to be particularly suitable for the man with a long penis, allowing him to adjust his length of thrust easily so as not to hurt his partner. This is a very real consideration when a man and woman have very different builds.

FIRST POSTURE

Second Posture

In this acrobatic-looking pose, the woman rests on her shoulders with her legs swung right up and over her head. This allows her partner to lean right over her and to have exceptionally easy access to her vagina. This can hardly be a comfortable position for the woman, but Sheikh Nefzawi, undeterred, recommends its use to the man whose "member is a short one."

This is a very practical method of making intercourse possible for the man who is particularly under-endowed, but I suspect that most women would find it too difficult or uncomfortable. In this event, the couple should consider alternatives to intercourse that will give satisfaction to both partners. These include masturbation, mutual masturbation, oral sex, and the use of sex aids.

SECOND POSTURE

Techniques for deep penetration

DEEP PENETRATION IS PARTICULARLY important to men. This is partly because the further the penis continues to travel down the vagina, the more the head and the coronal ridge (a highly sensitive area around the head of the penis) are stimulated. It's important to remember that at least at the start of penetration, the vagina remains partly closed all the way down to the cervix. So the woman must be fully aroused before attempting the postures for deep penetration as specified in The Perfumed Garden.

Third Posture

Here the man kneels between the woman's legs, then lifts one of her legs onto his shoulder and puts the other under his arm. This allows for very deep penetration, so make sure the woman is fully aroused and her vagina is ready to be penetrated so exceptionally deeply.

THIRD POSTURE

During arousal, the vaginal canal undergoes a process called "tenting," which involves the enlargement of its upper end to accommodate the deep-thrusting penis. Do not attempt to penetrate deeply before "tenting" has occurred, or the woman could be injured.

Sixth Posture

This is a classic rear-entry position that allows for deep penetration. It also has the advantage that, because the man is in a stable kneeling position, he has his hands free to caress his woman's back and breasts and to stimulate her clitoris. Or, he can hold her by the waist or hips and pull her back and forward on his penis.

SIXTH POSTURE

Trivia...

Why do we like rear-entry sex so much? Classic rear-entry sex generates a powerful, primal eroticism. During our early evolution, when we were more like our cousins the great apes, we would have copulated in this style. Anthropologists believe that the buttocks give out strong sexual signals. In fact it has been suggested that the human female developed such full breasts – far beyond those of any other primates – in order to imitate the visual appeal of the buttocks.

Ninth Posture

This is another version of rear-entry sex and one that lends itself to love-making while clothed as well as naked. These days, it's a love position that most people associate with making love on the kitchen table, on an office desk, or on some other unconventional surface.

In this version the woman can either lie face down across a bed with her knees on the floor, or stand and lean forward over it. The man straddles her legs from behind and grips her around the hips to facilitate thrusting.

NINTH POSTURE

Poses for artistic lovers

SHEIKH NEFZAWI SETS OUT several very convoluted, impractical sex positions that you'd think a couple would only want to carry out for esoteric or artistic purposes! However, there are also those that are more attainable.

■ **Some poses** *advocated by the author of* The Perfumed Garden *need more than average dexterity.*

The Stopperage

Drawing on the vocabulary of the wine trade, Sheikh Nefzawi quite clearly suggests corking up the woman's vagina with the male member.

The woman lies on her back with her legs raised in the air and her hands supporting her man's chest. He inserts his penis into her exposed genitals. By pressing the walls of the vagina together in this position and pushing the cervix forward, this position makes penetration difficult, and once inserted, the penis presses on the cervix.

There is a corresponding sensitivity of sensation – so much so that Sheikh Nefzawi warns the position is painful for the woman. He suggests it should be tried only by a man who has a short or soft member.

THE STOPPERAGE

The Stopperage is an excellent position for any man who suffers from partial impotence.

Frog Fashion

This is a strange (and perhaps difficult) position where the couple sit facing one another. As she grasps her knees and wedges her toes underneath his buttocks he moves forward with his legs on the outside of her body until he can penetrate her. Neither partner can move much but at the moment of orgasm (if you are lucky enough to get there) Sheikh Nefzawi suggests the man should grasp his woman's upper arm and draw her to him.

While this is a curiously secure and cosy position, it's probably one that's best left to amphibians!

FROG FASHION

The Tail of the Ostrich

In this position, the woman lies on her back and the man kneels up. He hikes up her legs so that she is resting on her shoulders and he can penetrate her from above. He can vary movement by raising or lowering his partner to alter the depth and angle of penetration.

I think this position smacks of male fantasy and has little to do with making sexual intercourse enjoyable for the woman. If she is happy to indulge her partner in what almost amounts to a fetish (she is, after all, virtually upside-down!) then all well and good.

Do not pursue the Tail of the Ostrich position for too long — it could be very tough on the woman's spine and neck.

Trivia...

Sheikh Nefzawi attributes a wealth of humorous nicknames to the many types of "vulva" he describes in The Perfumed Garden. Examples include "The voluptuous," "The crusher," "The glutton," "The hot one," and "The delicious one." He recognizes that just as all mouths and faces are different, so too are all genitalia.

THE TAIL OF THE OSTRICH

Fitting On of the Sock

More a type of foreplay than a true sex position, this is designed to arouse the woman for full penetration. While she lies on her back, her partner sits between her legs and inserts the tip of his member into her vulva which, with his thumb and first finger, he pulls gently closed around it. Moving his member gently back and forth, he rubs her outer lips, held there with his fingers until his secretion moistens her vagina. He then enters her completely.

This is an excellent method of using the penis as a dildo. Because it is so different from intercourse and so locally focused on the inside of her labia, including her clitoris, the woman may become extremely aroused prior to penetration.

FITTING ON OF THE SOCK

A simple summary

✔ There are hundreds of different ways of using sex to get closer to heaven.

✔ There are also hundreds of ways of using sex to demonstrate how much you adore a partner.

✔ The skills and experience of sex can be used therefore both to worship a partner and to get a sense of reaching a heightened place in your consciousness.

✔ Men and women have different but extremely attractive physical characteristics and part of growing more attached is to enjoy each other's differences wholeheartedly.

PART FOUR

THE *KAMA SUTRA* DISPENSES ADVICE ON COURTSHIP

SEDUCING THE EMOTIONS

Having talked about the physical things you can do to make your partner feel sexy, this section focuses on the *emotional* approach. The original *Kama Sutra* described only how the man might inspire confidence in his woman. But in this 21st century edition, the book's time-honored techniques are applied to both men and women.

In the following pages I describe how to make men and women feel happy and confident, *sexy* yet *stable*. The original text embraced the concept of polygamy. Today in Western society we don't marry more than one partner but we do have serial marriages. This section contrasts the ancient rules of behavior for several wives living together with the pitfalls of falling in love with other people's partners today. It is, according to the *Kama Sutra*, an age-old problem!

Chapter 16

Creating Confidence

MEN AND WOMEN WHO TRUST ONE ANOTHER can say and do anything. In order to get to this point of trust, you need to take things slowly. A leisurely pace pays off since complete confidence (that anything you say or do with your lover is acceptable) is a heady experience. And when you feel this good, sex becomes ecstatic. The truth is that not many people do feel that anything goes, particularly sexually. Invariably couples must deal with hesitations, setbacks, and legacies of past, insensitive relationships. But when you begin to trust each other the whole world becomes wonderful, and you'll find that there are no holds barred.

In this chapter...

✓ Abstaining from sex

✓ Talking up a storm

✓ Touching her intimately

✓ Touching him intimately

AT THE START OF A RELATIONSHIP, GET TO KNOW ONE ANOTHER SLOWLY IN ORDER TO BUILD UP TRUST

Abstaining from sex

IN ANCIENT INDIA, *the bride and groom were unlikely to have met before the ceremony. Or, if they had, they probably did not know each other very well. Making love with a complete stranger was potentially a brutal experience, so in a sensitive attempt to avoid such trauma, the* Kama Sutra *outlined clear methods of getting to know someone in the first days of marriage. Translated to our times, we could follow the same advice in the first stages of a new love affair. What follows is my extension of the teaching originally advocated by the* Kama Sutra, *but amended and updated to suit us all today.*

Why abstain?

If it is made clear that a partner is not going to make love to you, a layer of pressure is removed from the proceedings. Modern sex therapy works on exactly this basis.

Paradoxically, if making love is forbidden, you may want to all the more.

The other good reason for abstaining is that you need to get to know each other. You need to work at the early stages of love so that you can start to feel for each other. One of the best recipes for good lovemaking is to be so consumed with desire for your partner that you feel you simply have to have sex with them. If you know you're not allowed to, the feeling builds. On the other hand, if you think you ought to make love, the desire is never so great.

You don't have to spell this out to your new partner. Your behavior will indicate your sexual attitude. It's also a useful method of getting to know a partner's inner nature. The man or woman who can't cope with delaying intercourse and who wants immediate gratification will probably need immediate gratification for everything. In contrast the partner who demonstrates he or she is prepared to wait also demonstrates that you are worth waiting for. This is heart-warming and confidence-boosting.

■ **With arranged marriages,** *couples in ancient India, as today, needed time to get acquainted.*

Spending time together

So what do you do in this early period when you have met, when you know that you admire each other but you are not yet going to jump between the sheets? You hang out together.

You talk, you eat, you walk; you visit exhibitions, watch movies, or go to the theater. All of these activities are platforms on which you can build mutual knowledge. And you do this with warmth.

Making her feel comfortable

Use touch as part of your communication. Don't just say "I like you," give her a hug. When walking, demonstrate your concern for her well-being by slipping your hand under her arm. Don't be afraid of kissing her. But when you feel the temperature rise, deliberately withdraw. This lays the groundwork for building up sexual tension: A mild withdrawal can seem tantalizingly provoking. Because this behavior arouses mild anxiety, your partner's entire arousal level will be raised, readying her to be erotically receptive.

■ **Stay close to your partner** *when you're at a social gathering and don't be afraid to give her an affectionate kiss.*

If you accompany her to a dance or to a party, stand close. In a crowd, put a protective arm around her. Be open to any moves she makes to you. Many men are surprised when their woman spontaneously hugs, or puts an arm around them while watching a movie even though they may be simultaneously delighted. So accept her embraces with heartfelt pleasure.

Making him feel comfortable

Sit close to him in the bar. Snuggle up to him when you're having an intimate conversation. Don't be shy of telling him how much you like him.

Psychotherapist Phillip Hodson describes men as "praise-seeking missiles." The more nice things you can say about your man to his face, the more he'll like you for it.

If you sense that he's feeling crowded, don't be afraid to stand back and give him some emotional space. Try to find out how he's feeling – not everyone wants a partner who's with them all the time, however much they adore you. Feel strong enough in yourself to enjoy the time you spend away from him. This gives you both the opportunity to welcome the next date wholeheartedly.

MOVES THAT CONVEY WARMTH

1 Looking into a partner's eyes for longer than usual

2 Moving closer toward the other person than you would normally

3 Smiling more than usual, and looking in turn at various parts of your partner's body

4 Nodding your head in vigorous agreement

5 Sitting using open body language

6 Using hand gestures while talking that manage to take in the partner or that indicate an appreciation of him or her

7 Taking quick glances at the other person, moistening your lips with your tongue and widening your eyes a little while doing so

8 Making small touching movements. For example, when you're standing together, you could stand behind your partner and cuddle up against his or her body, putting your arms around their waist; you could put an arm around your partner; or you could caress and massage your partner's back

■ **Open, suggestive** *body language can be used to reinforce the beginnings of sexual attraction. This couple are smiling, looking into one another's eyes and sharing food in a particularly intimate way.*

Talking up a storm

IT IS HARD TO RELATE to someone without getting to know the inner person. One of the first ingredients of good lovemaking, therefore, is to talk. If you can't communicate openly with one another, it's unlikely that you'll get beyond the mechanics of sexual intercourse. The Kama Sutra's mission is to make sex as enjoyable as possible, so the great sex manual gives specific instructions for encouraging women to talk.

■ **Sharing wine** *and conversation is a great way for lovers to relax, as this antique Indian painting shows.*

Trivia...

Vatsyayana advised that if a man wanted to win over a very young girl (remember that in ancient India they married at a very early age) he should excel at children's games. He should impress "a damsel come of age" by his skill in the arts, and encourage a girl to love him by having recourse to her closest confidantes.

Getting personal

If a partner is reluctant to talk, one way of encouraging them to open up is to contribute something personal about yourself. Lead by example, and your friend will feel more inclined to follow suit. The most fertile subject for this sort of early conversation is family. Yours and your partner's. You'll need to know something about each other's backgrounds to gain an idea of how your families relate and how therefore you two may relate.

Eventually it will be important to talk about your feelings for each other and about your sexual emotions – always traditionally difficult subjects. If you can lay a foundation for opening up to each other, the same process can be used for getting sexual.

In order to have a really good talk, you'll need to:

1. Ask questions

2. Contribute personal information – but not hog the conversation

3. Keep the conversation on track instead of seizing every opportunity to talk only about yourself

A good conversation allows two people to have their say and to feel that they have said enough, without monopolizing the conversation or being a bore.

The art of listening

One of the skills of holding a good conversation is the ability to listen. Cast your mind back to the parties you have enjoyed most and invariably they will be the ones where you felt someone was genuinely interested in what you had to say. How did you perceive they were truly interested? You would have perceived their concentration because they:

1. Didn't interrupt

2. Murmured noises of appreciation and understanding

3. Looked at you without letting their gaze flicker halfway round the room

4. Used open body language toward you

5. Followed up your revelations by asking relevant questions that showed they had listened properly

6. Allowed you to talk yourself out

■ **Listening to your partner** *means giving them your undivided attention and really concentrating on what they have to say.*

Talking tender

Partners who come from families where affection is readily expressed will have no difficulty in spontaneously hugging, kissing, caressing, and saying "you're gorgeous," or "I really like you," or "you're extraordinarily attractive," or "I want you like crazy." But those of us with undemonstrative families may find it hideously hard to say a simple "I love you." Yet it is absolutely necessary that we all learn how to do this.

People can't know that you truly like them unless you tell them so. Unfortunately we don't possess telepathy, so we need to hear words of affection and tenderness.

Talking sex

One way of talking about sex is to look back at the type of sexual environment you were raised in and discuss it. You can talk about where you learned the facts of life, what your first experiences were, whether they were good or bad. What were your parents' attitudes toward sex? And do you agree with them? Sharing sexual memories with a partner helps you get to know each other better.

EXPRESS YOURSELF

If you find it hard to spit out the words of love, practice. Stand in front of a mirror and make passionate love to yourself. Tell yourself what a wonderful, enchanting, hot, sexy, man or woman you are. Say it – out loud. Say "I love you" three times a day. When you're with your partner (assuming of course that you feel the emotion) make sure you say "I love you," out loud, at least three times a week.

If you feel happier demonstrating your love in other ways, make sure your lover knows what you are saying. The man who built wonderful cupboards for his fiancée all over the house couldn't understand it when she thought he didn't love her. The cupboards were his way of showing he cared. But she needed a translation before she could appreciate his loving moves.

Below is a checklist of questions to discuss as part of your sex conversation. I'm not suggesting you ask all these questions in one intense session and subject your new partner to an exam. He or she might run a mile. Rather, just come out with your version of one of these questions when the occasion obviously lends itself.

1 Were your parents affectionate or aggressive towards one another?

2 What do you remember of incidents that may relate to your parents' sex life?

3 What was their attitude towards nudity?

4 What kind of hidden messages do you think you received from your parents about sex?

5 Were there any early sexual experiences that were embarrassing for you?

6 When and how did you first learn about sex?

7 What was your earliest sexual experience? Was it with someone of the same sex or of the opposite sex?

8 What have your subsequent sexual experiences and relationships consisted of?

INTERNET

www.nerve.com

This is a good-quality online sex magazine and discussion site. Check out nerve's *feisty articles, horoscopes, and photographic features.*

Touching her intimately

THERE ARE WAYS of slowly developing sexual intimacy. Vatsyayana suggests that for the first three nights of marriage the couple merely sleep together without the man touching the woman. Today, this would naturally pique the curiosity and the anxiety of a new wife but is appropriate during the early days of a modern relationship. The secret lies in not being overtly sexual but in still making small moves to foster intimacy. Here are Vatsyayana's suggestions for leading up to intercourse:

As you talk and caress, move on to kissing (see Chapter 9). Then slowly and delicately slide your hands on to the tip of her breasts but go no further. Wait. If she does not object and if she appears to like the touch, go on slowly, moving your hands further. Vatsyayana suggests that once the man has been able to touch her breasts, he kisses her again. Then he lets his hands drift softly to her navel and gradually goes further but does not seek intercourse immediately. If she objects, he could make suggestions that to make things fun and unthreatening the touch is turned into a game.

TOUCH TIPS FOR THE BREASTS

1 Softly drag your fingertips across the breasts

2 Gently squeeze her nipple between your finger and thumb and slide your fingers up and off. For extra sensation you can use both hands alternately so that the action and the sensations are continuous. Give your attention first to one nipple then the other

3 Trace patterns on her breasts. One sensational pattern is the spokes stroke. Here you think of the breasts as a wheel and, starting at the nipple, softly trace a finger out along each of the "spokes" to the outer edge of the breasts

■ **Spirals** *are also a sensational pattern to trace across your partner's breasts.*

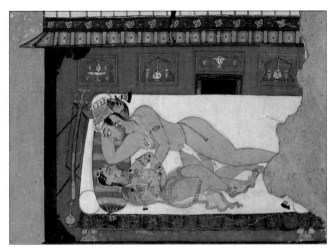

Vatsyayana's game consists of pretending that the touch has been performed by a girlfriend in the past and that the young woman's role, every time she is touched now, is to comment on how the touch feels and where she would like him to move his hand next.

Since in our society women are unlikely to have played suggestive touch games with their girlfriends, I suggest an alternative game that you can play with your partner based on a therapy exercise called the "map test."

■ **An Indian lover** *caresses his partner. The Kama Sutra advocates intimate touching as an erotic way to discover the sensitive areas of a partner's body.*

The Map Test game

The Map Test involves lightly stroking small areas anywhere on the body and asking the partner being stroked to give the touch a rating for erotic sensation on a scale of plus three to minus three. Think about the sensation in terms of both the sensuality of the particular body area and on the firmness or softness of the touch.

■ **When playing the Map Test game,** *remember to stroke just one small area of the body at a time. Lightly run your fingers over an area no larger than about 2 inches (5 cm) in diameter.*

The test is a method of building up a complete map of how each individual's body reacts sensually. It's a good idea to try this at some stage in the relationship because it offers valuable information about your partner's unique sensual reactions. For the purposes of a game however, you could turn the same testing touch into a "Who can offer the most sensual feeling competition?" This doesn't mean you can instantly dive for each other's genitals because, without the build-up of touching the rest of the body, you won't necessarily get the most intense response.

So how do you score? If something is good, rate it from zero to plus three. Something fantastically sexy would qualify as plus three. If there isn't much sensation, or it's unpleasant, grade right down to minus three.

Touching the genitals

Now the man lets his hands wander over her thighs and pubis and between her legs. All the time that he does this, he kisses her. He can kiss her on the forehead, the eyes, the neck; the entire gradual exploration of her body is accompanied by kisses.

The Map Test game can be extended by investigating the genitals in the same way that you explored the rest of the body.

■ **Keep kissing** *your partner as you intimately explore her body.*

Almost intercourse

So far these ideas correspond with tried and tested therapy methods of improving sexual relationships. Even now that the relationship has heated up, intercourse is not yet on the menu. Instead the man is advised to show how passionately attracted he is to the woman. Unsurprisingly her anxieties subside and her readiness for sex increases.

One form of sex therapy advises that the man slide his body over and around the woman's, including sliding his genitals over hers but without coming to climax. Only on the fourth day, when each feels much more intimate, may orgasm be experienced – but it should still be outside her body. It is only after you have covered all these stages that she will be psychologically ready for intercourse.

Touching him intimately

THE KAMA SUTRA is one-sided. It is written solely for the purpose of educating men on how to approach, instruct, and initiate their wives in the skills and joys of intercourse. There is very little instruction aimed specifically at the woman with her man's pleasure in mind. This next section is therefore an amalgam of hints thrown up by the original manual and possibilities inspired by today's ideas about lovemaking.

When she should take the initiative

Women still appear to be governed by the belief that men feel emasculated when women make the approaches. Yet surveys on the subject would suggest otherwise. One well-known telephone survey found that whereas women thought men would think them fast and loose for calling up to make a first date, men said they would be immensely flattered and delighted to be asked.

The consensus is that you won't know what will appeal to someone until you've tried it.

Moves a woman might make

You might:

1. Cuddle him

2. Put an arm around him at the movies

3. Cuddle up to him on the sofa

4. Lean against him at a party or dance

5. Dance very close

6. Give him a massage

7. Stroke him suggestively

8. Stroke your entire body over his entire body

9. Slide yourself on top and initiate sex

■ **This Tibetan statue** *celebrates the power of the female body over men.*

Respond with vigor

The *Kama Sutra* doesn't imply that every woman is a fragile flower. In fact, the normal female was thought to have as vigorous a response as a male. If he lovingly bit her for example, it was thought perfectly normal for her to bite back.

The Kama Sutra encouraged the use of loving slaps and blows regardless of gender.

There's also an entire chapter on how the woman may make love to the spent young man using such fetish objects as a dildo.

Inverted copulation

To help the man when he is exhausted and unable to carry on any longer, the woman is exhorted to climb on top of him and to rotate around his penis. By doing this she would stimulate the sides and outer areas of the genitals as well as getting pressure inside the vagina.

■ The *Kama Sutra* encouraged a woman to prolong sex even when her man became tired.

Inverted copulation allows the woman to drive herself on to satisfy her passion.

Another area where she can take charge of intercourse is when the man is not getting enough sensation from ordinary penetration.

This is where she might practice tightening and loosening the vaginal muscles so that she effectively milks his penis as he remains still inside her. To do this you need very highly developed vaginal muscles (see Chapter 12).

INTERNET

www.tantra.org/
kamasutr.html

Visit this Church of Tantra site to read more about role reversal positions and the love teachings of the Kama Sutra *in general.*

Acting the part of the man

There are several movements recommended for the woman to "act the part of the man" for occasions when her partner is tired, or as a variation for her own pleasure.

A favorite is The Top (see page 170), a position that needs great dexterity. While sitting astride her partner, the woman raises her legs to clear his body and swivels on his penis.

For more information on this and other movements where the "woman acts the part of the man" see Chapter 13.

■ **A woman can show** *her partner how strongly she feels about him by making the moves in initiating or prolonging sex.*

A simple summary

✔ Start sex slowly and be sensitive to each other's feelings. Abstain from intercourse until you feel intimate together.

✔ Talk to your partner. Get to know each other, and exchange information about each other's family histories and early sexual experiences.

✔ Combine your physical exploration of each other with a lot of passionate kissing. Make love in just about any and every way without actually having intercourse.

✔ It's not just the man who might take the initiative. The woman is encouraged to respond vigorously to start certain types of intercourse and not to hesitate in obtaining her own satisfaction if he is too tired to manage it himself.

Chapter 17

Courtship

BY PRESENT STANDARDS, the *Kama Sutra* does everything backward. In the original volume, after the sexual advice come words of wisdom, thoughts on courtship, the best presents to give, even tips on the romance of poetry. In our day, these thoughts are usually included at the beginning of a relationship manual. Wherever they fit into the text, however, they still offer inspiration to lovers who reckon they need all the help they can get when it comes to making an irresistible impression. Whether you're looking for ways to entertain and enthrall a partner, or simply show them how deeply you care, the following pages offer both lighthearted ideas and some sound advice.

In this chapter...

✓ **Games and diversions**

✓ **Giving imaginative presents**

✓ **The outward signs of love**

ROMANTIC WORDS AND LOVING GESTURES SHOW YOUR PARTNER THAT YOU CARE DEEPLY

Games and diversions

THE KAMA SUTRA offered training to young men whose brides-to-be were mere children when they first met. The man was advised to be kind and generous toward the young girl he was destined to marry in order to win her trust and love. Playing childish games was a way of establishing an early friendship between the couple. Modern psychologists would agree with this approach (only for grown-ups!) on the grounds that game-playing is a kind of rehearsal – a method of allowing you to make mistakes in a safe climate, so that you'll learn new skills for the future.

For the purpose of this book, I've transposed the idea of game-playing to adulthood. A game allows you to relax, laugh, and have fun. (In the previous chapter, a game was used to help the young woman grow comfortable with intimacy.)

Storytelling

Reading your lover a story at bedtime is an act of pure indulgence and is a time-honored method of giving a special treat. A story paves the way for relaxation and mutual appreciation. Of course, a story can also be erotic in its own right – and in case men think this an odd suggestion, bear in mind that women are aroused by sexy fiction.

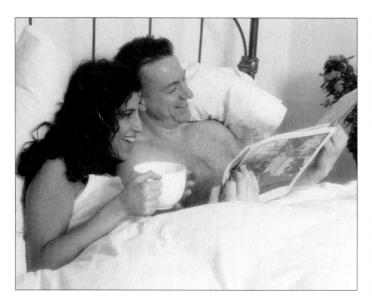

Don't worry if you don't feel able to conjure up a steamy blue tale at the drop of a vibrator. It's easy to find erotic fiction in books, magazines, and on the Internet.

■ **If bedtime** *with your partner tends to be cozy rather than sexy, why not spice it up by reading some good erotic fiction to one another.*

You'll find erotic fiction at the back of *Great Sex Guide* and *Sex Games*, both by Anne Hooper. There's *The Erotic Review,* which is an established magazine that publishes sexual fiction every month. Or you might like to read Nancy Friday's *My Secret Garden,* a collection of women's sexual fantasies.

INTERNET

www.eps.org.uk

Click here to browse the online catalog of the Erotic Print Society, set up in 1994 to cater for people "who appreciate the best in erotic art, literature, and journalism."

Guided fantasies

A guided fantasy can be a wonderful preliminary to good sex. Something about the intensity of lovemaking allows us to be childlike again and the simplicity of playing together triggers the best sexual experiences. This is a method where one of you tells a story and the other is encouraged to flesh it out in the mind. This means the story can be quite simple. If it helps, you can combine sensual touch with your storytelling.

The story doesn't have to be sexual but it should be sensual. By visualizing great sweeps of color, lush tropical landscapes, and bizarre and erotic clothes, you set the scene for arousal. Here are some possible storylines:

a A trip through a sultan's harem

b The capture and sale of a beautiful slave

c A journey into the ruby caverns of a far-off planet

d A hunt through leafy woods where you and a handsome rider become separated from the others

e The arranged marriage of a naive young girl to a handsome stranger

Do not embark on a guided fantasy every night of the week or it will lose its appeal. Think of it as a treat to be savored on special occasions.

■ **The more exotic and colorful** *the setting, the spicier your guided fantasy is likely to be.*

EXPLORING TABOOS

Some people worry that their fantasies are a sign of deviant sexuality. Fantasies about the same sex, or sex involving force, can make people feel worried about their unconscious desires. In fact, the most common explanation for fantasies is that we are naturally drawn to what we perceive as forbidden, naughty, or taboo. Rest assured that though these taboos are erotic in imagination, most of us would run a mile if they actually came true in everyday life.

Acting out a fantasy

Don't worry if you feel devoid of inspiration. There are lots of ways to start off fantasy acting:

1. Choose a favorite movie sex scene (such as the food scene in *9½ Weeks*) and re-enact it with the same props. Watch your sex scene in the mirror for cinematic effect

2. Write down some fantasy roles or characters (slave, teacher, virgin, or prisoner, for example) on pieces of paper. Or maybe you could think of a famous film role or star – then interact in character

■ **Acting out fantasies** *can preserve relationships by bringing novelty and excitement to people's sex lives.*

3. Pick a fantasy theme and decorate your bedroom in that style – for example, an oriental *Kama Sutra*-style boudoir, a Bedouin tent, or a den full of sex toys

Fantasy swapping

Revealing fantasies takes courage. You may fear shocking your partner or being the object of humor, ridicule, or even disgust. The way to overcome this is to make a pact to take turns swapping fantasies. Start gently and progressively spice up your stories. The only other rule is that your respective fantasies must be of equal "value." For instance, if your partner describes an exotic fantasy, then yours must be equally wild.

If you don't want to reveal your fantasies, then, on no account do so. Your privacy is sacrosanct so don't be bullied into sharing anything you'd rather keep to yourself.

If you are happy to divulge a fantasy but feel a bit nervous about doing so, choose one "strand" or aspect of your fantasy and explain that to your partner. The strand you choose should be symbolic and should capture the most erotic aspect of your fantasy. For example, if you fantasize about being forced to have sex by a stranger, tell your partner that you want him to make love to you when you are least expecting it and that he must continue his seduction of you even if you protest.

Don't forget. It is vital to build rules into fantasy sex games. Always have a prearranged code word that either of you can use at any point if you want the game to stop.

Giving imaginative presents

INDIAN LOVERS IN THE 4TH CENTURY *were extremely generous with gifts, and they gave them to just about everyone! Even a remote great-aunt of the girl being courted would have received a little something.*

The most popular gifts to the special lady herself were flowers because these constituted a type of code and each flower construed a different love meaning. Betel nuts, trinkets, games, toys, and even jewels were also offered. What's more, the artful lover might hide the present and tantalize his woman into looking for it. So present-giving through teasing became another way of getting close.

FLOWERS AND THEIR MEANINGS

- Blue hyacinths: *I love you tenderly*
- Jonquils: *Returned affection*
- Lilies: *Beauty and structure*
- Red tulips: *Love*
- Orchids: *Passion or beauty*
- Bluebells: *Everlasting love*
- Daisies: *Innocence*
- Violets: *Faithfulness*
- Garden roses: *Strong love and sexual attraction*
- Lilacs: *Sexual or romantic nostalgia*
- Amaryllis: *Straightforward sex*
- Daffodils: *Affection*

The importance of timing

Successful giving depends not only on the choice of gift but also on timing. There are certain presents that could be erotically explosive at an advanced stage of the relationship but disastrous if given just after you've both met. It's also wise to have a good idea of your friend's character: Giving an expensive bottle of champagne to a teetotaller would simply be embarrassing, while the gift of a weekend in a trendy New York hotel might be a nuisance for an avid football fan and season-ticket holder.

The first rule of giving is to avoid buying what you prefer and think about what your opposite number would really like.

■ **Chocolates** *are usually a popular present – but they won't be if your partner has just started a diet!*

Gifts for the start of something new

These are traditional straightforward offerings. Corny as it sounds, men and women like receiving sentimental cards, interesting books, flowers, and chocolates. You can either organize delivery or pitch up on the doorstep yourself. Of course, the 21st century also offers cyber methods of present giving. There are wonderful e-cards for every occasion, as well as florists, jewelers, and chocolate stores online.

INTERNET

www.interflora.com

www.godiva.com

www.bluemountain.com

Choose one of the above sites to order flowers, chocolates, or romantic electronic greetings cards.

■ **Saying it with flowers** *is an ideal way of showing affection, not only at the start of a relationship, but all the way through.*

What to buy when it's heating up

At this stage, presents can get more suggestive but should still be within the bounds of good taste and decency. This means that if either partner is slow to fire up, you're not going to outrage them. Indeed, the provocation that this intermediate type of gift offers may even help to set them alight.

You might consider giving silk boxer shorts, sexy books, suggestive cards, or erotic pictures. Most people like to have such presents handed to them in privacy by candlelight. But you could always e-mail virtual presents if you prefer.

When you're both at boiling point

Now you should be piling fuel onto an already fabulous blaze. It's also the time when you can go beyond the boundaries of good taste and go for the unashamedly bizarre and suggestive. This is the time for champagne, which you might try serving in the bath and pouring down your partner's face and chest as they attempt to drink. Then there's the gift of a good massage. Or perhaps you might offer an aerosol of whipped brandy cream or a tube of squashy chocolate body paint; apply it generously, then spend hours licking it off.

INTERNET

www.wrapit.co.uk

If you're looking for present ideas, this site provides a gift service "for modern couples." There are home, travel, adventure, and executive gizmo sections, among others.

■ **Champagne** *is an ideal gift once your relationship is really sizzling — especially when served in bed.*

221

Suggestive teasers

A sex shop or online sex store could supply you with a deliciously perfumed genital lubricant. Why not wrap this in red tissue and include a note saying "I'm longing to rub this between your legs." Crotchless panties may be the epitome of bad taste but boy, are they fun. And they feel kind of sexy to wear. Provided you think they will be received as joyfully as they are given, a set of nipple clamps, preferably donated halfway through intercourse, could prove to be dynamite!

INTERNET

www.passion8shop.com

This is a good place to go shopping for sexual presents.

Incidentally, one leading online sex store reported that nipple clamps were the year's best-selling items.

Gifts for when the friendship is off the wall

This is the time for serious sex toys. You have proved yourselves to each other, you know each other inside and out, you have no secrets, and you have explored every orifice, adoring every moment. Think giant strap-on dildo, edible lubes for oral sex, or his and hers butt-plugs.

Do not give heavy-duty presents unless you are absolutely certain they will be received in the spirit in which they are given! There are many partners who would run away if you were to misjudge their inclinations.

ANAL PLUG   VIBRATING PENIS RING

NIPPLE CLAMPS WITH WEIGHTS

The outward signs of love

VATSYAYANA HAD SOME VERY DIFFERENT IDEAS to us regarding what men considered attractive behavior in women. The sage believed that a woman should not show her willingness until her lover was clearly ready to make a move. He thought that any woman forward enough to initiate a move herself was likely to be an immoral character who would jump in and out of bed with many men.

Vatsyayana's advice to women was that although they shouldn't in any way initiate action – neither should they offer any resistance when a man got around to making a pass. He wisely advocated that a woman should watch the man carefully for signs of his feelings and gauge her own response accordingly.

Sexual preliminaries

"Do not anticipate your man's desires," Vatsyayana continued, "and let him show you how to love. Experience his loving as if it were something completely new for you. Appear reluctant, even when he kisses you. Respond only when he embraces you by force."

■ **Vatsyayana's advice to a woman** *was to allow the man to take the lead and be sensitive to his advances. Although a little reticence on the woman's part can heighten male desire, too much simply makes the woman appear unresponsive.*

Some of this of course might happen naturally, especially if it is the first time you have come sexually close. Vatsyayana seems to be hinting at the fact that sometimes keeping a little mystery about yourself serves as an aphrodisiac.

Don't overdo feigning reluctance. Most men agree that if you continue to kiss a woman who shows no response, it rapidly becomes boring.

223

Putting your partner first

If you really care about someone you suddenly become remarkably generous. You want to share yourself and so you make this clear by sharing objects, outings, meals. You spend time and money on this gorgeous person in a way you would never usually dream of. It's worth remembering this later in the relationship when the novelty has worn off and you don't feel so generous. Giving is an outward demonstration of love.

Showing you care

John Gottman, professor of psychology at the University of Washington, advises that even the most difficult marriages can be successfully negotiated provided that for every bad stroke you give you must offer at least five good strokes. A good stroke can be:

1. Saying "I love you"

2. Buying a book you know your partner wanted

3. Cooking a meal when you know your partner is exhausted

4. Offering a back rub

5. Giving your partner an appreciative hug

The right partner?

Vatsyayana believes it is better to choose a mate who is like you in social class and who possesses the temperament that will be most compatible with yours. This, he believes, is more important than marrying someone because they are rich.

■ **Giving your partner** *a warm hug is one way of showing that you're not taking them for granted.*

SOME 21ST CENTURY ADVICE

Go with your feelings and appreciate spontaneity. But be aware that, like anything else, you also need to learn how to make love. Probably the best way to learn is to invent lovemaking between the two of you.

Take kissing for example. If kissing feels like the right thing to do then go right ahead and do it, regardless of your gender. The same goes for touching, stroking, caressing. As long as it feels right for you and as long as your partner makes it clear he or she loves it, go right ahead.

Modern research on what makes the best relationship shows that:

1. Similarity in background is a bonus since you have the same expectations of future life

2. A good mate can be chosen by a matchmaker or met through a dating agency and that these relationships work as well and often better than marriages formed through random meetings

3. Similarity in temperament helps

4. A dissimilarity in temperament makes things harder but doesn't rule out a good marriage – provided you continue with the five-good-strokes-to-one-bad-stroke principle

■ **Couples with shared interests** *and a similar outlook on life tend to have more successful relationships than those with little in common and very different upbringings.*

Poetry in motion

The giving and receiving of love poems was of prime importance to the young men and women described in the *Kama Sutra*. Here is a little verse penned by Sir Richard Burton, Victorian editor and discoverer of the *Kama Sutra*, to a lovely Arabian who was probably his mistress. It's reprinted from *A Rage to Live – A Biography of Richard and Isabel Burton* by Mary Lovell.

> Her eyes were jetty, jet her hair,
> O'ershading face like lotus fair;
> Her lips were rubies, guarding flowers
> Of jasmine dewed with vernal showers . . .

If you can't string words together into successful poetic shapes, there are lots of love poems that you can borrow from. For inspiration take a look at *The Virago Book of Love Poetry*, edited by Wendy Mulford.

Showing appreciation

I've always felt the best sorts of appreciation are when a partner virtually unconsciously lets gasps, noises, or small cries escape, indicating that he or she is getting incredibly turned on.

Sounds can also help you gauge whether or not this is what you want. Do you like going quite so far, so fast? Or do you feel slightly uneasy?

Sounds of turn-on can act as a great aphrodisiac.

■ **Gazing at your** *partner with sincere feeling is one way of showing your appreciation.*

If you do feel rather overwhelmed, sounds provide useful information. They give you the option of slowing things down a bit and also convey to your partner a sense of your elusiveness (which can be powerfully attractive).

Gazing into your partner's eyes, burying yourself within their arms, going back for more, reacting to touch by wordlessly shivering, these are all methods of appreciation. But beware of sentences such as "Wow, you turn me on." Most of us want to be loved for ourselves, even at a sexual level. And the trouble with this sentence is that it conveys pure lust. It doesn't say "I desire you." Instead it says "I desire sex."

A simple summary

✔ Playing games together, even as adults, is still a wonderful, relaxed method of getting to know each other. Games enable you to learn more about each other's moods and temperaments. They also build confidence and trust.

✔ Offering your new partner (not to mention members of his or her family) gifts is a good psychological move. A present allows you to feel valued. A present from a son or daughter's new friend allows you to feel respected.

✔ It's important to let your partner know you are responding to their courtship but not, at the beginning, to go too far in your enthusiasm. This is on the grounds that reticence makes a person mysterious and desirable.

✔ It is important to offer a partner five "good strokes" to every "bad stroke." When he or she feels really loved and appreciated, it's easier to overcome the negative feelings that are brought to the surface when you misbehave.

✔ There's still room in the 21st century for a little poetry. According to Vatsyayana, poetry is a lover's staple.

Chapter 18

Choosing the Perfect Partner

VATSYAYANA DESCRIBES the suitable wife as being non-assertive, meek, and obedient. She should also be chaste, hard-working, not show her husband up in front of his friends, and generally manage his household to run like clockwork. In addition, she was supposed to learn from him the 64 skills, which may or may not refer to sexual skills. Since the thrust of the *Kama Sutra* is sex, it's pretty obvious that she was meant to catch up sexually as fast as possible! However, the implication is that she was sexually ignorant at the start of their relationship. The majority of Vatsyayana's ideas would not be considered desirable today.

In this chapter...

✓ Looking for perfection

✓ The high echelons of desire

✓ When you should reject a man

✓ A compromising position

THESE DAYS, EQUALITY IN ALL ASPECTS OF A RELATIONSHIP IS DESIRABLE

Looking for perfection

TODAY, MEN AND WOMEN are seen as being much more alike than in Vatsyayana's time. Regardless of their different outlooks on the world (the Mars and Venus points of view), these differences are generally thought of as just quirks of nature. Women no longer think that they should be passive in bed. Men might still want a supportive wife but also a partner who can hold her own at work, bring in the money, and, in some scenarios, support them rather than vice versa. We are well into the process of equalizing.

The perfect partner

It's pretty clear that our ideas of the perfect partner have shifted – a lot. We no longer expect, or even desire, a partner to be sexually ignorant. Generally, we like to think that a partner has some idea of what they are doing. And we really hope that they will enjoy doing it to us.

Where ideas about sex have changed enormously is in the realms of what exactly it is that *she* does. Twenty-five years ago the woman expected to be shown how to behave sexually and the man was meant to take the initiative. He was supposed to know exactly how to bring her to orgasm, whereas she was not expected to know any of these things.

This was extremely tough on the male. How was he supposed to understand the inner workings of an individual female when she possessed no insight into them herself? It was an enormous responsibility – worse, it was a double bind since it was actually impossible. Today, we want the woman to know about her body and its responses.

■ **An Indian man** *in the 4th century would not have thought of his wife or lover as his equal.*

By understanding her own body, a woman brings to a relationship valuable information about her individual arousal pattern.

Does the perfect partner exist?

Of course there is no such thing as the perfect partner. Nobody is or can be perfect. Every normal human being has downs as well as ups and there are always going to be times when one behaves less than perfectly. A large part of a good marriage lies in tolerating the difficult or unpleasant traits of a partner – and there really are no exceptions here.

It is very rare to find partners who are so compatible that they never argue at all. Where such unusual relationships exist, one theory is that they have little life in them.

It tends to be the arguments that provide the drama everyone needs in order to give meaning to life. We're talking disagreement here rather than major trauma. And the true perfect partner is someone who can see a partner's occasional tantrums simply as minor episodes; someone who is mature enough to continue to appreciate the lovely parts of the loved one that are currently hidden away (which isn't to say that this same perfect partner isn't capable of throwing similar tantrums).

Don't be mistaken. This is not an excuse to behave badly. As explained in the previous chapter, you need to offer five good strokes for every bad one. If you OD on the bad strokes you are likely to find yourself without any partner at all.

■ **Disagreements occur** *in every red-blooded relationship: What matters is that you're mature enough to accept the bad and appreciate the good points in your partner.*

The harm that perfection causes

If you are a perfectionist, you can have the most amazing sex life and still remain dissatisfied. For a perfectionist, sex has to be done not just right, but perfectly. And since sex is something generally performed by *two* people, that means that at least 50 percent of the sex remains outside your control. You can't ensure that the other person will "do" sex in the way you believe ideal.

Unless you can let go of the "ideal," you will always be discontented.

A perfectionist is one of the most discouraged people in the universe – someone whose confidence has been destroyed in childhood and who is constantly striving ever after. Unfortunately the perfectionist tends to project that discouragement onto their partner, who genuinely suffers. If a perfectionist doesn't have a good sex life, he or she may experience serious depression.

A useful mantra to hold onto when life isn't going too well is a teaching of psychologist Alfred Adler. He explained that although you cannot control events, you can have some control over how you react to them.

CASE HISTORY

Marge and Bill were a middle-aged couple whose sex life appeared to have ground to a halt. It was all Marge's fault, according to Bill. She spent so long tidying up the house before bedtime that by the time she got into bed, Bill was sound asleep. He had talked to her about leaving things, but she appeared incapable of doing so. Marge's side of the story was that Bill made an incredible mess around the house and never cleared up after himself. If she didn't attack the piles of clothes thrown around the room at bedtime, she'd only have to face them in the morning. She was quite worn out by her husband's untidiness and angry with him for the chaos he thrust upon her.

As a youngster, Marge could never please her over-ambitious parents and so she never felt good enough. She had taken on board the notion that to be acceptable she must do things perfectly. It had become a blueprint for emotional survival.

It is difficult to get rid of such entrenched ideas. Rather than try to achieve the impossible, it seemed best to get Marge to work within her personal blueprint. Instead of picking up after Bill, she agreed to sweep all his things into one corner of the room. It would be up to him to sort this out later. This left the rest of the room clear and Marge was able to climb into bed at an earlier time. She managed to deal with this by accepting that, just as she might be responsible for her own perfection, Bill was responsible for his. Bill was shamed by these conversations and actually made efforts to improve. Homework, consisting of sensual massage exercises, brought the couple back in touch (literally), and their sex life resumed.

The high echelons of desire

A LOVE PARTNER can be the most wonderful human being in the world. But if there is no spark of desire flickering between the two of you, you will find sex very problematical. The trouble with desire is that nobody quite understands how it works. Does it have to start in the mind? Or can it come from within the body? Is it purely hormonal? Or is it something to do with the mixture of connections two people make? And is there anything one can do about it?

INTERNET

www.oneplusone.org.uk

Visit this web site for more detailed information about marriage research.

Does it matter if sex is poor?

In a survey of couples with marriage difficulties, it was found that if sexual problems arising early in a marriage went unresolved for the first six months, slowly but surely the marriage tended to erode from within. In various surveys of long-time married couples, large numbers of men and women complained that they did not get the kind of sex they really wanted.

In many long-term marriages where sex has slowed down, couples nevertheless remain deeply attached.

■ **Sex in a marriage** *matters a great deal when you are young, but somewhat less so as you grow older together in an otherwise good relationship.*

233

What about desire?

Sex is a major part of a successful relationship and for sex to prosper you need desire. Vatsyayana offers two verses on the subject.

"Desire, which springs from nature, and which is increased by art, and from which all danger is taken away by wisdom, becomes firm and secure."

"A clever man, depending on his own ability, and observing carefully the ideas and thoughts of women, and removing the causes of their turning away from men, is generally successful with them."

Vatsyayana writes a lot about creating desire. Desire in the man, according to him, is created by a woman's flowing response, though she must not seem too easy. Desire in the woman is created by sensitive wooing, combined with physical moves to arouse her. Vatsyayana thinks that desire is a twofold process in that it is greatly led by a physical approach. This correlates interestingly with the latest sexological research on the subject.

Trivia...

To create desire in the most difficult of cases, Vatsyayana suggested an aphrodisiac made of the powder of nelumbrium speciosum (blue lotus) and mexna roxburghii mixed with ghee and honey. This had the power of making the man become lovely in the eyes of others, he wrote. But his potion wasn't quite as potent as he thought. Recent research on the blue lotus (also used in an ancient Egyptian love potion) shows that it does have a mild aphrodisiac effect, but only in the sense that it boosts energy levels. In fact it's very similar in its benefits to ginseng!

NEW RESEARCH ON SEXUAL DESIRE

The Kinsey Institute is working on the theory that there are not one but at least two brain centers involved in sexual desire. One is the "excitor," which is literally responsible for sexual excitement, and the other is the "inhibitor," which is responsible for putting the dampeners on things. How aroused you get depends on the balance between your "excitor" and "inhibitor."

If the "inhibitor" works too hard, the result is that you won't feel much desire. If the "excitor" works too much, you may get excited inappropriately. Scientists are working on drug therapies to regulate these centers. Women who find it difficult to become aroused can now use creams that enhance sexual pleasure by increasing blood flow to the genital area. Research is also being carried out into the use of Viagra for women. But most women will still need a lot of physical stimulation to climax.

Drumming up desire

So what do you do if, try as you might, you cannot turn onto your otherwise ideal partner? There could be various reasons:

1 **Lack of attraction:** It may be that this particular partner does not stimulate you sexually or arouse your imagination and may, therefore, simply be the wrong partner. You might decide to end the relationship and find a new partner – or to stay and accept that your sex life is unlikely to be very special

2 **Low hormone levels:** A very few people find that their testosterone levels are unusually low. This affects both men and women. Testosterone is now thought to be the hormone responsible for sexual interest and response. Testosterone replacement works for some

3 **Pushing the wrong buttons:** Some people simply haven't yet found the right way to be sexual together. Improving lovemaking so that it gives the partners greater rewards can kick-start desire in some cases

■ **Some partners** *may need training to help them discover one another's sensuality.*

Present clinical opinion favors a joint approach, usually sexual counseling plus some physical homework and, where it seems appropriate, an exploration of hormone levels.

A little magic

During Vatsyayana's time there was a complicated spell suggested for men who wanted to win a woman. This involved invoking the god *Kama* (the Indian Eros) and praying to him for help. The man begins the spell by pressing his thumb (the thumb equals the phallus in symbolic terms) against the woman with enough pressure to leave a mark on her skin. He must gather 21 pieces of *kudi* wood (*kudi* may be related to thorny acacias) and place them on a fire with their thorns facing east. Then three times a day for 3 days he must burn aromatic plants and ghee. For 3 nights he sleeps face downwards. He makes a clay model of the woman and shoots an arrow with owl feather fletching at the model. As the arrow pierces the image, the woman will come under his power.

Spells to help a man win over a woman probably worked by psyching up the male to such a degree of self-confidence that he ultimately appeared a different and much more attractive personality.

When you should reject a man

VATSYAYANA IS OF THE OPINION that outward appearance, "the forms of bodies and the characteristic marks and signs," is likely to lead you astray in your judgment of a good potential partner. Instead he thought you should judge people "by their conduct, by the outward expression of their thoughts and by the movements of their bodies." To be honest, he wrote this about women only, but it is a good premise that applies just as well to men.

When a woman falls in love

Gonikaputra, one of the writers often quoted by Vatsyayana, says that "a woman falls in love with every handsome man she sees and so does every man at the sight of a beautiful woman, but frequently they do not take any further steps." Here's what he goes on to say about women in love:

"In love, the following circumstances are peculiar to the woman. She loves without regard for right and wrong and does not try to gain over a man simply for the attainment of some particular purpose. Moreover, when a man first makes up to her, she naturally shrinks from him, even though she may be willing to unite herself with him. But when the attempts to gain her are repeated and renewed, she at last consents."

When a man falls in love

A man has much more of a head-rules-the-heart attitude to love, says the original script. "With a man, even though he may have begun to love, he conquers his feelings from a regard for morality and wisdom, and although his thoughts are often on a woman, he does not yield, even though an attempt be made to gain him over." I have to say that this is not my experience of men. Perhaps something has changed during the intervening 1,600 years!

If a man fails in his attempt to win the woman's affections, he is likely to leave her alone for the future, says Vatsyayana. If he gains her love, he often becomes indifferent to her. This is painting the gains of love in no-win terms. Perhaps that's because the *Kama Sutra*, which depends heavily on physical tactics, ignores the kind of mental stimulation that an intelligent partner desires.

The fact that the Kama Sutra focuses on the physical and not the intellectual approach to courtship is presumably because 4th-century women rarely received the education of their male counterparts and so their intellectual needs were dismissed.

REJECTING A MAN

So what are the main reasons for right-thinking women to reject a man? Below is the *Kama Sutra*'s list of 24 good reasons, many of which still hold true today:

- Affection for her husband (or someone else)
- Desire for children born in wedlock
- Lack of opportunity
- His lack of respect for her
- Too great a difference in rank or status
- Insecurity because the man is likely to be away too often
- Belief that the man is attached to someone else
- Fear that the man is incapable of secrecy (if this is an affair)
- Belief that she will come a poor second to his friends
- The apprehension that he is not in earnest
- Lack of confidence because he is an illustrious man
- Fear on account of him being too strong yet not in charge of his emotions, i.e. he might abuse her physically
- Feeling of inadequacy because he is smarter than she
- Previous friendship which prevents her from feeling desire
- Contempt of his ignorance of the ways of the world
- Distrust of his low character

- Disgust because he is incapable of understanding her love
- In the case of the elephant woman, the thought that he is a hare man, or a man of weak passion
- Anxiety that he might get into trouble through his passion for her
- Despair about her own imperfections
- Fear of discovery (if this is a secret love)
- Disillusion because of his poor grooming and shabby appearance
- Fear that he may be testing her then reporting back to her husband!
- The thought that he has too much regard for morality, i.e. he is too prim and proper

■ **In the 4th century,** *a woman was often one wife among several, but today women do not readily accept being second-best in a relationship.*

A compromising position

WHEN YOU ARE YOUNG, you see the world in terms of black and white. Gray isn't acceptable. But as you mature, you come to understand that reality means compromise – in other words much of life is gray and works well because of it. So don't think badly of yourself if you opt for a partner who is less than perfect. Take comfort if you find yourself behaving in a way that you never expected, because what is happening to you is perfectly normal. We can never always be happy. And we can never have entirely what we want. But if you enjoy the good things you have and put aside negative thoughts, you can end up with a very satisfactory life.

Vatsyayana's advice for effective courtship

If a woman shows aversion, he says, there are ways in which her lover may still improve his chances. If she is shy, for example, he can make a point of showing his love and affection for her so that her confidence grows. If there isn't enough opportunity to spend time together, then inventing some easy method of access would get over this. If she is overly formal, he could break down barriers by being extremely familiar. If she has a bad opinion of his character, he must find a way of showing that he really has a heart of gold. If he has neglected her, he can turn over a new leaf and pay attention, and if she is actually frightened, then he can reassure her and offer proper encouragement.

Let go of your ideals

Although it would be terrible to end up with someone you disliked or who repulsed you, it would be equally short-sighted to reject someone because they don't measure up to your every ideal.

One way of deciding whether to go or stay in a relationship is to list its advantages and disadvantages. If the disadvantages heavily outweigh the advantages, then you would be wise to disentangle yourself.

What really happens when you fall in love?

One of the problems is that love acts a bit like a dangerous drug. It totally clouds your vision, rendering you incapable of making a lucid judgment. Suddenly you find yourself with a partner who is mainly unsatisfactory – yet you cared about him or her so much originally. So what happened inside the body to point you in such a wrong direction?

Love works by giving the lover a cocktail of addictive hormones known as dopamine and noradrenaline, and a lot of phenylethylamine (PEA). It is these hormones, particularly PEA, that cause you to see your lover through rose-tinted glasses.

Trivia...

Psychological tests have proved that lovers actually view each other unrealistically, in what is called the "distorting mirror" syndrome.

The hormone phenyethylamine (PEA) basically makes you high. It creates an altered state of consciousness. You say and do things that you would never have dreamed of in ordinary circumstances.

This is great when the object of your love is worth the enthusiasm. But it can be disastrous when they are not. It's not surprising then that making any life-altering decisions when under love's spell could be considered unwise. Arranged marriage may not fit the romantic ideal, but it can provide good partnerships.

■ **Falling in love** *sends the senses reeling and the pulses racing – but have you really found the perfect partner or are you simply blind to their faults?*

■ **This traditional Indian wedding** *would probably have been arranged by relatives. Arranged marriages can be as successful as those based on romantic attraction because man and wife do not embark on their marriage with an unrealistic vision of their partner.*

Be realistic

What can you do to ensure you live happily ever after? First, understand that you cannot ensure this.

You can give your love affair excellent foundations. You can learn to build on the good sex between you, perhaps by acting out some of the 35 love positions considered advisable by Vatsyayana. But you won't always be happy. This is not a realistic expectation.

Accept that you two lovers are not the same person.

Because you are two people, you are different. Instead of wasting energy on fighting and thereby alienating each other, resolve to allow each other your differences. Try working your way round the differences. Come up with alternatives. If your partner wants to make love with you wearing rubber boots, agree to do so, occasionally. But in return they must give you a wonderful sensual massage once in a while.

Finally, don't feel that a compromise is a failure. Try to see the positive side. A compromise is a solution – an idea that works. It is an effective action plan, which you have been clever enough to design.

A simple summary

✔ There is no such thing as a perfect partner. If you hold out for this, you limit your choice and future happiness.

✔ A good partner should provoke you into feeling sexual desire.

✔ It is important for a couple to offer each other encouragement, appreciation, and respect, otherwise a love affair can die on its feet.

✔ When choosing the right man or woman, it is mature to steer a middle path. There will be drawbacks with any partner, but what counts are the good aspects of his or her character.

✔ One of the premises of a good relationship is that both partners learn to live with the less positive aspects of one another's characters.

Chapter 19

Dealing with Second and Third Wives

I N A DAY AND AGE when, in the West, we do not marry more than one person at a time, what is the point of including this anachronistic chapter? The answer is because it contains a lot of surprisingly useful material. We may not go in for multiple marriages but we do experience serial marriages. At least half of us (probably more) will marry at least twice. If there are children from a previous marriage, we are highly likely to have contact with the first partner, both our own ex-spouse and our new spouse's ex! What's more, jealousy and resentment may occur on all sides. As a result, something of real value may be found in looking at how women in the 4th century AD managed to handle the knowledge that they were not the only love of their partner's life.

In this chapter...

✓ Rules for the first wife

✓ Rules for the younger wife

✓ What can we learn from multiple marriage?

AN EX-SPOUSE'S HAPPY REMARRIAGE CAN BE HARD FOR A REJECTED PARTNER TO ACCEPT

Rules for the first wife

MOST OF US KNOW that when you remain continually angry with someone, sex is inevitably disrupted. You don't usually enjoy going to bed with someone you're furious with, so it makes sense to work at keeping a marriage as happy as possible. That way, there's a good chance that the sexual side will survive. Vatsyayana's counsel to a wife was not only to get on well with her husband but to maintain good relations with the entire household – including his other wives. A lot of his advice sounds very harsh – especially if the first wife doesn't manage to get pregnant. But there are also strategies for overcoming such misfortune.

Be unselfish

From the very beginning, writes Vatsyayana, a wife should endeavor to attract the heart of her husband by continually showing him her devotion, her good temper, and her wisdom.

This is a good starting point and no doubt if Vatsyayana were living today he would add that the same might be expected of a husband. However – and this is where he got tough – if the woman does not bear her husband any children she should take it upon herself to tell him to marry another woman. Doesn't this make you value *IVF* treatment program more than ever?

DEFINITION

IVF stands for in-vitro fertilization, the assisted conception procedure in which an egg is fertilized in a test tube and later implanted into the uterus.

INTERNET

www.medicine.ox. ac.uk/ndog/ivf

www.infertilitydoc shop.com

Find out more about IVF treatment – embryo freezing, patient safety, chances of success – and other infertility treatments at these sites.

When the second wife is married and brought to the house, says Vatsyayana, the first wife should give her a position superior to her own, and look upon her like a sister. In the morning, the elder wife should forcibly make the younger one decorate herself in the presence of their husband, and should not mind all the husband's favor being given to her.

Act like an elder sister

If the newer wife does anything to displease her husband the elder one should not neglect her, but should always be ready to give her most careful advice, and should teach her to do various things in the presence of her husband. (We could even be talking about sex here.)

"Her children she should treat as her own, her attendants she should look upon with more regard even than on her own servants, her friends she should cherish with love and kindness, and her relations with great honor."

But what happened if, despite the younger wife's fecundity, the husband still favored the elder wife? The rivalries and jealousies don't bear thinking about. And the more wives there were, the greater the competition and the likelihood of warring factions developing. Two wives joining forces against a third or fourth could have been a recipe for war.

On the positive side, however, women like living with sympathetic women. In a time when such huge differences were perceived between the sexes, co-wives probably lent one another lots of support. One wife might have been glad to take on the household chores and leave a grumpy husband to be "managed" by another. In a way, they were like wives to one another.

■ *"Sister-wife" describes someone who's a tower of strength and support to a friend. In Vatsyayana's day, the wives of a household often bonded in a similar fashion.*

When there are many other wives . . .

Three or four wives may have been the limit for the lower classes (mainly because of the expense!) but would not have sufficed for a 4th-century king. He would have boasted many wives and concubines, since the harem was an accepted upper-class way of life.

INDIAN NOBLES HAD MANY WIVES

In these circumstances the rules changed dramatically. The elder wife, said Vatsyayana, should associate with the one immediately next to her in rank and age, and should instigate the wife who has recently enjoyed her husband's favor to quarrel with his present favorite.

After this she should sympathize with the former, and having collected all the other wives together, should persuade them to denounce the favorite as a scheming and wicked woman, without, however, committing herself in any way.

The purpose of creating strife within the harem was to even out the power held among the women so that they became more equal, and no one wife could gain total control. On examination it turns out to be a carefully considered system of management.

245

Encouraging quarrels

If the favorite wife happens to quarrel with the husband, then the elder wife should take her part and give her false encouragement, and thus cause the quarrel to be increased. If there is only a little quarrel between them, the elder wife should do all she can to work it up into a large quarrel. Here she is operating on the "divide and rule" principle – the elder wife doing her best to be chief ruler.

Cutting your losses

Unsurprisingly, not all these cunning schemes worked. When they didn't have the desired effect, Vatsyayana's advice was, if she finds that her husband still continues to love his favorite wife, she should then change her tactics, and endeavor to bring about a conciliation between them so as to avoid her husband's displeasure.

I wonder how many warfaring strategies present-day second wives can relate to when it comes to dealing with their husbands' former partners?

Rules for the younger wife

AT THE BEGINNING OF HER MARRIAGE, *a younger wife – as current favorite – would have been in a position of relative power within the household. However, she had to be careful to preserve her precarious status: She would have needed to be prepared to deal with a group of angry, even embittered, women who would be gunning for her.*

Start by being circumspect

According to Vatsyayana, the younger wife should regard the elder wife of her husband as her mother, and should not give anything away, even to her own relations, without her knowledge. She should tell her everything about herself, and not approach her husband without her permission.

Whatever is told to her by the elder wife she should not reveal to others, and she should take care of the children of the senior even more than her own. (Only a man could seriously write this.)

Don't tell tales

When alone with her husband she should serve him well, but should not tell him of the pain she suffers from the existence of a rival wife (it might make him feel guilty and that must be avoided of course). She may also obtain secretly from her husband some marks of his particular regard for her, and may tell him that she lives only for him, and for the regard that he has for her.

■ **The younger wife** *should not be a snake in the grass and tell her husband of an older wife's misdeeds, said Vatsyayana.*

She should never reveal her love for her husband, nor her husband's love for her to any person, either in pride, or in anger, for a wife that reveals the secrets of her husband is despised by him. As for seeking the regard of her husband, Gonardiya (another sage of the past) says that it should always be done in private, for fear of the elder wife.

Cultivate sympathy for the elder wife

If the elder wife is disliked by her husband, or is childless, the younger wife should sympathize with her, and should ask her husband to do the same, but should surpass her in leading the life of a chaste woman. (It is, of course, much easier to be altruistic towards an elder wife when you know you are the preferred partner.)

This is the breadth of Vatsyayana's advice on multiple marriage and it reveals an inner knowledge of the jealousies and tensions that could easily develop. But instead of focusing on the women working together and finding a shared sisterhood, it mainly pits women against women. This in itself is a system of divide and rule, with the ruler being the husband, whom the wives are exhorted to leave out of their squabbles.

■ **In Vatsyayana's time,** *multiple marriage could lead to rivalry among wives. Today, the trend towards serial marriage can create similar jealousies.*

247

What can we learn from multiple marriage?

IN SPITE OF THE ARCHAIC and non-PC methods of negotiating your way through a household of rivalries and jealousy, there are lessons to be taken from the marriage section of the Kama Sutra. *These seem to me to be lessons of pragmatism, humility, and respect.*

Pragmatism

Between the lines, Vatsyayana is also saying that it is pointless sustaining constant hurt because an accident of fate means you have to cope with rival wives. You will be happier in yourself if you accept the situation and get on with life. This doesn't mean you have to become a doormat – quite the opposite.

He suggests you make it extremely clear to the sister-wives where your powers lie and what respect is due to be accorded to you. He also, in other sections of the book, writes matter-of-factly of wives taking lovers where their husband has, for whatever reason, proved unsatisfactory.

Humility

Whichever wife you are in the pecking order, he makes the point very clearly that it is not a good idea to throw your weight around and make life unpleasant for others. This is because, one day, it may be your turn to lose power and so become vulnerable to the others.

Vatsyayana's message is to do as you would be done by.

However the one exception he makes to this is with the elder wife whom he obviously sees as being owed something. To her he suggests the power of widening a split between the husband and a favorite wife and one can only assume that this is because he truly believes that any seniority in the house should be ascribed to the first wife and not to a newcomer. It is generally sensible to appoint a leader rather than have everyone jostle for first place. More gets achieved, as a result.

Respect

Harmony within a household depends largely upon respect. Without respect, nothing will work. And the management of respect is a great skill, which should be used in any team, be it at work, at play, or in a multiple marriage.

One of the reasons secrecy is so often advocated in the *Kama Sutra*, regardless of whether or not the reasons are good, is because secrecy allows you to preserve respect. It is easy for us, in the here and now, to be dismissive of this somewhat dubious attitude and say "so what?" But think about it. Women have options today to lead their own lives if marriage doesn't work out.

In the days of the Kama Sutra, women were utterly dependent upon their men. If they were thrown out of a marriage they would have to go back to their father's household with no guarantees they would be welcome or even accepted.

Trivia...

Since the advent of women's liberation in the 1960s, women have developed some very different ideas about each other. Rather than seeing other females as constant rivals, they value each other as friends in an entirely new sense. For the first time in Western history women are independent of men and their self-sufficiency has had the effect of drawing them together.

■ **The end of a marriage** *isn't the end of the road for today's independent women, although it would have been for their dependent 4th-century counterparts.*

First and second wives can be friends

So what might we get out of all this today?

First and second wives should try to be friendly when young children are involved. Rather than making civil contact virtually impossible, it is wise to accept that there must be reasonable behavior for the children's sake. If there are no children, then the picture changes. Unless there are special reasons for doing so, there is no particular need to remain in touch.

But the possibilities go further. In many marriages, the former wife and the present wife manage to become excellent friends and to support each other. After all, unlike any other of their friends, these two have the clearest idea of what the other has put up with or is presently coping with. It's a bond, and it doesn't have to be a negative one.

■ **Whatever their position** *in the household, multiple wives in Vatsyayana's day would have had to get along with their rivals as best they could and be pragmatic about their situation.*

We might perceive that it pays to work on getting along well with any former or later wives of your husband, and any former or later husbands of your wife.

A simple summary

✔ Although we no longer go in for multiple marriage, we do subscribe to serial marriage. This means that we may yet learn something from Vatsyayana's rules.

✔ First wives are surprisingly advised to divide and rule if there are second and third wives. This is presumably because it is a way of controlling the distribution of power in a multiple household.

✔ First wives are also expected to give way with absolute humiliation should a husband decide, for whatever reason, that he wants another spouse.

✔ If there are several wives, the elder wife is advised to team up with the second wife to present a united front to the newcomer.

✔ The younger wife is instructed to regard the elder wife as a mother and to defer to her in most things. She is advised to act circumspectly and not to boast of any special favors she might receive from their husband.

✔ None of the wives are supposed to upset their husband and all of them are expected to be loyal to him.

✔ We can learn from this that pragmatism, humility, and respect are valuable emotions to be brought into play in marriage.

✔ First and second wives can be friends and should try to remain friendly, especially if children are involved.

Chapter 20

Other Men's Wives

IN THE DAYS OF THE *KAMA SUTRA*, adultery was considered a relatively commonplace occurrence. This easygoing attitude stemmed partly from the prevalence of arranged marriages (which might provide unsatisfactory sex partners) and partly from the culture of the time where men enjoyed great sexual freedom which most women were denied. For the sake of curiosity, here are the *Kama Sutra*'s descriptions of why and how to seduce another man's wife. But please don't act upon them yourself!

In this chapter...

✓ Tales of adultery

✓ The best seducers

✓ A clandestine affair

✓ Playing by the rules

WHERE OTHER MEN'S WIVES ARE CONCERNED, NOTHING BEYOND FRIENDSHIP IS ACCEPTABLE TODAY

Tales of adultery

THE KAMA SUTRA STATES that "any woman is fit to be enjoyed without sin." In fact, that didn't mean that any woman was fair game, since women of higher castes were expressly forbidden to commit adultery. Remember the notion of kama? It meant that men felt obliged to practice sex in order to obtain the overall status called moksha. So men slept with women of lower castes for pleasure and as a way of pursuing their philosophy.

Thinking of the consequences

Before the would-be seducer took the plunge and slept with a woman, he was asked to give serious consideration to the following:

1. What the real chances were of something happening

2. Whether or not the woman in question was fit for sex

3. What dangers could result from establishing a relationship

4. What the future effect of such a union might be (for example, could children result or could the man's or woman's marriage be threatened?)

■ **Seducers through** the ages have sought novel ways of bedding the woman of their desires.

How could a man justify sleeping around?

Vatsyayana believed that a man might resort to the wife of another, "for the purpose of saving his own life, when he perceives that his love for her proceeds from one degree of intensity to another."

According to Vatsyayana, if a young man wants a woman badly enough, he ought to be able to have her. In essence, it's a spoiled child's philosophy!

■ **Vatsyayana's advice on** *the consequences of adultery still holds true today. Sleeping with another partner can threaten a marriage and cause the end of a happy family life.*

Testing times

There are ten degrees of
intensity that are supposed to
help you decide whether or
not you want a new partner
badly enough to actually make
the move. These are:

1. Love of the eye

2. Attachment of the mind

3. Constant reflection

4. Destruction of sleep

5. Emaciation of the body

6. Turning away from
   objects of enjoyment

7. Removal of shame

8. Madness

9. Fainting

10. Death

■ **People considering** *adultery may find themselves in
constant reflection, distancing themselves from the day-to-day
routine of normal life.*

IS SHE WORTH IT?

When it came to gauging whether or not the object of your affections actually
merits your attention in the first place, Vatsyayana believed that "the forms of
bodies and the characteristic signs of love are erring tests of character." It is better
to judge women by their conduct, by the outward expression of their thoughts,
and by the movement of their bodies – not by their outward appearance. Since we
now know that men are particularly attracted by the visual, it's probably worthy
advice. Interestingly, women tend to judge character above appearance anyway.

Different kinds of love

Sanskrit scholars believed there were four kinds of love. They thought the type of love you experienced would affect the relationship you had, and, conversely, that the relationship you had would affect the kind of love you experienced.

You, your style of loving, and your relationship were believed to be inexorably intertwined. This would be true of a marriage, a love affair, or even a liaison with a courtesan. The four kinds of love are described as follows:

1 The love that results from continuously doing something so that it's habitual or like an addiction – such as a love of hunting, drinking, or sexual intercourse

The Sanskrit scholars' writings on the addictive type of love may be one of the earliest descriptions of sex addiction.

2 The love that stems from the imagination, which might include a love for mouth congress (oral sex) for some, and a love of kissing, embracing, and so on for everyone. We're talking about good old-fashioned enjoyment of sexual activity here

3 The love that results from a belief of true and mutual love on both sides, which proves to be genuine. This is a specific love where each partner looks upon the other as his or her very own

4 The love that results from the perception of external objects. This may sound as if it's about kinky sex, where the love object is a hiking boot for example, but it's actually referring to a kind of aesthetic appreciation – the enjoyment of looking at a particular object or person and appreciating their beauty

Does it matter what kind of love you feel? The *Kama Sutra* thought so. Why? Perhaps because if you could identify the sort of love you were feeling, you could more sensibly plot your future. The future, and the way you lived your life, were very important.

■ **A habitual need** *for sexual intercourse, likened to an addiction, was one type of love.*

THE MOST ATTRACTIVE LOVERS

The men most likely to succeed with women, according to the *Kama Sutra*, are those who are:

- Aware of their weak points
- Desired by other women
- Good friends to other females
- Admired for their strength (Bull-men)
- Liberal-minded
- Enterprising and brave
- Better educated and more attractive, interesting, and intelligent than a woman's current partner
- Powerful, well-dressed, and living in magnificent style

■ **Good sportsmanship in a man** *is a magnetic attraction to certain women. Sportsmen, such as polo players and baseball players, are irresistible in some women's eyes because their sport is associated with masculinity and wealth.*

The best seducers

MEN IN THE 4TH CENTURY *must have been very competitive – they actually categorized adultery in terms of success or failure. They were very clear on the male character traits that made them great seducers. What's more, they rated women in terms of easiness. The harder it was to seduce a particular woman, the greater the male considered his success.*

So just what qualities did these Casanovas possess to give them such luck with the opposite sex? The list is a long one. It starts with men who are good lovers and know a lot about lovemaking skills. It includes men who are good storytellers, and men who have known a woman since childhood so that she will feel trust and comfort in their presence. High on the list are men who make their women feel confident. So, too, are men who send their women presents!

■ **Attentive men** *who woo women with presents and make them feel desired and special are more likely to succeed in the game of love.*

Men who have never previously loved any other women are also, perhaps surprisingly, thought of as successful seducers.

The secret of success today

Devotees of the popular TV series *Sex and the City* might think that life in the 21st century is not much different to that in 400 AD. An interesting, powerful, very attractive man who also happens to have something of a reputation as a lady-killer is likely to be very appealing to the modern woman.

It's an age-old recipe of characteristics – but extensive research into love and attraction has confirmed that, as far as women are concerned, it is a perfect mix.

If you're interesting, powerful, attractive, and reputed to be a good lover, you're lucky enough to possess all the attributes of sexual attraction. But don't despair if you don't have them all – just one will do.

The gulf between the sexes

Believe it or not, John Gray, author of *Men are from Mars, Women are from Venus*, wasn't the first to come up with the idea that the sexes think differently. Vatsyayana, all those hundreds of years ago, was well aware that in order to enjoy sex to the full, men and women need to take different approaches with each other.

"The ways of working, as well as the consciousness of pleasure in men and women, are different. The difference in the ways of working, by which men are the actors and women are the persons acted upon, is owing to the nature of the male and the female," says Vatsyayana. So how do men and women differ in their consciousness of pleasure?

A man thinks, "this woman is united with me" and a woman thinks, "I am united with this man," says Vatsyayana. Of course, that may have been true 1,600 years ago, but times have certainly changed. I wonder how many women in the world think like that now?

INTERNET

www.marsvenus.com

Visit John Gray's site and click on seminars and workshop for an interactive class based on his book.

A clandestine affair

IN WILLIAM SHAKESPEARE'S comedy As You Like It, *one of the characters signals his contempt for another by saying, "I bite my thumb at you sir." It's a gesture that we wouldn't necessarily understand these days, just as we wouldn't recognize some of the 4th-century body signals and physical movements that were* etiquette *for the man wooing a married woman. Moustache-pulling, for example, apparently played a crucial role. Makes it almost worth growing one, doesn't it?*

DEFINITION

Etiquette *are rules or customs setting out the correct or acceptable way to behave in one's social life.*

Surreptitious signals

Says the *Kama Sutra*, whenever the man and woman do meet, the man should be careful to look at her in ways that reveal his state of mind to her. He should:

1. Pull about his moustache

2. Make a sound with his nails

(3) Cause his own ornaments to tinkle

(4) Bite his lower lip

In case these activities do not make his intentions clear enough, he is also advised to talk about her to his friends when she is looking at him.

He should show off his liberal-mindedness and his appreciation of enjoyments (to give her an upbeat impression). Also, to make it obvious that he visibly springs to life in her presence *only*, he should look weary and feign indifference when sitting next to any other woman in the party.

A conversation with two meanings

While carrying on a conversation with a child or another adult, the man could be seemingly talking about someone else while actually making reference to the woman he loves. In this way he can declare his love, but covertly.

■ **To seduce a woman**, *the 4th-century man was advised to show off his appreciation of life's pleasures, just as a man today might boast a knowledge of fine wines.*

He might also draw marks in the dust with his stick that have meaning only for her, which could be rubbed out instantly should anyone else come near.

Using covert wooing tactics was part of an elaborate game which, since the outcome was not predictable, would have given a man the genuine thrill of the chase and a woman the excitement of being pursued.

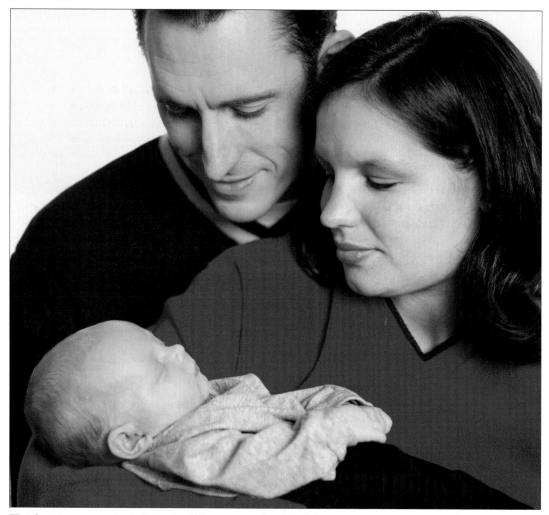

■ **Admiring a woman's baby** *could be a way to her heart, according to Vatsyayana, especially if her husband wasn't being as attentive and loving as he could be.*

Caresses that speak volumes

Next, Vatsyayana suggests that the man should fondle and caress one of the children in the party, especially if he or she happens to be sitting on his love interest's lap. He might even kiss the child in her presence and place a sweet in the child's mouth, caressing the youngster on the chin before withdrawing his hands. All the time, he should be looking at the woman he desires.

She would understand that these caresses being bestowed on the child were really intended for her. In her imagination, she would experience the touch for herself and, if at all interested in the man, would probably become very aroused.

RUTH'S STORY

"I was feeling very lonely in my marriage. My husband was always at the office and, since I was now at home bringing up our small children, I felt isolated. I remember going to a family friend's party where the couple's small children were running around. I was tired and as I sat on one side of the room, I looked across at our host, whom I considered very attractive.

He was sat with his five-year-old daughter on his knee and, as he talked to the woman next to him, was stroking his daughter's arm. I remember thinking what a sensual man he was – there was great delicacy in his touch.

He wasn't doing this for my benefit – he'd hardly noticed me at that point. But it was enough for me to want to know him better and without consciously doing so, I subsequently tried to get closer to him.

About a year later, we did start up an affair and he was just as sensually dynamic as I had imagined. I've never forgotten watching that stroking and wondering how it would feel if it were being done to me."

■ **The tenderness and affection** *shown by a man toward his children can be a good indication of the type of lover he will be with his partner.*

Playing by the rules

EVEN WHEN SEDUCING another man's wife, there were rules to be followed if you wanted to succeed. Vatsyayana, stressing the psychology of the situation, explained there were certain moves that were guaranteed to kill a budding affair stone-dead and should be avoided at all costs. Most important, there were certain women who should be given a wide berth because they could seriously ruin your future.

Rule one – one at a time

When a man is endeavoring to seduce a woman, he should not attempt to seduce any other woman at the same time. If a woman were to discover that her lover's strategy was to seduce a handful of women in the hope that at least one might succumb, she would hardly feel special, would she? This kind of behavior would also show up the man in a far from flattering light. Who would respond to someone with such a questionable reputation?

Rule two – keep her affections

After he has succeeded with the woman and enjoyed her for a considerable time, the man is advised to keep her affections by giving her presents that she likes – but may then begin to ply his attentions elsewhere. A sense of loyalty appears to be unheard of. And the possibility of the relationship ripening or deepening over time doesn't seem to be taken into account at all.

On one level it means he would avoid becoming too attached to his lover, so the inevitable break-up wouldn't be so painful for him. But on another level it means that he would never experience more than a series of shallow affairs. He would be likely to safeguard his legitimate marriage this way but unlikely ever to feel fully satisfied.

Rule three – be prudent

When a man sees the woman's husband going to some place near his house, he should not enjoy the woman then, even though she may be easily won over at that time. This sounds like common sense. On the one hand, there is always the real possibility that the husband might change his mind and come home. On the other, even if he doesn't intend to return home, the adulterous couple won't know that.

INTERNET

www.geocities.com/
SouthBeach/Lounge/
9071

For fascinating facts, advice, and books about extramarital affairs, go to Adrian's Adultery site.

Lovemaking while listening with one ear for the equivalent of the key in the latch is stressful. I'd love to think that the rule of prudence was also devised to safeguard the woman in question. But I suspect it was for the benefit of the lustful young male.

Rule four – choose a partner with care

A wise man, having regard for his reputation, should not think of seducing a woman who is apprehensive, timid, untrustworthy, well-guarded, or possessed of a father-in-law or mother-in-law. Such women could bring disaster since they could jeopardize the secrecy of the affair so that the seducer would be in real danger of being found out. Even though this wouldn't greatly alter his social standing, it would certainly ruin his chances with subsequent women.

A simple summary

✔ Morals worked differently in the 4th century. Man thought it a duty to himself to gain sexual experience.

✔ Women of a higher caste were expected to remain faithful, but women of a lower caste were considered to be fair game for adulterous relationships.

✔ Rather than disliking the idea, many women in arranged marriages were eager to experience an affair.

✔ There was an entire body language of seduction that could be employed in public, yet so that only the woman in question could understand its meaning.

✔ While Indians in the 4th century didn't think twice about seducing and enjoying partners married to other people, we don't share this same belief today. So although we may read the seduction instructions with interest and curiosity, we are not advised to practice them.

PART FIVE

THE *KAMA SUTRA* GIVES US A DIFFERENT TAKE ON SEX

TIMELESS KAMA SUTRA SKILLS

THE LEGACY OF THE *KAMA SUTRA* is multifaceted. It gives us *alternative* ways to look at sex over and above the recreational view we tend  to take in the 21st century. It offers us a *long-term* view, not of how sex has changed but of how solutions to sexual difficulties have altered.

Sex problems seem to be *perennial*. Throughout the ages, men have mourned the loss of their potency and women have needed a sympathetic approach and a lot of wooing to enjoy what happens in bed. However constant the words of the *Kama Sutra*, they still need modernizing. So the entire section on potions and aphrodisiacs has been updated to include the newest methods of sex therapy and sexual medicine. This volume concludes by returning to the overall theme of the original – *spirituality*. When sex works wonderfully well, doesn't it feel spiritual?

Chapter 21

The Art of Pleasing Your Lover

IF YOU POSSESS NO CLUES about your partner's personality and emotional preferences, it won't matter if you make love standing upside down or on top of an elephant, sex won't work too well. On the other hand, if you have examined your lover's character and the way he or she thinks and acts, then you are in a good position to modify your own behavior to please. Try to make the most of skillful lovemaking techniques. Building up knowledge about sex in general – and your partner's sexual needs and desires, in particular – is potentially highly rewarding.

In this chapter...

✓ Understanding your man's emotional character

✓ Understanding your woman's emotional character

✓ Rapturous lovemaking

✓ The use of sorcery

A REAL UNDERSTANDING OF YOUR PARTNER'S NEEDS WILL GREATLY ENHANCE YOUR SEX LIFE

Understanding your man's emotional character

THE NOTION THAT THERE ARE *men and women who correspond to types of animal (as discussed in Chapter 11) is an idea that's introduced in the* Kama Sutra *and fleshed out (literally) by Kalyana Malla, author of the* Ananga Ranga. *Although the descriptions start by focusing primarily on the size of the male's penis, Kalyana Malla does take the idea much further by linking physical stature with personality characteristics. Here are Malla's "three orders of men."*

The Shasha, or Hare-man

"The *Shasha* is known by a *Linga* [penis] which in erection does not exceed six finger-breadths [about 3 in/7.5 cm]. His figure is short and spare but well proportioned in shape and make; he has small hands, knees, feet, loins, and thighs, the latter being darker than the rest of the skin.

"His features are clear and well proportioned; his face is round, his teeth are short and fine, his hair is silky, and his eyes are large and well-opened. He is humble in his demeanour; his appetite for food is small, and he is moderate in his carnal desires. Finally there is nothing offensive in his *Kama-salila* [semen]."

The Vrishabha, or Bull-man

"The *Vrishabha* is known by a *Linga* of nine fingers in length [4½ in/11.4 cm]. His body is robust and tough, like that of a tortoise; his belly is hard, and the frogs of the upper arms are turned so as to be brought in front.

"His disposition is cruel and violent, restless, and irascible, and his *Kama-salila* is ever ready."

■ **The Bull-man** *is described as being physically tough and having a cruel and violent nature.*

The Ashwa, or Horse-man

"The Ashwa is known by a *Linga* of twelve fingers [about 6 in/15 cm]. He is tall and large-framed, but not fleshy, and his delight is in big and robust women, never in those of delicate form. He is reckless in spirit, passionate and covetous, gluttonous, volatile, lazy, and full of sleep. He cares little for the venereal rite, except when the spasm approaches. His *Kama-salila* is copious, salty, and goat-like."

■ **The large-framed** Ashwa *male was well matched with a big woman.*

■ **The Horse-man** *was considered well-endowed (bearing in mind that people were generally much smaller than we are today), lazy, and tired most of the time.*

The ancients seem to have had a somewhat negative view of male personality types. If men were judged by Kalyana Malla's criteria today, life would be rather depressing for women!

Understanding your woman's emotional character

KALYANA MALLA *divided women into four types, ranging from the calmest, most dignified, and most desirable to the loudest and most unpleasant.*

The Padmini, or Lotus-woman

"Her face is as pleasing as the full moon; her body, well-clothed with flesh, is soft as the *Shiras* [a tall, fragrant tree] or mustard flower; her skin is fine, tender and fair as the yellow lotus, resembling, in the effervescence and purple light of her youth, the cloud about to burst.

"Her *yoni* [vulva] resembles the opening of the lotus-bud, and her love-seed [*Kama-salila*, the water of life or, more prosaically, her vaginal secretion] is perfumed like the lily which has newly burst. She walks with swan-like gait, and her voice is low and musical as the note of the *Kokila* bird [the Indian cuckoo]; she delights in white raiment, in fine jewels, and in rich dresses."

■ **An opening lotus-bud** *represents the* yoni *of the Lotus-woman, with her delicate skin, dignified posture, and fine clothes.*

The lotus was considered to be an aphrodisiac, so it might be said that the Padmini was bursting with sex appeal, while also possessing purity and dignity.

The Chitrini, or Art-woman

"She is of middle size, neither short nor tall, with bee-black hair, thin, round, shell-like neck; tender body; waist lean-girthed as the lion's; hard, full breasts; well-turned thighs and heavily made hips. The hair is thin about the *yoni*, the *Mons Veneris* being soft, raised, and round.

INTERNET

www.icircle.com

Visit this site to get a good idea of women's interests in and concerns about sex and relationships.

■ **The Art-woman** *sounds fit, possibly athletic, well-shaped for child-bearing, yet sophisticated.*

"The *Kama-salila* is hot, and has the perfume of honey, producing from its abundance a sound during the venereal rite. Her eyes roll, and her walk is coquettish."

The Hastini, or Elephant-woman

"She is short of stature; she has a stout, coarse body, and her skin, if fair, is of dead white; her hair is tawny, her lips are large; her voice is harsh, choked, and throaty, and her neck bent. Her gait is slow, and she walks in a slouching manner; often the toes of one foot are crooked. Her *Kama-salila* has the savor of the juice which flows in spring from the elephant's temples."

The *Hastini* showed all the signs of feeling inferior, hence the bent neck and the slouching walk. Yet her throaty voice and large lips also indicate someone with a very earthy, sexy temperament. With rest, sunshine, and some humane treatment, the Hastini woman could get to look a lot more attractive and turn out to be very loving.

The Shankhini, or Conch-woman

"She is of bilious temperament, her skin being always hot and tawny, or dark yellow-brown; her body is large, her waist thick, and her breasts small. Her *yoni* is ever moist with *Kama-salila*, which is distinctly salt, and the cleft is covered with thick hair."

The *Shankhini* is sickly and sometimes feverish, in both health and temperament, while her body size appears out of control. She perhaps suffers from an eating disorder, which in turn probably means she also suffers from serious mood swings.

■ **Conch-woman** *lacks the good looks, dignity, and pleasant scent of Lotus- and Art-woman.*

EVALUATING YOUR PARTNER'S CHARACTER

Assuming that you are interested in your partner on a long-term basis, you would be wise to make certain that you're compatible before making any commitment. The following mini-questionnaire is applicable to both men and women:

1 Does he or she drink a lot? And if so, does he or she drink alone? If the answer to either question is "yes," think twice about getting involved. Men and women with even mild alcohol problems can become violent, abusive, and out of control, while men may experience problems achieving an erection and/or fathering a child

■ **Shared social drinking** is a pleasant part of most relationships, but if one of you drinks too much, or alone, rifts may occur between you.

2 Does his or her family background match yours? This is more important than it sounds. Even when the sex is wonderful, if you have instinctively different methods of coping (based on your differing family backgrounds), you are likely to feel irritated, resentful, or angry. This can result in the breakdown of sexual relations and cause a great deal of bad feeling

3 Is he or she lazy? If so, you will end up doing everything – and unless you are thrilled to be in total control, you will grow to regard him or her as a dead weight. If you lose respect for your partner, you may stop desiring him or her sexually

4 Do his or her ideas about managing money match yours? Differences of opinion in this area can wreck a marriage. If his or her bank account is permanently in the red, or if he or she borrows and never bothers to pay back, steer well clear. It will be your hard-earned riches that are wasted next. It doesn't matter how great the sex is if you're about to lose the roof over your head!

Rapturous lovemaking

WHEN EROTIC SENSATION *reaches such a height that you can make almost any movement and feel pure thrill, The Perfumed Garden suggests some spectacular positions to please your partner and push him or her right over the top. Fortunately and wisely, author Sheikh Nefzawi also appreciates that position isn't everything. The kind of movement you make during intercourse has a lot to do with the sensation you receive.*

The Alternate Movement of Piercing

In this unusual variation on sitting positions, the woman's role is an entirely passive one; after penetration, her partner moves her back and forth instead of thrusting from the pelvis. He can do this by alternately pulling her towards him and then letting her drop back slightly or, as Sheikh Nefzawi suggests, she can sit on his feet and he can move them to carry her backward and forward.

This is a thought-provoking pose. It could work only if the man were both an athlete and a yoga master and his partner so very small that she could be shifted about as suggested. However, the next position suggested is physically possible and, because of the unusual angle of entry, might give the man a most provocative buzz!

ALTERNATE MOVEMENT OF PIERCING

The Rainbow Arch

In this position, the woman lies on her side with her top leg raised. The man slips his body over the lower leg with his head facing her back and penetrates her from this angle. This has the advantage that the woman might feel stretched wide open by the angle and the man might feel very aroused by snuggling up against his woman's buttocks.

The disadvantage is that the woman might soon lose circulation in the lower leg. Because of the shape that is formed by the entwined lovers, this position is also called "drawing the bow."

RAINBOW ARCH

Love's Fusion

This is a face-to-face, side-by-side position that permits the man to thrust vigorously and the woman to move with him if she chooses. Many men and women are turned on by the sensation of their partner's legs entwining their own. Just lying together, weaving patterns with lower limbs, can be very arousing.

LOVE'S FUSION

FURTHER MOVEMENTS OF LOVE

In addition to the movements of love outlined in Chapter 15 for use during intercourse, Sheikh Nefzawi also recommends the following:

a **Love's Tailor:** "The man, with his member being only partially inserted, keeps up a sort of quick friction with the part that is in, and then suddenly plunges his member in up to its root"

b **The Toothpick in the Vulva:** "The man introduces his member between the walls of the vulva and then drives it up and down, and right and left. Only a man with a vigorous member can do this"

c **The Boxing-up of Love:** "The man introduces his member entirely into the vagina, so closely that his hairs are completely mixed up with the woman's. He must now move forcibly, without withdrawing his tool in the least"

The use of sorcery

VATSYAYANA WAS OF THE OPINION *that using sorcery to win over your man – or woman – was perfectly acceptable. His "health" section at the back of the* Kama Sutra *lists some very unpleasant-sounding recipes – some of which would probably have been extremely bad for your physical well-being. Although some of his advice is reproduced here, it is not meant to be followed. It's doubtful that it would work as a form of magic – and it could be dangerous!*

How to hold onto your man's affections

The woman is advised to use a spell that invokes the power of *Indrani*, the personification of marital bliss. She throws beans (symbolizing the testicles) on the head of the man. An effigy of the man is made and the woman throws burning arrows (symbolizing the phallus) around it. This procedure will bring the man to her.

So now you know! A little extra magical advice has it that if the couple desire a pale-skinned son, they must drink milk and eat rice cooked in milk.

How to sleep with countless women

Crush together *shringataka* (a substance never heard of by this author!), jasmine, and wild fig with licorice, sugar, and milk. Cook the mixture over a low fire with clarified butter (ghee) before dividing it into cakes. Eat the cakes and you'll be sleeping with hordes of women!

■ **Potions** *could seriously enhance a man's sexual powers.*

How to ruin your rival's chances

This is a very useful spell to help any woman who has been supplanted in her husband's affections to destroy her rival's *bhaga*.

The woman must obtain some of her rival's hair, a discarded toothpick, and a garland worn by the victim. These three are wrapped in a piece of sacrificial cow's hide and buried under three large stones. Remnants of the garland are then ground up and mixed with a few remaining strands of hair, bound with black thread. These bundles are buried under three stones. When they are dug up, the rival's *bhaga* will dry up.

These potions are described merely for your entertainment — they are not intended to be used!

> **DEFINITION**
>
> *The term* bhaga *had two meanings: "luck" and "vagina." To ruin a rival's* bhaga *was to render her barren, and thus, in the 4th century, absolutely useless as a wife.*

A simple summary

✓ Kalyana Malla, author of the *Ananga Ranga*, describes three types of men in terms of their sexual characteristics, physical stature, and personality.

✓ He divides women into four physical and emotional types of varying degrees of desirability.

✓ If you really want to please your partner, it is sensible to know something about your partner's character and emotional make-up.

✓ But it is also wise to learn a practical store of sex positions that offer maximum sensation as well as variety and fun.

✓ Sheikh Nefzawi, author of *The Perfumed Garden*, outlines six outstanding methods of using the penis inside the vagina to great effect.

✓ Beware of sorcery – it may have worked in the 4th century AD but it won't work today!

Chapter 22

Keeping Love Alive

THE PROBLEM OF INFIDELITY was never resolved in the 4th century AD, nor – 1,600 years later – has it been resolved today! In ancient times, there was one rule for upper-class women, who simply weren't allowed to have lovers, and another for lower-class women, who were expected to have them. Men automatically believed they might pursue any woman they desired. There were also double standards for upper-class women in that it was fully expected that wives of wealthy personages would look for lovers if their marriages were unsatisfactory. Today, men still want freedom and women have more freedom; as a result, infidelity remains a problem.

In this chapter...

✓ Fidelity and infidelity

✓ Talking the same language

✓ The meaning of intercourse

✓ You give my life meaning

TODAY WE EXPECT A PARTNER TO BE FAITHFUL, BUT MANY RELATIONSHIPS ARE ROCKED BY INFIDELITY

Fidelity and infidelity

IN AN IDEAL WORLD WE WOULD all remain faithful to our partners. *Our measure of fidelity is sex. If we have sex with someone other than our partner, we are voting with our genitals. To the "wronged" individual, such a vote is particularly painful and humiliating because it implies that he or she is no longer special. And it becomes even more complicated when the unfaithful partner declares that he or she values you very much and has no desire to break up the marriage – it was only sex! What are we supposed to make of this?*

The painful statistics

Fifty years ago, a single act of extramarital sex would have been enough to provoke a divorce. Today we don't immediately telephone the lawyers.

One in two marriages in the US and one in three in the UK end in divorce. Of course, infidelity is not the cause of every marriage break-up, but it's fair to say that many people in relationships do experience the "sin" of wanting someone else.

We believe instead, unpleasant though it might be, that it is probably normal occasionally to want to experience sex with other people, if only out of a sense of curiosity. So we do our best to rise above one or two isolated incidents and focus on improving the relationship with our husband or wife.

■ **Couples may vow** *to be faithful on their wedding day, but it isn't unusual for one or both partners to have an affair at some stage in the relationship.*

Can you safeguard against infidelity?

There are women who believe that if they allow their husband to have his own way in everything, their marriage is guaranteed to last because he'll have absolutely no need to look elsewhere. There are men who believe that if they give their wife the freedom to enjoy a partially separate lifestyle, which includes dating other people, she'll have no need to move on. Sometimes these options work. Often, however, they don't.

So what can you do to ensure that your marriage has a reasonable chance of survival? You can:

1. Talk problems through in a non-accusatory fashion

2. Remember that all marriages have ups and downs – and being down is just a phase

3. Bear in mind that, for a marriage to last – even when there is a lot of drama and quarreling – it needs five good "strokes" for every bad one

INTERNET

www.infidelitysupport network.com

Infidelity Support Network offers professional advice and support for those who have experienced infidelity. The site features online counseling and a daily self-assessment progress report.

What about sex?

When one person has an affair, he or she may sometimes stop having sex with the spouse. It is vital to remember that even if there has been a sexual gap, sex can not only resume but become pleasurable and reassuring again. Some partners find that the revelation of an affair so arouses their adrenaline that sex becomes practically compulsory. Others find that their anger and hurt make them turn off completely.

If an affair proves a tough hurdle to leap, sex enhancement exercises may well help a couple overcome it.

The *Kama Sutra* could be invaluable in helping a couple to revive their sexual relationship. If you follow the early lovemaking advice and use this to slowly rekindle your passion, you could not only learn how to touch again but also discover new patterns of lovemaking that you might both need.

SENSATE FOCUS

The following sex therapy routine can help couples to improve their methods of lovemaking. Enjoyment of touch – not orgasm – is the object of the exercise.

1. Massage each other but do not touch the genitals

2. Massage each other, this time including the genitals

3. Spend more time on the genitals but don't forget the rest of the body

4. Once you feel certain you can regain sexual excitement through touch (even if it is lost momentarily), move on to intercourse. Do not try for orgasm yet

5. When you get to the intercourse stage, don't be afraid to continue to use your hands on genitals even while you are thrusting

6. Once you think that intercourse feels sustainable, then you can include orgasm

7. If at any stage you feel you have moved on too fast, go back a step

■ **Taking time** *to explore each other's bodies through touch before moving onto full intercourse will enhance your lovemaking.*

Talking the same language

HOW DO YOU KNOW IF YOUR PARTNER *really understands what you are saying? Thanks to our individual backgrounds we all have different understandings of the same situations. A family in which everyone shouts and screams as a way of communicating might be seen as lively and conversational by one person, yet might come across to someone else as being angry and in constant conflict. Both interpretations are common. Imagine the problems, then, when two very different interpretations are supposed to lead to sex.*

Making the conversation really work

Good communication follows a structure. Before you scream and say "I haven't got time for this," just take a quick look at the best way to converse and think about whether or not your conversations follow this pattern.

For conversation to work successfully – or, in other words, for both of you to feel the other has taken notice of what you are actually saying – make sure you allow each other room for the following:

1 One person must be able to talk without interruption

2 The other person must listen properly and show that they are paying attention by nodding, making sounds of agreement, and maintaining good eye contact

3 If a problem is being voiced, both parties must be prepared to negotiate. This doesn't mean caving in and agreeing to unworkable solutions. Conversely, you should be looking for a workable way forward that is of mutual value

4 Both parties must then act on whatever has been agreed, otherwise the conversation will have been meaningless and the relationship will erode further

■ **If your partner** *tries to interrupt you while you're talking, ask them to wait until you've finished before they have their say.*

Showing respect

Some conversations feel more enriching than others. If you are trying to create feelings of love and tenderness, it should be obvious that this requires that you let your partner know how much you value and respect them. It is through the use of language that respect – and unfortunately, disrespect – is demonstrated. Even though an individual may respect his or her lover, it seems all too easy to lapse into speech patterns, learned during childhood, that put the other down. Yet there are simple ways in which you can foster respect.

It's easy to speak disrespectfully even when you don't mean to – so think about what you're saying before you actually say it.

My partner never listens

If the problem in your relationship is that one of you feels that the other never listens, the following exercise will help you both learn to listen and respond properly when the other initiates a conversation.

The basis is that any communication you make must be in three stages:

1. The first speaker makes a statement

2. The second speaker replies, making a direct response to what the first speaker has said

3. The first speaker must respond to that reply, and what he or she says must in some way relate to it

THE "MAY I?" EXERCISE

This is a useful exercise if you tend to speak before you think about what you're saying. Rather than simply launch into a conversation or automatically give your point of view, get into the habit of asking "May I?" first.

This will give you time to think before you say anything impulsive. You should also learn to preface advice with "May I tell you something?" and to accept the answer willingly, whether it is "yes" or "no."

Making compromises

The art of breaking an impasse lies in accepting that there has to be a compromise. To make this work:

 a Don't promise the impossible

 b Show that you take your partner seriously

 c Make a promise about future behavior – but make sure it's one that you know you will be able to keep

 d Be sure that you keep the promise

Showing love

Communication is not only about how you talk. It is also about body language, touch, and gesture. To remind you: five good strokes to every one bad stroke is reckoned to make an argumentative relationship still workable. Your good strokes are supposed to show love. Here are some suggestions for how to show love:

a Hug

b Pat

c Caress

d Say "I love you" regularly

e Leave loving messages around

f Make brief but loving phone calls

g Act thoughtfully in a way that shows you have been thinking about what your partner would like

■ **Gestures can be louder** *than words, so frequent loving phone calls are a great way to show how often your partner is in your thoughts.*

The meaning of intercourse

ANOTHER METHOD OF IMPROVING *your relationship is to understand the meaning of intercourse. The Kama Sutra has already made it clear that intercourse can be used physically, emotionally, and spiritually. In the 21st century, we also use it for several other reasons.*

There are four common reasons besides love and desire why people pursue sex: as a comfort; to stave off loneliness; to vent pent-up energy; and to acquire status or prestige. Even if our reasons for having sex are negative, it doesn't mean that the sex cannot be fulfilling and joyful. Sex can in itself be a healer. Experiencing climax is actually a method of bonding. Still, it's useful to get a handle on the reasons why your particular partner might be using sex.

Sex for comfort

Just as people eat for comfort, they can also wish to have sex for comfort. When life is depressing, sex might be the single positive successful activity we undertake. Men and women can "grow" through sex. So a common scenario arises when a partner with no confidence learns in their first long-term partnership that they are really good at sex. This is the beginning of building up confidence generally.

■ **When the world appears a dark** *and gloomy place to be, good sex can be the best antidepressant. It takes your mind off your troubles and makes you feel cared for and wanted.*

An antidote to loneliness

When someone is depressed, they feel a sense of having a hollow space inside. This space may have been created because the individual's parents failed to praise or make them feel good about themselves. Filling the hollow space is behind much sexual activity, especially compulsive sex. So-called sex addicts are actually very lonely people who are desperately seeking another person to fill up the space.

If we grow up without a spark of encouragement and are always forced to see ourselves as failing, it is hardly surprising that we feel empty.

The problem is that it is hard for the other partner to become mother, father, and sex therapist rolled into one, which means that many such intense relationships fail. If the needy partner can see that his or her loneliness is a leftover from childhood (and not a sign of a lagging partner) and willingly enters therapy to work through pain, the partnership stands a good chance of survival.

■ **Some people fill** *the emptiness they feel inside by having as much sex as they can – good or bad.*

Letting off steam

Of course, intercourse expresses positive as well as negative feelings. Ironically some people feel swamped by their partner's exuberance. They feel their sense of control threatened, and react by withdrawing and creating some space between themselves and their lover. This is pretty dismaying if you happen to be initiating sex at the time.

SHOWING SENSITIVITY

Consider British author A. A. Milne's characters, Winnie the Pooh and Tigger. Tigger was extremely lively and quite literally bounced at people. If he bounced at Pooh (Pooh being a rather lumbering bear), Pooh tended to step back and lose balance. Metaphorically, that's how our partners feel when we bounce at them. It doesn't matter that our exuberance is joyful – we are not taking their feelings into account. The moral is: Be sensitive to your partner. Look before you bounce.

The power of status

Jackie Mason, the comedian, made a good point recently when he remarked on the fact that, although dozens of very young, beautiful girls will say how incredibly attractive they find an 80-year-old millionaire, it's extremely rare to find young, beautiful girls saying the same about an 80-year-old garbage collector.

There is indeed something about a partner's status that feels as if it rubs off. And this status can be a powerful motivator in promoting a love affair.

Unfortunately, although you enjoy a partner's lifestyle, this doesn't guarantee that you will enjoy sex with that person.

INTERNET

**www.allexperts.com/
getexpert.asp?category
=856**

This well-established question-and-answer site dispenses advice for couples in older/younger relationships. A panel of volunteer experts are available to respond to problems online.

CASE HISTORY

Susan was an exceptionally attractive woman with a high-powered career in banking and staff directly answerable to her. Susan had married a man who was 20 years older, very charming and respected in her community.

Susan's parents had been happy about the marriage and she was a loving daughter who lived up to her parents' expectations.

The trouble was that Susan thought her husband was pretty exceptional too, and found herself so in awe of him that she was incapable of being her real self. She couldn't relax. Because she could not "let go" enough to have a climax, her sex life with her husband suffered and the marriage slowly ground to a halt.

The divorce proved surprisingly liberating. Although she felt she had failed in her parents' eyes, Susan began an affair with a younger man who looked up to her. This gave her an aphrodisiacal sense of power and her sex life blossomed.

You give my life meaning

THE PRAGMATIC, LEVEL-HEADED VIEW of sex in the Kama Sutra *offers us something we could learn from now. Most men and women going into relationships in the 21st century do so hoping to find good reasons for living. We look for fun, companionship, a mutual partner in child-rearing, someone to contribute toward our own identity. And these are all reasonable, normal desires.*

We are all unique

But in the rush to find that special partner we tend to lose sight of something. That something is the fact that we already possess a unique character. As thinking, feeling individuals we give our lives a meaning all of our own. But it's nice to have another person in our lives, in fact it's preferable to have another person beside us.

It's vital to remember that inside our own heads we can only be ourselves. We can never be our partner. There is a real sense in which we must recognize our aloneness and grow to feel comfortable with it.

■ **Although we** *all hope to share our life with a special partner, it's important we don't lose our individuality.*

Solitude and intimacy

The soap opera *Sex and the City* brilliantly epitomizes the struggle between solitude and intimacy. To some people, the series is merely a crass collection of oversexed and oversensational dilemmas, screened for our titillation and little else. But to dismiss it in such a way is to lose sight entirely of the unwritten script – the conflict that lies underneath the upfront sexual behavior. The drama is looking for new ways of not just living a sex life but also of feeling good about it and good about yourself. Underneath the explicit scenarios, the series explores sexual politics in an experiential but serious manner.

INTERNET

www.hbo.com/city/

Click on this address for the latest news and gossip about Sex and the City.

Learning to love yourself

One belief emanating from the 1980s is that, in order to enjoy a fulfilling intimate relationship with a partner, you first need to possess a good intimate relationship with yourself. This includes:

a Feeling okay when you don't currently have a partner

b Enjoying your own company

c Enjoying sex with yourself

d Feeling strong enough about yourself and your worth to say no to a potential partner who doesn't shape up

e Feeling unafraid to acknowledge sexual likes and dislikes (however extreme these might be) to a partner

The hidden message of the Kama Sutra

Where does it say all this in the *Kama Sutra*? It doesn't in so many words – and certainly not to women. It does help the man find and keep a desirable wife. With

■ **Feeling comfortable** *and happy in yourself is important if you are to enjoy a fulfilling and successful relationship with a partner.*

that under his belt, so to speak, it then leads him by the hand on to all the other aspects of life, all of which are sexually linked. It advises on his household, on his cultural life, on the management of his extramarital affairs, on following the sexual example of the monarch, and on the formation of male character. In other words, it teaches the man how to realize his personal characteristics and to expand them. He is learning to be a strong male individual.

The entire text of the original Kama Sutra aims to give the young male reader strength of character and helps him shape his life as he desires.

If the *Kama Sutra* were to be written for the first time today, it would not illustrate this aspect only for men, it would undoubtedly do the same for women. And what would it say to women?

Advice to women might read as follows:

a   Don't hold back. Put yourself in the way of life experience

b   Take calculated risks but prepare the ground carefully beforehand

c   Be unafraid of seeking and experiencing sexual relationships and look upon them as an adventure and a "growth" area

d   Be confident in seeking what feels right for you, but at the same time be sensitive to the feelings of others and listen to their needs

e   Above all, put in a lot of practice on reaching for "heaven" through sexual enjoyment

■ **Everybody can** *enjoy a full and satisfying sex life when they have the confidence to experiment and try new experiences.*

A simple summary

✔ There are no guarantees that a good sexual relationship will last.

✔ If you communicate well and demonstrably show love in the face of difficult times, your long-term prospects are positive.

✔ Gaining insight into what sexually motivates your partner, be it extreme neediness or exuberance, will help you deal sensitively with that partner.

✔ It is great to derive meaning from your partner and from your sex life with your partner.

✔ But it is also vital to derive meaning and strength from your own individuality.

✔ Sex can be a wonderful experiential platform from which to discover your strengths and weaknesses.

Chapter 23

Arousing a Weakened Sexual Power

THE ODDS ARE that everyone will experience a sex problem at some time in their life. Yes, *everyone*. However, most temporary sexual difficulties don't matter a bit. It is normal to experience occasional sexual failure. Both the *Kama Sutra* and *The Perfumed Garden* recognized that sexual powers wax and wane according to age and health. Some of the remedies suggested in the ancient texts were helpful, others were downright unpleasant and not remotely likely to improve matters. But many of the sexual positions advocated then would aid a troubled couple today.

In this chapter...

✓ Ancient troubleshooting techniques

✓ Treating impotence today

✓ Overcoming premature ejaculation

✓ Dealing with a lack of desire

✓ Inability to experience orgasm

THE *KAMA SUTRA* SPELLS OUT WAYS TO REVIVE A FLAGGING SEX LIFE

Ancient troubleshooting techniques

"IF A MAN IS UNABLE to satisfy a Hastini, or Elephant woman, he should recourse to various means to excite her passion. At the commencement he should rub her yoni with his hand or fingers, and not begin to have intercourse with her until she becomes excited, or experiences pleasure." This is a promising beginning to the Kama Sutra's troubleshooting section since it is by far the best way to assist women to climax.

Supplementing the lingam

The *Kama Sutra* recommends that the man whose penis is not large enough to satisfy his woman should put on an *apadravyas*. One form of *apadravyas* was known as the *Kantuka* or *Jalaka*, which was an open-ended tube, outwardly rough and studded with soft globules, that fitted on to the penis and tied at the waist. Or there was the option of the penis bracelet, made from soft metal and with a knobbly surface, that could be wrapped around the penis.

> **DEFINITION**
>
> *An apadravyas was a sex aid fitted on to or around the penis to supplement its length or thickness. They were made of a variety of materials, from buffalo horn to silver or copper wire.*

In southern India, men practiced penis piercing, enlarging the hole until it was big enough to be perforated by a large rounded *apadravyas*. This had the effect of making the head of the penis absolutely huge, which was likely to give a partner great pleasure even if the man wearing it found it difficult to get an erection.

The asparagus cure

And what about those unfortunates suffering from erection problems? Asparagus featured in several recipes that promised that the man might enjoy innumerable women.

Alternatively, by plastering his penis with a burning ointment and then having intercourse, a man was (apparently) guaranteed an erection and total sexual enslavement of the woman! Trying this today would simply guarantee a trip to the hospital!

■ **Asparagus was** *considered a general cure-all for men suffering from erection or impotence problems.*

Contracting the yoni

In the 4th century, most women wanted to keep their *yoni* as small as possible in order to offer the greatest possible friction to their man. The *Kama Sutra* recommends one ointment made from a fruit that apparently helped to keep the *yoni* contracted throughout the night. Another concoction, made by pounding together the roots of several flowers, including the blue lotus, was said to enlarge the *yoni*.

> ### Trivia...
> *Such was one Brahmin's extraordinary sexual reaction to being stung by a wasp (no prizes for guessing where), his young wife insisted he should be stung over and over again! Aagh!*

Ancient sex therapy

Should a man become so worn out by being on top during intercourse that he is unable to climax in that way, the woman is encouraged to lay him down on his back and give him assistance by acting his part.

Several specific woman-on-top positions were described to help lead the lagging male to orgasm (see Chapter 13). These were considered especially helpful for older male lovers with little stamina, who needed extra friction to increase sensation. Women were also encouraged to use their vaginal muscles to help him to orgasm (see Chapter 21).

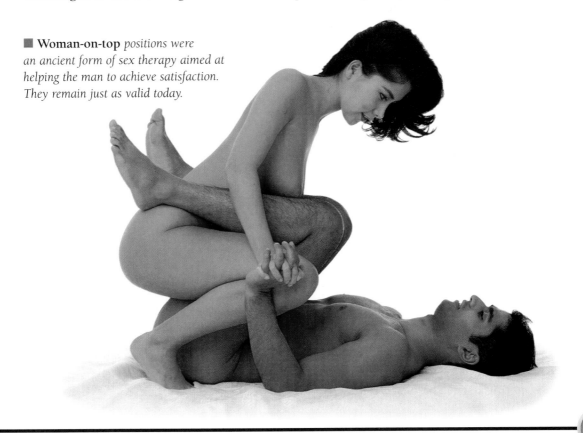

■ **Woman-on-top** *positions were an ancient form of sex therapy aimed at helping the man to achieve satisfaction. They remain just as valid today.*

Treating impotence today

YOU COULD, OF COURSE, MUNCH ON *asparagus if you have erection problems, but it's highly unlikely to provide a complete cure. Fortunately, these days there are various solutions to this dismaying difficulty. If impotence is "relationship specific," classic sex therapy exercises can help. When the problem seems to be physical, Viagra can work well. Alternatively, certain sex aids can be highly effective for men who don't like the idea of swallowing pills.*

Do-it-yourself sex therapy

Try the sensate focus exercises (see Chapter 22) over a period of several weeks, gradually leading up to intercourse. When it comes to intercourse, the woman should be on top and, instead of thrusting, she should concentrate on moving just enough to keep him erect. Orgasm is not the goal here; the woman should be able to contain her man's penis for at least 15 minutes before orgasm is considered desirable.

■ **Impotence need not** *cause a rift in a relationship – there are many ways of overcoming the problem, which can be pyschological or physical. The main emotions that induce pyschological impotence are fear, anxiety, and guilt.*

How Viagra works

Viagra is a small blue pill that helps men gain and maintain an erection in two ways. First, it relaxes the penile muscles so that blood flows into the penis to form a solid erection; second, it stimulates the brain to produce a certain reaction that, when the man has erotic thoughts, causes the penis to become erect.

Unfortunately Viagra isn't for everyone. Doctors warn that the drug may cause serious heart problems for some people and there have been some deaths associated with taking the drug.

Do not use Viagra without having a cardiac check-up first.

INTERNET

www.mensclinic.com

www.impotenceworld. org

Try these two web sites for more information about impotence and erectile dysfunction, and treatment options for sufferers.

A new impotence solution

A new anti-impotence drug, Uprima, has a similar success rate to Viagra in that it works for one in two men – but trials suggest it has fewer side effects.

Unlike Viagra, it can be used "with caution" by men taking heart medication. Uprima works by stimulating parts of the brain involved in the erectile process. It is dissolved under the tongue and takes about 15–20 minutes to have an effect.

Venous leakage

A small percentage of men suffer from a condition called "venous leakage," which occurs when the "locking system" at the base of the penis is damaged. As a result, blood that flows into the penis to form an erection flows out again almost immediately. Often, the simplest solution is a medically designed ring that fits snugly around the base of the penis and keeps the blood in place.

Another treatment that works for some men is testosterone supplementation. Taken in pill, patch, or gel form, supplements of this hormone help restore desire and erection.

Overcoming premature ejaculation

PREMATURE EJACULATION *is most often a problem for young men. It is associated with anxiety, inexperience, and having sex under conditions where the man is anxious to get the act over and done with quickly. Fortunately it is one of the easiest sex problems to overcome.*

Do-it-yourself therapy

The following simple do-it-yourself training scheme can help to solve the problem of premature ejaculation in most cases. I'm not suggesting you attempt all five stages in one session – just master one step at a time, as and when it's convenient for you.

1. Masturbate with a dry hand until you can last for 15 minutes

2. Masturbate with a wet hand until you can last for 15 minutes

3. Ask your partner to masturbate you with a dry hand until you can last for 15 minutes

4. Ask your partner to masturbate you with a wet hand until you can last 15 for minutes

5. Combine masturbation and intercourse

Slowing your lover down

Start by practicing the basic "sensate focus" exercises (see Chapter 22) over a period of 2 to 3 weeks – but stop short of intercourse. Once you have enjoyed these, you may move on to genital exploration. If at any time your lover signals that he is about to have an orgasm, you can give him the *penile squeeze*.

You can then massage him again until he regains his erection. This will help him to feel confident in maintaining an erection without ejaculating – and once he begins to believe he can last much longer in bed – he'll be able to do so!

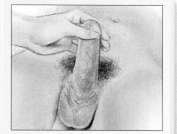

DEFINITION

The **penile squeeze** *is an exercise for men who suffer from premature ejaculation. When your partner says he is going to come, grasp his penis and press firmly just below the glans. Hold until his urge has been suppressed.*

Moving on to intercourse

When he can last for about 15 minutes without ejaculating, sit astride him and thrust gently while he remains immobile on his back – until he can last for 15 minutes. Again, he should signal when he thinks he is reaching the "point of no return" so that you can climb off and reapply the penile squeeze. You then remassage him and sit astride again.

Once this part of the exercise is working, you remain sitting astride him but now he thrusts gently until he can last for 15 minutes. Finally, you both thrust until he can last for 15 minutes.

Are you an extreme case?

If you are among the tiny percentage of men whose problem is so acute that self-training or training with a partner doesn't work, you might draw some comfort from new possibilities offered by drug therapy.

Drugs that calm down anxiety (such as beta-blockers) also seem to slow down premature ejaculation. So it's worth asking your doctor for advice.

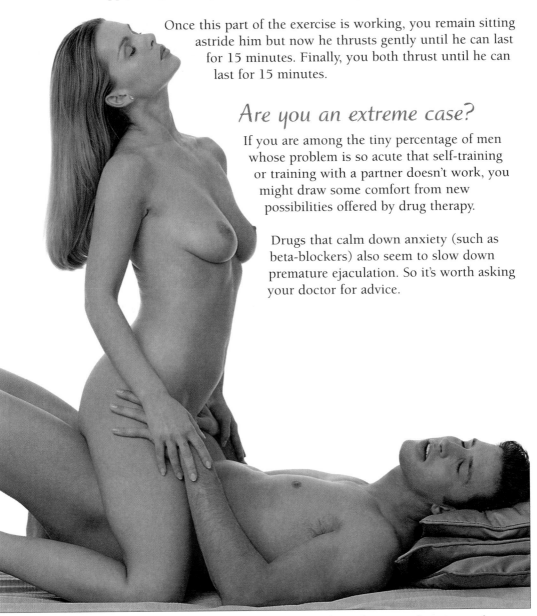

■ **When attempting** *to overcome premature ejaculation, remember to keep your thrusting gentle. The aim of the exercise is to slow your partner down and avoid overexciting him.*

Dealing with a lack of desire

FINDING YOURSELF UNABLE TO TURN ON appears to be the sex problem of the new millennium. These days we work too hard and get too little time off in which to rest. As a result, stress levels build up. Constant stress is bad for men and women: It kills sexual desire. So is there anything you can do about it, barring the obvious remedy of taking more time off for relaxation?

Mismatched desire

If you're happy with sex on an occasional basis and you meet someone who wants sex more regularly, your mismatched desires could cause a problem. One way of dealing with this is to make an agreement or a sex contract.

AGREEING A SEX CONTRACT

The following arrangement has the advantage of making you both feel you have some choice in whether you have sex, even if the final results are much the same.

(1) You choose whether or not to have sex on three days of the week

(2) Your partner chooses on the other three days of the week

(3) Sunday is up for grabs

A more up-to-date method of dealing with mismatched desires might be to take some of the newer drugs. Phentolamine aids sexual arousal and beta-blockers lower it. (By the way, these drugs are available by prescription only.)

You've always had a low sex drive

Perhaps you have never really had much interest in sex – yet you would like to experience desire. You feel just the same as anyone else. You want a loving partner and, ultimately, a family life.

Not to worry. These days there is a cocktail of hormones available to assist your condition.

Supplemental hormones such as testosterone and DHEA can put the zip back into your love life.

Talk to your medical practitioner if you think that hormone supplementation may help you.

Your partner doesn't turn you on

Perhaps you have found yourself lusting after that good-looking colleague in the office but no matter how hard you try, you cannot turn on to your old man or your old lady back home.

INTERNET

www.sexology.org/

www.sieccan.com

Sex Therapy Online and the Sex Information and Education Council of Canada offer information on therapy.

This is called partner-specific lack of desire and calls for some work with a relationship counselor. In the days of the *Kama Sutra,* a man in this situation would simply acquire a new wife and not bother too much about upsetting the old one.

We don't have that option in the 21st century (or not so easily, anyway) so we need to look at both emotional and physical reasons for partner-specific boredom.

■ **A loss of desire** *for your partner could be a sign of boredom. Counseling may be needed to help you get to the root of the problem.*

Are you taking medicine?

A little-publicized cause of loss of sexual desire lies in the prescription drugs you may be taking. So check out the medicine cabinet. Drugs that lower sexual desire include:

- Some antihistamines (as in allergy medications)
- Cold remedies
- Travel sickness pills
- Some antidepressants and beta-blockers
- Too much estrogen
- Strong tranquillizers
- Sleeping preparations such as barbiturates

Alternative therapies and "natural" supplements can have unwanted side effects, including lowering sexual desire.

Always check with your doctor before coming off any medication since you may need the medication more than you do the return of sexual desire. However, if you discuss your dilemma with your doctor, he or she may be able to prescribe an alternative medication with no side effects. It's worth trying.

Inability to experience orgasm

SOME WOMEN ARE UNABLE *to experience climax through intercourse or, less commonly, through masturbation. They may find it difficult because they have not yet discovered what works for them. Or they may suffer from inhibition, finding it hard to "let go" with their partner. Then again, they may need stronger stimulation than they have so far been lucky enough to receive.*

Very occasionally some women lack an adequate supply of natural testosterone – the hormone that sexologists now believe is responsible for sexual desire and arousal.

Many women do not spontaneously learn to masturbate as young girls. Teaching themselves to do so in later life often results in climaxes.

> ### Trivia...
> The famous Hite Report (1976) found that while only 30 per cent of women climax during sexual intercourse, as many as 82 per cent climax during masturbation.

Finding your first orgasm

There is a self-massage program aimed at helping women experience orgasm. This involves several stages:

 Take a warm bath

2. In a warm room, give yourself a massage and pass your hands lovingly over your body, excluding the genitals. Just note which types of touch feel good and which feel ordinary

3. On another occasion, repeat steps 1 and 2 but take the self-massage further to include the genitals. You are not trying for orgasm, you are simply exploring yourself to discover sensation. If you find that particular movements or particular areas feel good, then build your touch upon these areas

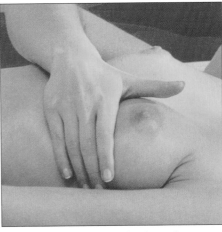

■ **Gently caress your body** *to discover which types of touch feel good, and where.*

■ **Progress to exploring your genitals** *and finding out which are your most sensitive areas.*

4 Over time, cut down the body massage and step up the genital massage. Remember, you are not aiming for orgasm. This doesn't mean you should actively work to prevent it should you feel it happening. But it doesn't matter if it doesn't arrive

5 If you do not reach orgasm spontaneously in this way, invest in a vibrator and use it in the same way as you have been using your fingers

6 If you do climax, next take your new-found information about yourself into your relationship and help your partner to stimulate you in the way that you have been stimulating yourself

Trivia...

There's no truth whatsoever in the old but persistent myth that female masturbation leads to concupiscence (unbridled lust) or nymphomania. The urge to masturbate is now known to be completely natural in both men and women.

INTERNET

www.hite-research.com

Click here for more details of the famous Hite Report on Female Sexuality and the need for clitoral stimulation.

■ **Don't keep** *all your intimate self-knowledge to yourself – show your partner what you've learned and how best to turn you on.*

That little extra

Vibrators offer stronger stimulation than fingers and many women need the extra speed and strength of oscillation in order to come. If this self-pleasuring program doesn't work, it may be that you need the assistance of testosterone supplements to give additional sexual sensation and arousal. If you also think you might be quite inhibited, the drug phentolamine (medical prescription only) helps release inhibition.

Fortunately our drugs are more up-to-date than those of the *Kama Sutra*, but the principles of learning trust, sexual skills, and special technique (such as the penile squeeze) still hold good for us as well as for the 4th-century Indians!

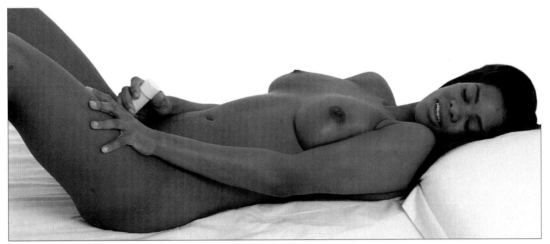

■ **For women** *who find it difficult to achieve climax, the intense clitoral sensations brought on by using a vibrator can help bring them to orgasm.*

A simple summary

✓ The idea of using sex aids and medicines to sustain erection is nothing new.

✓ Although some of the remedies in the *Kama Sutra* may have worked, most of them probably didn't. Present-day treatments are likely to be much more reliable.

✓ The best sex aids are a mixture of talking therapies, practice of sex behavior programs, certain medications, and the growth of trust and intimacy.

Chapter 24

Safe Sex

ALTHOUGH SEXUAL DISEASES were in existence when the *Kama Sutra* was written, Vatsyayana makes no mention of them. Present-day sex manuals always include a chapter on sexual health and especially on safe sex. People have always sought to avoid such infections, but the practise of "safer sex" is a recent phenomenon. What has prompted this change in sexual behavior is primarily the dramatic spread of AIDS (Acquired Immune Deficiency Syndrome) as well as other less dire sexually transmitted diseases (STDs).

In this chapter...

✓ Why do we need safe sex?

✓ Lovemaking and AIDS infection

✓ Alternatives to intercourse

✓ Erotic condom techniques

CARRY A CONDOM AND PROTECT YOURSELF AGAINST SEXUALLY TRANSMITTED DISEASES

Why do we need safe sex?

THE BASIS OF *safe sex* is the avoidance of exchanging bodily fluids (semen, vaginal secretions, and blood), because this exchange is the most common way in which sexually transmitted disease (STD), especially HIV infection, is passed on. The most effective way to minimize the risk of transmitting HIV during intercourse is to use a latex condom in combination with a spermicide.

> **DEFINITION**
>
> *The term* safe sex *describes sexual activity that is least likely to expose the participants to infection by HIV (Human Immunodeficiency Virus), which is the cause of AIDS, and other sexually transmitted diseases.*

Minimizing risk

When complete trust exists between partners, and each is confident enough of the other's sexual history to be reasonably sure that there is no risk of sexually transmitted disease, especially HIV infection, safe sex is irrelevant.

New sexual partners, however, should always practice safe sex until they know each other well enough to be sure that infection is unlikely.

Could you have HIV?

The easiest way to find out whether you have the HIV virus is to go for an HIV test at one of the many specialist clinics (look in the telephone directory under AIDS Testing.)

HIV AND THE DEVELOPMENT OF AIDS

When HIV enters the bloodstream, it attacks the immune system – the complex mechanism that enables the body to defend itself against disease. This damage eventually leaves the body vulnerable to other infections and liable to contract otherwise rare illnesses, including certain types of cancer and pneumonia.

When a person with HIV begins to be affected by such illnesses, he or she is said to have developed AIDS. It is these illnesses, not the HIV infection itself, that eventually cause the death of an AIDS sufferer.

■ **At the start of a new relationship,** *safe sex is an important issue. When you don't know someone well and are unsure about their sexual history, it's vital to take precautions against STDs.*

However, be aware that if you undergo the test in your real name and it shows that you have the virus, this may seriously damage your chances of getting life insurance, a mortgage, or any other long-term finance.

■ **Certain primates** *have suffered from a similar disease to AIDS for years, but the disease appears to be a new one for humans.*

Will we all ultimately get AIDS ?

AIDS has spread at a frightening rate from Africa to many other parts of the world within two decades. Many uncertainties surround the disease and many theories have been proposed over the years. One theory is that people in very hot countries such as Africa may be particularly prone to the illness for genetic reasons and that Westerners are less likely to contract the virus, or at least its most common strain.

However, most experts agree that the virus is spread mainly by unsafe sex (regardless of genetic predisposition); if you are in contact with the virus, then, whether you take protection or not, you are at risk of contracting it. The moral of the story is: Don't have sex irresponsibly – take the necessary precautions for your own safety.

Stephen O'Brien, Ph.D., of the National Cancer Institute has recently found that people of European ancestry carry a genetic substance that confers protection against the most common AIDS virus. However, the results of such experiments do not mean that Western people can become complacent – they can, and do, contract HIV infection.

Sex tourism

Certain parts of the world that specialize in sex tourism, such as regions of Thailand and certain African states, now find themselves with an epidemic of AIDS. In Russia, at present, thanks to the breakdown of the old Soviet system, the ensuing poverty, and the subsequent increase in prostitution, AIDS and tuberculosis are spreading rapidly.

The problem is so big in Russia that warnings are given out to both the Russian public and its visitors – a Russian message to curious visitors reads: "Go on holiday with a partner. Don't sample the foreign wares, however tempting."

Lovemaking and AIDS infection

IF AIDS SPREADS SO EASILY, are there any men and women in particular who are best avoided? And are some sexual activities more "dangerous" than others? One known fact about HIV is that your risk of contracting AIDS increases with the more casual sex you have. Another known risk factor is infection with other sexually transmitted diseases.

The following would be deemed high-risk sexual partners:

1. An intravenous drug user who shares needles

2. A partner with a history of many sexual (especially homosexual or bisexual) partners. An infected (HIV-positive) man can transmit the virus to his sexual partners – of either sex – in his semen. And a woman who is infected with HIV can pass the virus to her sexual partners in her vaginal secretions

3. People such as hemophiliacs, who have contracted the disease from their (necessary) blood transfusions

INFECTION AND INCUBATION

When a person is infected with HIV, the virus will be present in his or her blood. It will also be present in the semen of infected males and in the vaginal secretions of infected females. Anyone coming into intimate contact with these infected bodily fluids, as can happen during unprotected sexual intercourse, will be at high risk of contracting the virus themselves.

Once HIV has entered the blood, there is as yet no way of eradicating it, and AIDS will usually develop in about 8 to 10 years. You cannot, however, contract HIV from simple, everyday contact with someone who is infected. For example, you cannot catch it by shaking hands with them or from their coughs or sneezes, or by touching objects they have used.

Once may be enough

The ease with which infection can pass from one person to another during unprotected intercourse is clearly illustrated by numerous cases in which a single sexual contact with the infected person has been enough to infect someone with HIV. People have unwittingly contracted HIV through unprotected sexual contact with drug addicts infected with the virus as a result of sharing needles with others. Married women have been infected with HIV by husbands who caught the virus through heterosexual or homosexual affairs or after unprotected sex with an infected prostitute. Married men, too, have been known to contract HIV from wives infected during an affair.

A careless attitude

Many people erroneously think that AIDS is not a heterosexual problem (believing that it applies only to homosexuals) and refuse to take precautions. Others who are aware of the dangers of HIV often underestimate them, and anyway they find it impossible to ask a partner to use a condom or to consider whether he or she may have encountered the virus.

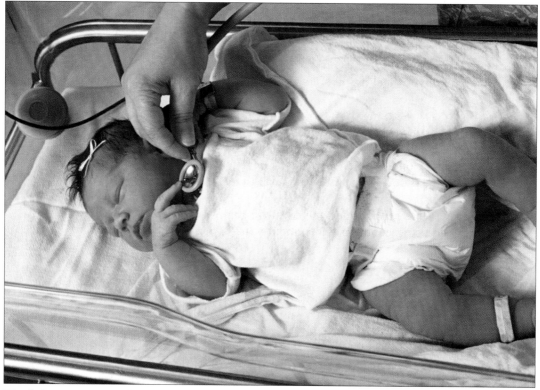

■ **While many HIV-infected mothers** *do not pass the infection onto their babies, there have been numerous cases of the virus being transmitted in this way.*

On the other hand, a few people are overfearful of getting AIDS and go for repeated blood tests, even when they know they cannot possibly have caught the virus.

Some people have such an intense anxiety about contracting AIDS that it becomes a type of phobia.

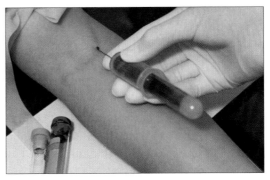

TAKING BLOOD TO TEST FOR AIDS

How to ask for safe sex

When developing a relationship with someone new, try getting comfortable with small aspects of sexuality at the beginning. Tackle these slowly, with the easiest discussion first. Remember that self-disclosure is a good way of approaching something difficult.

Try phrases such as:

1. "I feel very nervous about asking this question, but it's something that's very important to me"

2. "What are your feelings about safe sex?"

3. "I know some people think women (or young people) shouldn't carry condoms but I think it's very important. I carry them. Do you?"

4. "I've often wondered about the value of taking an AIDS test. I can see that it could be very important. But I've never done it so far. Have you?"

5. "I know some people think me a bit overcareful, but I really only feel safe with sex when using condoms. How about you?"

Saying "no"

It might be that the end result of your delicate and carefully negotiated discussion is that your partner refuses to use condoms or other safe sex practices.

You might say "no" to unprotected sex by saying something like: "I like you immensely and I'd love to go to bed with you, but I feel so strongly about safe sex practices that, in the circumstances, I'm going to have to call it a day. But why don't we try and stay really good friends?"

Alternatives to intercourse

WHEN YOU REACH THE STAGE *of knowing you don't want to have penetrative sex but you do want sex of some sort, you might be happy to consider several other activities. But before you disappear in a welter of mutual masturbation, be aware of the risks involved.*

Various activities, sexual and otherwise, are set out below in three categories, according to the risk of HIV infection.

High risk

- Vaginal sexual intercourse without a condom
- Anal intercourse with or without a suitable condom
- Oral sex, especially to climax
- Any sexual activity that draws blood (accidentally or deliberately)
- Sharing penetrative sex aids, such as vibrators
- Inserting fingers or hands into the anus

Medium risk

- Vaginal sexual intercourse with a condom
- Love bites or scratching that breaks the skin
- Anal licking or kissing

INTERNET

www.cdnaids.ca

www.aidsinfonyc.org/ network/index.html

These sites offer detailed information and advice on all aspects of AIDS and its treatment.

THE FACTS ABOUT SAFETY

People often fear that the following activities can transmit sexual diseases, including HIV. However, these fears are entirely unjustified because all the following are risk-free:

- Bites from blood-sucking insects
- Sitting on toilet seats
- Swimming in public pools
- Using other people's bed linen or towels
- Swallowing another person's saliva (assuming there are no cuts or sores in your mouth)
- Sneezing
- Cheek-to-cheek kissing
- Shaking hands or cuddling
- Sharing a glass or silverware
- Being a blood donor (in developed countries where the needles used are sterilized)

■ **Wet kissing** *is a pleasurable sexual occupation that is risk-free provided neither partner has bleeding gums, mouth ulcers, or cold sores. Dry kissing poses no risk.*

- Sexual activities involving urination
- Mouth-to-mouth kissing if either partner has bleeding gums or cold sores
- Cunnilingus using a latex barrier
- Fellatio using a condom

No risk

- Dry kissing
- Wet kissing (provided neither partner has bleeding gums, mouth ulcers, or cold sores)
- Stimulating a partner's genitals with your hands, or having your genitals stimulated
- Self-masturbation

So what could you do instead of intercourse?

Think seriously about fantasy and masturbation. For example, you and your partner could take it in turns to describe sexual fantasies to each other while you both self-masturbate, or while you masturbate each other. You could both use vibrators (individually) or use vibrators on each other (provided you don't share them).

■ **Fellatio is a high-risk activity** *if you don't know your partner's sexual history. Using a condom lessens the risk of becoming infected with STDs, but doesn't eradicate it altogether.*

Safe oral sex

Since there is a reasonably high risk of infection, oral sex should be avoided unless you take careful precautions to prevent contact with semen or vaginal fluid.

While a condom will prevent contact with semen during fellatio, a latex barrier is needed to prevent contact with vaginal fluid during cunnilingus. Both types of protection are available at drug stores.

Massaging each other's whole body, including the genitals, is another option but as is the case with oral sex, contact with bodily fluids such as semen and vaginal secretions should be avoided, especially if you have any skin cuts into which the fluids could penetrate.

Erotic condom techniques

THE CONDOM *is not only an effective form of contraceptive, it also acts as a barrier to infection, especially with sexually transmitted diseases (STDs). Some couples, however, are reluctant to use condoms because they think that interrupting lovemaking is unromantic and unerotic. Yet by following a few simple rules, a woman can turn the mundane act of slipping a condom on to her partner's penis into a sensual experience.*

Choosing condoms

As a general rule buy name brand condoms and always check the expiration date on the package. Avoid the strangely shaped condoms with knobbly edges and clitoral "ticklers." Although they may heighten the sensation, they are, alas, not as safe because they do not fit the penis tightly enough and so may slip off, allowing semen to leak into the vagina during intercourse.

CONDOM SAFETY TIPS

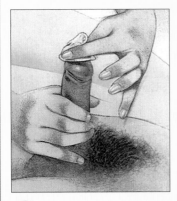

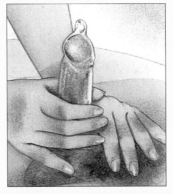

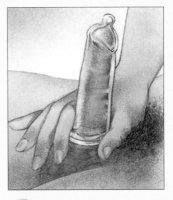

1 Squeeze out the air

Gently press the tip of the condom between finger and thumb to ensure it contains no air – an air bubble could cause it to split during intercourse

2 Slip on the condom

Put the condom on the tip of the man's penis with one hand and roll it down the shaft with the other. If he is uncircumcized, pull back his foreskin first

3 Roll it all down

Ensure the condom is rolled right down. The man should withdraw his penis soon after climax, holding the condom in place to prevent leakage

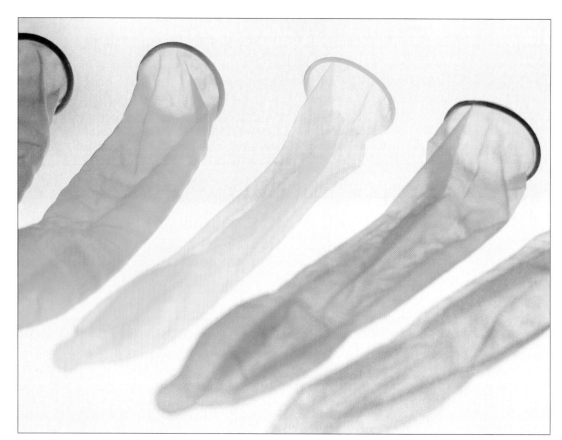

■ **Modern condoms** *are available in the thinnest layers of latex and a wide range of colors, flavors, and textures to add variety and fun to lovemaking.*

Does "Sir" require a fitting?

One great method of turning condom-wearing into a sex game is to pretend that he is shopping for penile dress ware and you are the fitting room attendant. To make the donning of the condom as erotic as possible you might begin with a brief but sensuous genital massage. Then change your hand action from genital massage to genital masturbation as a preliminary to fitting the condom on to his penis. When actually slipping the sheath on to him, use slow, sensuous movements, to make the occasion as erotic as possible.

Never unroll the condom before fitting it.

INTERNET

www.condomania.com

Check out this web site for a fantastic variety of sheaths.

The Thai massage parlor method

In Oriental massage parlors, masseurs who give their customers fellatio practice a skillful technique. As they fellate, they place the condom just inside the mouth and, held in place by the tongue, slip the sheath over the penis as part of the oral massage. Hands, of course, can be used to give added sensation by masturbating during fellatio and to unroll the sheath down the shaft at the same time. Thai women are said to do this so expertly that their client has no idea it has happened. You might invest in some special flavored condoms so that you get some fun out of this too.

Trivia...

A frequently asked question is whether or not lesbians can get HIV. It is possible that women can transmit the virus to other women but it is extremely rare. There have been, so far, only a tiny number of cases reported.

A simple summary

✓ We need safe sex techniques in the 21st century because absolutely anyone might have been unfortunate enough to contract AIDS. And so far, AIDS is ultimately fatal.

✓ However, there are certain lovemaking methods that minimize the risk.

✓ One of the safest methods is to use condoms since these provide a barrier against infection.

✓ Contrary to fears, it is possible to fit a condom on to your partner so that the experience becomes a sensual one. Thai massage parlour women provide a useful example.

✓ Condoms are the easiest contraceptives to get hold of, are widely available in drug stores and supermarkets, and can be bought in a variety of brands and flavors.

Chapter 25

The Kama Sutra's Legacy

THE ORIGINAL TRANSLATOR of the *Kama Sutra*, Sir Richard Burton, considered it "a work that should be studied by all, both old and young . . ." Elucidating on this point, he added, ". . . the former will find in it real truths, gathered by experience, and already tested by themselves, while the latter will derive the great advantage of learning things, which some perhaps may otherwise never learn at all, or which they may only learn when it is too late to profit by learning."

In this chapter...

✓ Wise words then – and now

✓ The importance of Burton's liberal ideas

✓ Where the world remains medieval

✓ Has the sexual revolution fully arrived?

✓ Burton's afterword

THE *KAMA SUTRA* CAN HELP COUPLES TODAY TO FIND SPIRITUALITY THROUGH SEX

Wise words then – and now

HUMAN BEINGS MAY HAVE NOTCHED UP thousands of years of sexual experience, but we don't seem to have learned very much. What hasn't helped is that generations – especially in the West – chose to cloak sex in privacy – forcing each new generation to start learning about sex from the beginning again. It was fortunate that Vatsyayana had the foresight to commit the Kama Sutra to writing because the sexual wisdom of the 4th century is just as eagerly sought-after now as it was then. In this high-speed, high-tech, high-stress age, the ancient manual has much to teach us.

The need for speed

In this modern age of instant gratification, shorter attention spans, and desire for speed, we may not be enjoying sex as much as previous generations. This isn't to say we don't experience orgasm – at least 80 percent of us manage it one way or another. But we don't always find sex as special as we should. Sometimes we come away from lovemaking feeling disappointed. We don't feel that we've enjoyed the sensual feast or the rush of excitement we'd anticipated.

■ **In the days of** *the* Kama Sutra, *sex was unhurried and languorous. In our high-speed modern age, time is a luxury many of us cannot afford.*

Sometimes we may have enjoyed that adrenalin rush by accident. Perhaps we're among the lucky few who have had the luxury of idling in bed, spending time slowly building up towards an explosive climax so resounding that it blows our minds. And during that cataclysm we truly feel lifted to a higher plane, if only for seconds.

The feeling of floating off to a higher place happens as a result of changes in the brain as we climax.

But suppose we don't reach this ultimate experience? This is where the ancient wisdom of the *Kama Sutra* proves as useful as any present-day sex manual. First it introduces the concept of stages of love – it sets the equivalent of a graduation program.

Second, it makes it clear that *kama* is one of the three ingredients that lead men (and women) to a better place (*moksha*). And although the *Kama Sutra* preceded the evolution of Tantric theories, the sex practices outlined were clear forerunners of Tantric sex. Tantric sex itself is an extension of the notion of *kama*. (This is not as circular as it sounds.) And Tantric sex is definitely about reaching an "infinite state" through the medium of sexual intercourse.

In search of heaven

These ideas all lead to the possibility that by missing out the notion of the "better place" in the 21st century we create a gap in our lives. The gap may be the result of losing the "meaning" that wonderful sex provides.

So perhaps, in its own uniquely practical way, the *Kama Sutra* offers us, all these centuries later, a formula for slowing things down, hotting things up, and guiding us toward that "better place." If we want to find heaven in bed (although there are no guarantees), does the *Kama Sutra* offer us the chance of discovering it? I would like to think so.

In the 21st century, by learning from the wisdom of the 4th century, there is the real opportunity of rediscovering forgotten knowledge. And with that knowledge we might once again experience sexual spirituality.

■ **Spending time** *just being sensual with one another and not rushing into intercourse makes sex, when it happens, far more pleasurable.*

The importance of Burton's liberal ideas

EVEN THOUGH WE HAVE NOT YET *caught up with the spiritual beliefs of the* Kama Sutra, *there are other ways in which Sir Richard Burton's legacy has proved "world changing." He was the first to break through those old Victorian taboos of repressive sexuality.*

Sir Richard Burton's courage in publishing sexual writings at a time when he knew he would be socially ostracized was considerable. Even his wife Isabel, although she pretended to know nothing of the contents of her husband's manuscripts, was clearly familiar with his work, which in itself was revolutionary for that time.

Sir Richard Burton believed that women were naturally as sexual as any man. Few Victorians thought like this.

Burton set the ball of sexual change rolling. It took a very long time to undo the sexual repression of the Victorian age but it is possible, that without Burton's courage, it might not have happened in our lifetime. His books were the wave that caused ever-widening ripples over the next 150 years.

Thank you, Richard

All lovers, capable of being yourselves and being naturally sexual as a part of being yourselves, can thank Sir Richard Burton for his legacy. Without his pioneering vitality you might still be using the Victorian mindset.

Now it's okay to be sexual

In the West we think that we are all entitled to do as we like sexually, barring, of course, activities that would harm anyone. Most of us would say it is fine to be sexual but would reserve the right to choose just how we practice this.

But if we want to be sexual to the ultimate degree as laid out in the *Kama Sutra*, this means following the manual's distinct "stages of love" as follows:

1. Women must be wooed subtly and over time

2. Sensuality must be matter-of-factly but sensitively introduced

3 The build-up to sex should be infinitely various, including hugging, pressing, kissing, scratching, biting, and even inflicting blows

 4 A woman is expected to know about the many sexual positions, even if she has not yet experienced them

5 Any properly knowledgeable individual must know and have practiced the 24 basic sex positions in order to understand how to love

 6 Sex can be carried out in a completely matter-of-fact mood yet still lead to wonderful sensual experience

Where the world remains medieval

IN THE WEST, high-quality sex manuals are often given as birthday or engagement presents to friends of both sexes. Yet in some parts of the world, such as in Afghanistan where the fundamentalist Taliban rule, not only would women never be given such a book, they would never be given a book at all since they are not considered of value. Denied basic rights, such as the right to an education and to decent medical facilities, they are seen as a kind of chattel.

It's ironic that in medieval times, it was in the sexually sophisticated East that the uncouth crusaders, learned the rudiments of hygiene and sexual sophistry. Of course, the Taliban nation is particularly extreme.

■ **The crusaders** *were a barbaric bunch who lived in cruel medieval times. Unfortunately, in parts of the world where a medieval attitude persists, barbaric customs are still practiced.*

Modern Indians and Pakistanis enjoy the same kind of sensual pleasures as their ancient ancestors, even though there is a veneer of prudishness.

Imagine if penises were cut off!

Cutting off a man's appendage is not a pleasant thought is it? Yet in this supposedly advanced day and age, the equivalent of this is done to thousands of women in the name of culture.

> ### DEFINITION
>
> *A clitoridectomy is a procedure to excise the clitoris, also known as female circumcision. It is usually carried out in primitive, unhygienic conditions and is extremely dangerous – often leading to serious bleeding, infection, and death. In certain cultures, this practice is a matter of family honor since it is believed that an uncircumcised girl is unmarriageable. However, the underlying ethos of clitoridectomy is control of women through reducing their sexual response.*

There are many parts of Africa in which *clitoridectomy* is practiced. The *Kama Sutra* would be useless for women who have undergone this procedure since they would be able to feel little sexual sensation and whatever feeling there was would be extremely painful.

Condemnation of this barbaric practice has been widespread and campaigners around the world have been working, with the backing of the World Health Organization, to persuade the relevant authorities to abolish the procedure. But change comes slowly and even in major modern cities worldwide where female immigrants have settled, circumcision specialists continue to practice.

What can I do?

It's all too easy to simply do nothing. After all, how can anyone be expected to dissuade an entire nation from practicing a centuries-old custom? But you can have an influence by making your views known.

If, as a man, you cringe at the idea of having your penis cut off as an eight-year-old, why not find out which countries condone clitoridectomy and write to or e-mail their high commissions or embassies? You could even write in protest directly to the appropriate government ministers.

If, as a woman, the idea of having your clitoris excised and your vagina sewn up with huge stitches and no anaesthetic makes you flinch, spare just a little time and get to the word processor. Please.

> ### INTERNET
>
> www.amnesty.org/ailib/intcam/femgen/fgm9.htm
>
> *Click here for detailed information about countries in which clitoridectomy is practiced and on worldwide and local organizations that are campaigning against it.*

Has the sexual revolution fully arrived?

UNFORTUNATELY THERE IS STILL A LONG WAY *to go. The sex revolution won't have fully arrived until women all over the world are granted freedoms such as control over their own bodies, a decent education, and parity with men. And as long as there are taboos surrounding sex, how can it be fully accepted as healthy and normal?*

■ **If the *Kama Sutra*** *were read as avidly as some of the hottest bestsellers, people's knowledge and understanding of sex might advance considerably.*

Sex as an agent of change

If you suggested putting the *Kama Sutra* on the required reading list for primary schools – or even secondary schools – you would be drummed out of town. You don't see it on the curriculum at colleges either. And yet, why not? Sex is a natural human drive. Why should it be considered so explosively dangerous that it must be "swept under the carpet?"

Stop and think for a moment. It is only by demystifying something that it becomes "normal." Men and women tried hard to change things in the 20th century with some significant results. But clearly there is still a way to go. Hopefully by making the reading of such classics as the *Kama Sutra* normal and acceptable, this liberating climate will continue to improve. It is even possible that the ancient classic could help to pioneer sexual, political, and social change in the near future.

And the change won't only be in teaching and learning the 64 methods of lovemaking and the 24 sex positions detailed in the *Kama Sutra*. It will include the healthy acceptance of sex as a natural drive. And it could lead to a profound sense of spirituality – a heartwarming thought.

Burton's afterword

SIR RICHARD BURTON PAYS HOMAGE to Vatsyayana, saying that the Kama Sutra's author "must also have had a considerable knowledge of the humanities." In summing up the Indian classic, Burton adds: "Many of his remarks are so full of simplicity and truth that they have stood the test of time and stand out still as clear and true as when they were first written, some 1,800 years ago."

Burton continues by commenting on the depth of Vatsyayana's wisdom: "Vatsyayana states that he wrote the work while leading the life of a religious student (probably at Benares) and while wholly engaged in the contemplation of the Deity. He must have arrived at a certain age at that time, for throughout he gives us the benefit of his experience, and of his opinions, and these bear the stamp of age rather than of youth; indeed the work could hardly have been written by a young man."

■ **Sir Richard Burton,** *here depicted in Arab dress in 1854, honored Vatsyayana by describing him as a genius and author of a great classic.*

A work of genius

Burton concludes his homage to Vatsyayana with the words: "The works of men of genius do follow them and remain a lasting treasure. And though there may be disputes and discussions about the immortality of the body or the soul, nobody can deny the immortality of genius, which ever remains as a bright and guiding star to the struggling humanities of the succeeding ages."

Burton's eulogy to Vatsyayana reads as follows:

So long as lips shall kiss, and eyes shall see,
So long lives This, and This gives life to Thee.

A simple summary

✔ Even though the publication of the *Kama Sutra* and the other books under the imprint of the *Kama Shastra* Society were a small beginning, their influence has trickled through and lent itself to the beginnings of sexual revolution in the 20th century.

✔ The *Kama Sutra* offers us a sexual path to spirituality as well as a practical path to great sex.

✔ Because we pass little sexual information down from one generation to another, there will always be a need for books like the *Kama Sutra*.

✔ It is regrettable that there are parts of the world where barbaric customs are still practiced, such as appalling sexual surgery on women.

✔ It's important that pressure is brought to bear on countries that condone clitoridectomy to put an end to this cruel oppression of women.

✔ The addition of the *Kama Sutra* to the required reading list of students might further the sexual change that has already begun.

Glossary

Ananga Ranga Translates as meaning "stage of the Bodiless One", a reference to the story of how Kama, the Hindu god of love, became a bodiless spirit when his physical body was burned to a pile of ashes by a stare from the third eye of the god Shiva.

Androgyny The state of having the characteristics of both male and female in one individual.

Apadravyas An ancient Indian sex aid that was fitted on to the penis in order to facilitate penetration.

Aphrodisiac Any substance that increases or enhances sexual desire and stamina. The word derives from the Greek goddess of love (and sex), Aphrodite.

Areolae The brown, slightly bumpy areas that surround the nipples.

Atavistic Reversion to primitive type.

Ayah A nursery maid who has practical responsibility for child-rearing in wealthy households.

Bhaga "Luck" and "vagina". In the 4th century a rival's *bhaga* would be ruined by rendering her barren, and therefore useless as a wife.

Brahmin A priest, and next to the king, considered the highest social class in Hindu India. Brahmins were venerated because people believed that they were "purer" than members of other castes and that they alone were capable of performing certain vital religious tasks. There are still Brahmin priests today, particularly in southern India.

Caste The Indian class system. Caste is indicated by a mark worn on the forehead that reveals whether an individual is high or low caste. Traditionally, lower caste people do not expect preferential treatment while those of high caste do.

Chakras Centres of energy that occur at seven points in the astral body, which the yogis believe surrounds and permeates the physical body. Six chakras are located along the equivalent of the spine in the physical body, while the seventh crowns the head.

Clitoridectomy The excision of the clitoris, usually carried out under primitive conditions of hygiene, and also known as female circumcision. It is extremely dangerous and often leads to serious bleeding, major infection, and death. The procedure is carried out as a mark of family honor because it is believed that a girl who is not circumcised will be unmarriageable. However, the underlying ethos to clitoridectomy is control of women through reducing their sensuality.

Clitoris A tiny, bud-shaped area at the head of the labia. It both transmits and receives some of the most erotic feelings that a woman can experience.

Condom A latex sheath worn over the penis to prevent conception or the transmission of STDs. There is also a female version of the condom, which is placed inside the vagina.

Courtesan An extremely cultured and talented female who would not only command high fees for sexual relationships with high-caste men but would also contribute generously to the arts. Courtesans would also sing and dance.

Cunnilingus A form of oral sex done to the woman, in which the clitoris is manipulated by tongue.

Dildo An object shaped like an erect penis that is used for sexual stimulation and for massage. Early versions of the artificial penis were made from bone; later they were made from china or thick glass.

Erogenous zones Areas of the body full of particularly sensual nerve endings. Obvious examples are the genitals, lips, and breasts, but there are many other, more unexpected, sites on the body that respond thrillingly to stimulation.

Essential oils Easily evaporated volatile substances occurring naturally in some plants.

Etiquette Rules or customs setting out the correct or acceptable way to behave in one's social life.

Fellatio The form of oral sex done to the man, in which the penis is manipulated by mouth.

Foreplay Sexual stimulation that takes place before sexual intercourse. Foreplay includes kissing and touching various parts of the body.

G-spot A supersensitive area on the vagina's front wall, about a half to two-thirds of the way in. If pressed firmly (by the penis or a finger) a powerfully erotic sensation is created. Research indicates that not all women possess a G-spot, but many of those who have one know that it can trigger orgasm.

HIV Human Immunodeficiency Virus (HIV) is the virus that causes AIDS (Acquired Immune Deficiency Syndrome). The virus is most commonly transmitted through bodily fluids such as blood and semen during unprotected sexual intercourse with an infected partner. Infection can also occur through sharing hypodermic needles with infected intravenous-drug users. AIDS sets in when the immune system becomes severely depressed, exposing the infected person to serious and often catastrophic infections.

Impotence A sexual problem in a male in which he is unable to get an erection, or in some cases cannot maintain one.

Infidels Peoples of the Islamic east in medieval days, which included a mixture of Arab, Turcoman, Kurdish, Jewish, and other cultures.

IVF In Vitro Fertilization (IVF) is assisted conception where the egg (or eggs) has been fertilized in a test tube and later implanted into the uterus.

Jaghana The part of the body from the navel downward to the thighs.

Kama Sutra A compilation of writings by various authors about sex. It is not a pornographic book but a simple statement of how sex – one of the most important aspects of ancient Indian life – can be enjoyed. The book, in its present form, has endured for at least 1,600 years and is regarded as one of the great Indian classics.

Labia The fleshy outer lips surrounding the vagina.

Libido An individual's sexual drive or energy.

Lingam A penis.

Masturbation The act of stimulating your own genitals erotically, using either your hands or a sexual device.

Missionary position The basic sex position with the man on top.

Moksha A spiritual release from life or liberation.

Opprobrium Disgrace, reproach, or imputation of shameful conduct, infamy – anything that brings reproach.

Orgasm Also known as climax, orgasm is intense sexual excitement that builds up during masturbation or sexual intercourse, reaching a crescendo of extreme sexual pleasure. Physiologically, orgasm is a release of the muscular tension and engorged blood vessels that have built up during sexual excitement.

Pederasty Sexual relations of male with male, often also meaning sex with boys.

Penile squeeze An exercise for men who suffer from premature ejaculation. The penis is grasped and firmly pressed below the glans until the urge for orgasm has been suppressed.

Perineum The area between the anus and the testicles, or between the anus and the vagina. It is often very sensitive to being touched or stroked.

Premature ejaculation The inability of a man to delay his orgasm for long enough to allow his partner to experience full sexual pleasure.

Pubococcygeal (PC) muscle The muscle located between the front of the hip bones (the pubis) and the tail of the spine (the coccyx). It helps maintain the tone and control of the vagina, anus, and penis.

Purdah The separation of the female members of a household from the men. In practical terms, this meant that they occupied separate portions of a house or compound and had little or no contact with males.

S and M A type of sexual activity that involves both sadism and masochism. A sadist likes to dominate and punish, whereas a masochist enjoys being submissive and receiving pain.

Safe sex Sexual activity that is unlikely to expose the participants to infection by sexually transmitted diseases, including HIV (Human Immunodeficiency Virus), which is the cause of AIDS.

Sex flush Reddening of the skin on the face and chest that appears during extreme sexual excitement and fades after orgasm.

Sexology The study of sexuality and the sexual interactions between humans. The scientists who engage in this study are called sexologists.

Shastra Scripture or doctrines.

STD The umbrella term "STDs", or "sexually transmitted diseases", covers a wide range of infections that can be spread through direct sexual contact. An older term, "venereal disease", or "VD", refers to the "classic" sexually transmitted diseases, such as gonorrhoea and syphilis. STDs encompass latter-day diseases, including HIV and some forms of hepatitis, which are often spread through sexual contact. *See also* HIV.

Uttana-bandha Positions in which the woman lies on her back and the man enters her while kneeling between her legs. They are also called supine postures.

Viagra A current drug treatment for impotence. It helps men gain and keep an erection.

Vibrator An electrical or battery-driven vibrating device used for sexual stimulation and massage. It is often shaped like a phallus.

Yoni A vagina.

More resources

Useful addresses

ADVICE AND COUNSELING

Family Resources Warm Line
Provides nonmedical parenting advice, support, and referrals.
Telephone: (800) 641-4546

EDAP (Eating Disorders Awareness and Prevention)
Advice, information, and counseling on eating disorders.
Telephone: (800) 931-2237
www.edap.org

RAINN (Rape, Abuse, Incest National Network)
For victims of any kind of sexual assault. Call the number below to be automatically connected to a rape crisis center in your area.
Telephone: (800) 656-HOPF
www.rainn.org

HIV/AIDS ADVICE

AIDS Hotline (US Department of Health and Human Resources)
General information about AIDS and HIV, referrals provided.
Telephone: (800) 342-AIDS
www.aidshotline.org

AIDS Treatment Information Service
Information on treating HIV, referrals available.
Telephone: (800) HIV-0440

The Multicultural AIDS Coalition
Douglas Park
801-B Tremont Street
Boston, MA 02118
Telephone: (617) 442-1622

Project Inform Treatment Hotline
Information and referral for HIV-infected individuals.
Telephone: (800) 822-7422
www.projinf.org

SEXUAL HEALTH

Herpes Resource Center
Information on the prevention
and treatment of herpes.
Telephone: (800) 230-6039

National Sexually Transmitted Disease Hotline
Answers to questions about STDs,
and referrals to local clinics.
Telephone: (800) 227-8922

American Social Health Association
News on personal and sexual
health issues and information
on STD prevention treatment.
PO Box 13827
Research Triangle Park, NC 27709
Telephone: (919) 361-8400
www.ashastd.org

SIECUS (The Sexuality Information and Education Council of the US)
Provides information about all
facets of sexuality.
130 West 42nd Street,
Suite 350,
New York, NY 10036
Telephone: (212) 819-9770
www.siecus.org

PREGNANCY AND CONTRACEPTION

National Abortion Federation Hotline
Provides advice about abortion and
pregnancy and reproductive laws, and
offers information about the facilities
available to women.
Telephone: (800) 772-9100

Planned Parenthood, Inc.
For birth control services, pregnancy
tests, parental care, STD education
and treatment, AIDS tests, and
HIV counseling.
810 Seventh Ave
New York, NY 10019
Telephone: (800) 829-7732 or (800)
230-7526
www.ppnyc.org

Further reading

Becoming Orgasmic: A Sexual and Personal Growth Program for Women
Julia R. Heiman, Joseph LoPiccolo (Simon & Schuster)

Exploring Human Sexuality
Karen Klenke-Hamel and Louis Janda (D. Van Nostrand)

Men are from Mars, Women are from Venus
John Gray (HarperCollins)

More Joy...An Advanced Guide to Solo Sex
Harold Litten, Rod Shows (illustrator) (Factor Press)

Principles and Practice of Sex Therapy
S. Leiblum and R. Rosen (Guilford, New York, 2000)

The 7 Steps to Passionate Love
William Van Horn, MD (Greenleaf Ents.)

Sexual Ecstasy: The Art of Orgasm
Margot Anand (Putnam Publishing)

The Complete Kama Sutra
Alain Danielou (Park Street Press, Rochester, 1994)

The Illustrated Manual of Sexual Aids
Evelyn Rainbird (Minotaur Press)

Women's Orgasm: A Guide to Sexual Satisfaction
Georgia Klein-Graber, RN, and Benjamin Graber, MD (Warner Books)

Other Anne Hooper titles

Anne Hooper's Sexual Intimacy

Anne Hooper's Ultimate Sexual Touch

The Ultimate Sex Book

Great Sex Games

K.I.S.S. Guide to Sex
(All published by Dorling Kindersley)

The Body Electric
(Pandora Books)

A Thinking Woman's Guide to Love and Sex
(Robson Books)

Women and Sex
(Sheldon Press)

Sex on the Web

THERE'S A VAST AMOUNT of information about the Kama Sutra and about sex in general on the Web. The following contains some of the most useful and interesting sites. Please note that due to the fast-changing nature of the Net, some of the below may be out of date by the time you read this.

www.aidsinfoyc.org/network/index.html
This is the site for the AIDS Treatment Data Network, a non-profitmaking, community-based organization. The site offers information on all aspects of AIDS and its treatment.

www.allexperts.com/getexpert.asp?Category=856
This well-established question-and-answer site dispenses advice for couples in older/younger relationships. A panel of volunteer experts is available to respond to problems online.

www.amazon.co.uk
Visit this site and click on the sex or erotica sections to order copies of any of the sex books mentioned on pages 64–65.

www.amazon.com/exec/obidos.ISBN%3D1573922056/societyforhumansA/105-7105617-8333505
If you're interested in finding out more about Victorian erotic literature, click on the Amazon address for details of book sales.

www.amnesty.org/ailib/intcam/femgen/fgm9.htm
Click here for detailed information about countries in which clitoridectomy is practised and on worldwide and local organizations that are campaigning against it.

www.annsummers.co.uk
Click on online shopping to view Ann Summer's comprehensive catalog of sex aids and toys.

www.aromashoppe.com
A Canadian site offering mail-order essential and massage oils.

www.beautycare.com
Offering a variety of cosmetic dental care products for sale online, this site also gives useful beauty tips.

www.bettydodson.com
Visit Betty Dodson's site to see her collection of sex books, videos, and vibrators. The site's other sections include feedback forum, sexual politics, and sex humor and satire.

www.bibliomania.com/4/-/frameset.html

This site provides literature from all over the world for free. To read the *Kama Sutra* online, simply click on research and select non fiction/Vatsyayana/Kamasutra.

www.bluemountain.com

Blue Mountain's electronic greeting cards cover an array of subjects from "love messages" to "events and milestones."

www.calmness.com/chakras.htm

This site features information on the seven main chakras and how they affect our bodies, both physically and psychologically.

ww.cdnaids.ca

The site of the Canadian AIDS Society provides a wide range of web site links and toll-free hotlines for people seeking confidential HIV-related information.

www.comeasyouare.com

This Canadian site offers mail-order sex aids and other items, including massage oils.

www.condomania.com

Check out this web site for a fantastic variety of sheaths. The online catalog also features a lively selection of novelty sex aids.

www.dk.com

For details of Anne Hooper's books, visit Dorling Kindersley's web site. Click on the health section, then on the sex section.

www.dkonline.com/dkcom/dk/massage.html

Visit this site for a step-by-step account of how to give a relaxing foot massage with scented oils.

www.emmaus.on.ca/BESTCO/

This is the site for the Board of Examiners in Sex Therapy and Counseling in Ontario. It provides a referral directory to help locate a qualified sex therapist in the province.

www.eps.org.uk

Click here to browse the online catalog of the Erotic Print Society, which was set up in the UK in 1994 to cater for people "who appreciate the best in erotic art, literature, and journalism."

www.etchingspress.com

This small Australian-based independent publishing firm offers a wide selection of erotic literature.

www.fetishhotel.com

Visit this site for an extreme adult experience (no juveniles).

www.geocities.com/SouthBeach/Lounge/9071

For fascinating facts, advice, and books about extramarital affairs, go to Adrian's Adultery site.

www.godiva.com

The Godiva Chocolatier's site features recipes and an online catalog of gifts to suit all occasions.

www.goodvibes.com

Click on Antique Vibrator Museum to see examples of vibrators from 1869 through to the 1970s.

www.halcyon.com/elf/altsex/cunni.html
Visit this site for more information and advice on cunnilingus.

www.halcyon.com/elf/altsex/fella.html
Find the answers to the most frequently asked questions about fellatio at this site, and pick up some tips at the same time.

www.hbo.com/city
Get all the latest news and gossip from the hit television show *Sex and the City*.

www.here-now4u.de/engthe–kamasutra–of–vatsyayana.htm
Click here to read Carla Geerdes' article "The Kamasutra of Vatsyayana," which gives an overall view of the classic book.

www.hite-research.com
Find out more about the famous Hite report on Female Sexuality and the importance of clitoral stimulation.

www.iashs.edu
This is the site of the Institute for Advanced Study of Human Sexuality. It is the only graduate school in the US, and one of the few in the world, approved to train sexologists.

www.icicle.com
Women's interests in and concerns about sex and relationships are sympathetically explored.

www.indiana.edu/~kinsey
The web site for the Kinsey Institute for Research in Sex, Gender, and Reproduction supports interdisciplinary research and the study of human sexuality. The Institute was founded by Alfred Kinsey in 1947.

www.impotence.org.uk
The Impotence Association offers up-to-date information, advice, and support to sufferers and their partners.

www.impotenceworld.org
Check out the web site of the Impotence World Association for more help with this medical condition.

www.infertilitydocshop.com
This site gives information about all aspects of infertility and provides links to American medical specialists.

www.infidelity.com
Infidelity Support Network offers advice and support for those who have experienced infidelity. The site features online counseling and a daily self-assessment progress report.

www.inform.umd.edu/ENGL/englfac/WPeterson/VICTORIAN/weblinks.htm
Find out more about life in Victorian times at the web site of William Peterson (a lecturer at the US University of Maryland). There are links to sites connected with Victorian literature and culture.

www.interflora.com
Interflora's site enables you to order bouquets to be delivered around the world.

www.isidore-of-seville.com/burton/index.html

Visit this site for information about the life and travels of the explorer Sir Richard Burton.

www.islamcity.com/education/ihame/10.asp

Click here for more information about the history of the crusaders and their importance in the development of trade between Europe and the countries of the eastern Mediterranean.

www.ivillage.com

Relieve the stresses of day-to-day living with ivillage's 10-step online yoga routine. Click on "Print-and-Go Yoga" to try this basic, do-anywhere plan.

www.kamat.com

For text and photographs of erotic Indian temple carvings, go to this address, scroll down the page and click on "Erotic Arts of India" under the heading "What's Popular."

www.krsnabook.com/ch24.html

Learn more about Indra, the Hindu king of heaven, by reading Chapter 24 of the biography of Krishna online. Written by the founder of the Hare Krishna movement, the book is a collection of stories about the life of Krishna, who lived in India 5,000 years ago.

www.lush.co.uk

Go to this site and click on Products, then Soap, to see some extraordinary soaps for sale.

www.marsvenus.com

John Gray's site allows you to join in an interactive class based on his bestselling book *Men Are from Mars, Women Are from Venus.*

www.massagefree.com

Learn how to give the perfect massage with the help of pictures and detailed descriptions of different techniques.

www.medicine.ox.ac.uk/ndog/ivf

The Oxford Fertility Unit's guide to IVF treatment provides information on topics including embryo freezing, patient safety, chances of success, and costs.

www.mensclinic.com

The site of the Canadian Men's Clinic Limited offers information about erectile dysfunction, impotence, and treatment options. There are three locations in Canada: Toronto, Ottawa, and Vancouver.

www.nerve.com

This is a good-quality online sex magazine and discussion site. Check out nerve's feisty articles, horoscopes, and photographic features.

www.oneplusone.org.uk

Visit the site of One Plus One, an organization that monitors contemporary marriages and relationships, for more detailed information about its research.

www.parkstpress.com

Visit this site to order Sir Richard Burton's translation of the three classic Eastern love texts: *The Illustrated Kama Sutra, The Ananga Ranga,* and *The Perfumed Garden.*

www.pleasuregarden.co.uk

The Pleasure Garden's site offers a selection of sex books, videos, and adult toys.

www.sexology.com

Visit the Sex Therapy Online site to learn more about human sexuality. Expert therapists give advice and support online.

www.sieccan.com

The site of the Sex Information and Education Council of Canada provides links to sex information and sex therapy sites.

www.soapcentral.com

Visit Soap Opera Central for the latest news on the top American soaps.

www.tantra.com

This site has articles and advice on Tantra, details on Tantra workshops, plus a section for beginners.

www.tantra.org/kamasutr.html

Visit this Church of Tantra site to read more about role reversal positions and the love teachings of the *Kama Sutra* in general.

www.thriveonline.oxygen.com/sex/gspot.html

Find out how the G-spot functions and discover some facts and fictions associated with this sensitive hot spot.

www.unmissabletv.com/tx/soaps

Click on to the unmissable TV site for features, star profiles, and updates on British and Australian soaps, including *Coronation Street*, *EastEnders*, *Brookside*, and *Neighbours*.

www.virtualkiss.com

Click here to find out more about magic moments of momentous kissing.

www.worldhealth.net/index.shtml

The World Health Network's site provides information on specialist anti-aging medicines and lists practitioners from 60 countries.

www.wrapit.co.uk

Visit Wrapit's web site for a comprehensive catalog to buy gifts online.

www.yogasite.com

This is an online yoga resource center featuring detailed information on yoga postures, retreats, and styles.

www.yogauk.com

Yoga Village UK's site provides information on yoga events across the UK and yoga-related shopping. Visit this site to find teachers and classes in your area.

Index